Gifted Response

Gifted Response:
The Triune God as the Causative Agency of our Responsive Worship

Dennis Ngien

MILTON KEYNES ● COLORADO SPRINGS ● HYDERABAD

Copyright © 2008 Dennis Ngien

14 13 12 11 10 09 08 7 6 5 4 3 2 1

First published 2008 by Paternoster
Paternoster is an imprint of Authentic Media
9 Holdom Avenue, Bletchley, Milton Keynes, Bucks, MK1 QR, UK
1820 Jet Stream Drive, Colorado Springs, CO 80921, USA
OM Authentic Media, Medchal Road, Jeedimetla Village,
Secunderabad 500 055, A.P., India
www.authenticmedia.co.uk

Authentic Media is a division of IBS-STL U.K., limited by guarantee, with its Registered Office at Kingstown Broadway, Carlisle, Cumbria CA3 0HA. Registered in England & Wales No. 1216232. Registered charity 270162

The right of Dennis Ngien to be identified as the Author of this Work has been asserted by him in accordance with the Copyright, Designs and Patents Act 1988.

All rights reserved. No part of this publication may be reproduced, stored in a retrieval system, or transmitted in any form or by any means, electronic, mechanical, photocopying, recording or otherwise, without the prior permission of the publisher or a licence permitting restricted copying. In the UK such licences are issued by the Copyright Licensing Agency,
90 Tottenham Court Road, London, W1P 9HE

British Library Cataloguing in Publication Data

A catalogue record for this book is available from the
British Library

ISBN: 978-1-84227-610-5

Cover Design by James Kessell for Scratch the Sky Ltd.
(www.scratchthesky.com)
Print Management by Adare
Printed and bound in Great Britain by J.H. Haynes & Co., Sparkford

This book is Dedicated to Scholars,
My mentors in Scholarly and Spiritual Pursuits:

James I. Packer, an Evangelical Giant
Jürgen Moltmann, a Reformed Theologian
David Demson, a Reformation Scholar
William E. Hordern, a Lutheran Theologian

Table of Contents

Foreword Ralph Del Colle — ix

Acknowledgments — xiii

Introduction — xv

1 The Spirit "Worshipped and Glorified" as the Perfecting Cause of Our Worship in Basil of Caesarea's *De Spiritu Sancto* — 1

2 The Necessary Reason for Worship: On Praising the Superlative Deity in St. Anselm's *Proslogion* — 35

3 Participation in the Constitutive Kiss: Worship in Bernard of Clairvaux's *Song of Songs* — 63

4 Worship as Radical Reversal in Martin Luther's *Theologia Crucis* — 105

5 The Trinitarian Dynamic of Worship in John Calvin's *Institutes* (1559) — 136

Bibliography — 170

General Index — 180

Foreword

Dennis Ngien, noted for his systematic acumen in his contributions to historical theology, continues his exploration of trinitarian theology in this volume. In a previous work, *Apologetic for Filioque in Medieval Theology* (Paternoster, 2005), he explored the Spirit's procession among the great figures of that period: Anselm, Richard of St. Victor, Thomas Aquinas, and Bonaventure. Also, as a Luther scholar – see his *The Suffering of God according to Martin Luther's Theologia Crucis* (Lang, 1995) and *Luther as a Spiritual Adviser: The Interface of Theology and Piety in Luther's Devotional Writings* (Paternoster, 2007) – he now combines his love for the Reformers with a close reading of the Fathers and the leading lights of the Middle Ages. The scope of this book follows a longer trajectory beginning with Basil of Caesarea in the Christian East and moving to the medieval era and then the Reformation. Anselm of Canterbury and Bernard of Clairvaux are the representatives of the former with Martin Luther and John Calvin as the voices of the latter. Ngien's focus is worship, specifically, how worship is our participation in what he terms God's causative agency. His sensibilities are classically Protestant, always underscoring how the creature redeemed by grace is a passive recipient of God's grace that enables our response in worship. Not that Ngien intends this work as an apologetic for sixteenth-century Protestant magisterial theology, although one need not doubt where he stands. I suggest a richer reading, one that is the fruit of his hermeneutical lens, and where Ngien the theologian is at his best.

Lex orandi, lex credendi, as our author states, is assumed in this study. That prayer and doctrine are mutually related and that the causal relation proceeds from the latter to the former is not so much argued as it is illustrated in each of the chapters. Hence the reader is not driven to the comparison of various liturgical rites and the developing doctrinal tradition but is invited by the author to meditate on the implications of respective theological works from each of the representatives. The result is not a potpourri of voices but variations on the singular theme.

Ngien is a seasoned guide in pursuit of this theological center. One appreciates the wisdom of his choices, and not only for their ecumenical implications. Precisely because of his reiteration of the theme we discover what binds them together in the deep structure of their thought. It is not incidental that a Greek Father, two Latin doctors, and two Reformers all identify trinitarian agency as central to Christian worship. It may not be too bold to suggest that despite varieties in liturgical rites and differences in the doctrine and theologies of grace, Ngien's excavation of their relevant understandings of divine agency offers a sound basis for ecumenical consensus, all the more because of its application in worship. For it is the Church at prayer and praise in service of Word and Sacrament that best signifies its instrumentality in the work of salvation.

One need only follow the logic of the chapter titles to register the richness of this work and what it could mean for the worshipping church. Basil of Caesarea's *De Spiritu Sancto* proffers the Holy Spirit as the "perfecting cause" of worship. That Christian perfection is the aspiration of a true disciple (Phil. 3:12–14) all Christians accept. However, differences in theologies of grace and the doctrine of sanctification abound not only between the Eastern and Western churches, but also between Catholic and Protestant and between Lutheran and Wesleyan. However, if the Spirit is the "perfecting cause" of our worship, Christians may discover that the ancient *sursum corda* – "lift up your hearts," that signature doxological moment of all Christian prayer – is indeed the operation of grace that situates all ecclesial communities in the divine presence. One may debate the modalities of passive receptivity and its relationship to human liturgical praxis – without minimizing Ngien's intent in utilizing passive receptivity as his theological leitmotif – nevertheless, it bespeaks unity in the Spirit for all churches when they call upon the name of the Lord in their assemblies.

Following on to St. Anselm's *Proslogion*, his "Superlative Deity" allays any fear that talk of Christian worship may degenerate into an account of human religious consciousness. Projections of spiritual aspiration hardly lead to worship in spirit and truth. Indeed Ngien's characterization of Anselm's famous proof – God is "that than which nothing greater can be thought" – as his fiduciary formula, underscores its formative dimension for faith. The constant purification of faith in regard to its object requires transparency within liturgical praxis, namely, the recognition that God is also the necessary subject of worship, eliciting the praise of which God alone (as illustrated by the formula) is worthy.

Doxology is also participation in God of which mystical union is the fruit. The poetic spousal imagery of Bernard of Clairvaux's *Song of Songs* reveals how the causative agency of Christian worship proceeds from the intratrinitarian relations of divine love. The "constitutive kiss" (Ngien's phrase) of trinitarian embrace is pneumatic in its agency and is mediated by the crucified Christ. Here contemplation emerges as the inner core of worship as the Christian is caught up in the sacred humanity of Christ, passional wounds and all. Such wounds are not that distant from the soteriological concerns of the Reformers.

Ecumenical convergence is best situated in the poverty of the exchange between Christ's righteousness and our sin. Therefore, Martin Luther's *Theologia Crucis* assures us that this is God's way to us. Its radical reversal indeed presents a different staurological focus than Bernard's passional mysticism. And certainly one may debate whether Luther's *theologia crucis* and the passional spiritualities of medieval and Baroque Catholicism are entirely compatible. That is another discussion. What Ngien offers is the necessary and prior consensus that justification under the cross and participation in Jesus' sufferings in the imitation of Christ must be seen as the witness of God's work in us. If that be the case then spiritualities of the cross, Eucharistic mysticism, and the proclamation of the cross in Word and Sacrament are closer than has sometimes been judged.

Saved by the scandal of this cross with all of its contradiction and paradox the Church also becomes the site of trinitarian mediation from above to below and below to above that John Calvin's theology of worship exemplifies. The conclusion of the book with a strong affirmation of this double-movement in worship attending as it does on the theological necessity of the

Ascension ensures the fruit that the Church desires, namely, the knowing and active participation of the priesthood of all believers – the priesthood of the faithful in Catholic parlance – in worship. Such is the fruit of an attentive reading and reception of what this Reformer, as with the other theological doctors, continues to offer the Church through the legacy of their thought and their faith.

Such a quick run through the path charted by Ngien's scholarship and theological passion is but a glimpse into the eschatological dynamic that is the foundation of all liturgical doxology. The Church of Jesus Christ lives from and for this reality, a new creation born from the God who is love and who is pleased to receive our worship. One can therefore say, and happily so, that edification as well as illumination is the gift of this text. For that we can be grateful to its author.

Ralph Del Colle (PhD)
Associate Professor of Systematic Theology
Marquette University, Milwaukee, Wisconsin;
Editor, *International Journal of Systematic Theology*

Acknowledgments

I would like to extend my deep gratitude to Dr. Ralph Del Colle of Marquette University for his magnanimous foreword. I am also very grateful to the following notable scholars for their enthusiastic commendations: Gerald Bray of Beeson Divinity School, Jeremy Begbie of Ridley Hall, Cambridge University, Oliver Crisp of Bristol University, Anthony Cross of Oxford University, and Robin Parry, the Editorial Director of Paternoster. Thanks are also due to Matthew Knell for his invaluable copy editing work.

With minor variations, Chapter One has already appeared in *Eusebeia* 8 (Fall, 2007): 19–53, Chapter Four appeared in *Reformation* 12 (2007): 1–32, and Chapter Five appeared in *Ephemerides Theologicae Lovanienses* 84 (2007): 23–51. I am grateful to the editors of these journals for allowing me to reuse them here.

I would like to offer a personal note of thanks to the constituency of the Centre for Mentorship & Theological Reflection, for their generous financial support. I would like to express my appreciation to Drs. Michael Haykin of Southern Baptist Theological Seminary, Jeffrey Greenman of Wheaton College, the faculty members of Tyndale Seminary, and many pastors and students, for their unfailing encouragements and prayers. And I cannot fail to mention Hugh Rendle and his library staff, for their joyful service rendered to the author.

Last, but not least, I am immensely indebted to Ceceilia – my dearest life-companion and a real comrade in the gospel ministry – for creating time and space so that I could concentrate on research and writing. Praise God for his enablement, without which this book would never have been completed!

Glory to God in the Highest!

Dennis Ngien
March 10, 2008
Toronto, Canada

Introduction

Much of the contemporary Church's emphasis on worship has been concerned primarily with what *we* do in the act of worshipping God. The focus has been on the "how-to" aspect of worship and the discussion has been largely devoid of theological underpinning. This book seeks to fill that dangerous gap in the literature by means of an analysis of the theo-logic of worship in the major thinkers of each period, beginning with the patristic through the medieval to the Reformation: Basil of Caesarea, Anselm of Canterbury, Bernard of Clairvaux, Martin Luther and John Calvin. The unifying theme that runs through these theologians is that *worship is God's gift, in which we participate*. It is primarily God's causative action in us, and secondarily our corresponding response to him, the former being logically prior to the latter. The chief motive of worship is grace – that the God who initiates his movement toward us in order to make worship through the Son in the Spirit possible is the same one who draws us into the heavenly sanctuary through the Son in the Spirit. In worship, the fundamental position in which God places us must be observed – namely, we are passive recipients of what God actively gives freely and unconditionally.

The causal connection between doctrines and doxology is assumed in this study. Thus the doctrines of Christ, the Holy Spirit, salvation, Trinity, grace, Word of God and Eucharist – all of these interpenetrate systematically and none can be viewed independently of the others – are significant for a proper theological understanding of worship. With each chapter standing on its own, the riches of the historical sources related to each theologian will form the substance of our reflections on the subject.

Chapter One focuses on Basil of Caesarea's *De Spiritu Sancto*, in which he argues that not only is the Spirit the legitimate object of worship, the one who receives our praise, but also the perfector, the one through whom worship offered in the Son joins with the heavenly choir of angels. Just as the Son belongs rightly to the Godhead, so also the Spirit is placed within the same Deity, not under or outside it. Because the Spirit enjoys the natural union and intimate communion with the Father just as does the Son, he is equally rendered that which rightly belongs to God alone: glory and worship. The double-movement of the Trinity constitutes the condition of the possibility of true worship: God descends to our flesh in the Son, revealing his gracious will in the Spirit; conversely the Spirit draws us through the Son to the worship of the Father. Worship is truly ours insofar as it participates in the unitive movement of the Spirit through the Only-begotten to the Father.

Chapter Two focuses on Anselm's *Proslogion*, in which the import of the fiduciary utterance, "that than which nothing greater can be thought," is of such great force that God must be *believed* as such, and thus *worshipped* as such. God is the divine superlative because his nature demands it, and causally it creates in us a worshipping response that is rationally fitting. The moment of understanding is precisely the moment of doxology. The initial result in Anselm's search for God was an awareness of God's distance, which is finally overcome by an apprehension of the Triune God. In worship, God is to be experienced through enjoyment, for the very purpose of insight is nothing other than the fullness of joy which is promised by the Son, and is communicated to our hearts by the Holy Spirit.

Chapter Three focuses on Bernard of Clairvaux's sermons on the *Song of Songs*, in which worship is comprehended in the groom's kiss, which is shared with the bride in the efficacy of the Spirit, the unitive kiss between the Father and Son. The mystical union with Christ via contemplation of the sacred image of Jesus' humanity, particularly his passion, is a foundation for the worship of our Savior as the Bridegroom of the soul. The bride in a spiritual union with the Son as her groom in the Spirit is the basis of her entrance into the holy of holies. Hence the Spirit is the power of efficacy in this double movement, and also in the

Church's worship: only in the kiss (Spirit) is the worship offered in the groom able to reach the Fatherly sanctuary; conversely, the Spirit causes us, those whom he sanctifies, to engage in the loving contemplation of the groom's wounds through which our being and activities – our praise and thanksgiving – reach the glorious countenance of the Godhead.

Chapter Four seeks to show how the theme of worship is ontologically constitutive of Luther's *theologia crucis*, his foundational theology. The creatures, of their own reason and strength, cannot ascend to heaven, obligating God and causing him to be gracious. Thus worship is grounded in the theology of radical reversal, in which God alone must begin and lay the first stone, without any entreaty or desire of the creatures. God is the causative agency of our responsive worship of him. Yet our worship reaches the heavenly sanctuary not by means of our response but by Christ's efficacious response (imputed to us through the Holy Spirit). Worship then is a performative action in which God is both subject and object. In addition, hearing God's Word via human speech (preaching), an instrument of divine power, and taking it to heart, is worship at its highest.

Chapter Five fleshes out the trinitarian dynamic of worship in Calvin's *Institutes* (1559). Calvin's theology of worship largely appears in his commentaries, sermons, and letters. However, it is arguable that Calvin's scholarship on this topic also occurs in his more polemical *Institutes*. Christ's mediation is the theological basis of the believer's active response to God: in his person, in his Name, our worship has access to God. Christ's priesthood is for us so that we might recover our own. God the Son has conquered the inaccessibility of true worship, and abolished the distance between God and us. With Basil, Calvin stresses the double-movement in worship: the God-humanwardness, in which God first descends to us in his Son, reveals himself by the Holy Spirit as the object of our worship; and the human-Godwardness, in which the Spirit elevates us to Christ's Ascension, to participate in the incarnate Son's communion with the Father that is understood as worship.

Chapter One

The Spirit "Worshipped and Glorified" as the Perfecting Cause of Our Worship in Basil of Caesarea's *De Spiritu Sancto*

Introduction

The most important work on the Holy Spirit in the fourth century came from the pen of Basil of Caesarea.[1] The immediate occasion of Basil's *On the Holy Spirit* was a dispute with the Pneumatomachians (the "Spirit-fighters") over the doxology he introduced, glorifying the Father *"with* the Son, together *with* the Holy Spirit."[2] Basil's treatise was probably aimed at his former mentor, Eustathius, whose subordination doctrine of the Spirit was widespread.[3] *On the Holy Spirit* is Christocentric in its focus, but trinitarian in its

---

[1] Richard Hanson, "The Divinity of the Holy Spirit," *The Church Quarterly* 1 (1969): 300.

[2] David Anderson, introduction to *Basil the Great: On the Holy Spirit*, tr. David Anderson (Crestwood, NY: St. Vladimir's Seminary Press, 1980), 1.3. Hereafter cited as *On the Spirit*. See also Saint Basil, *De Spiritu Sancto*, tr. Blomfield Jackson, in vol. 8 of *The Nicene and Post-Nicene Fathers*, Second Series, eds. Philip Schaff and Henry Wace (Grand Rapids: William B. Eerdmans, 1989). Hereafter cited as *De Spiritu Sancto*. See Tom A. Noble, "Gregory Nazianzen's Use of Scripture in Defense of the Deity of the Spirit," *Tyndale Bulletin* 39 (1988): 106.

[3] Robert Letham, *The Holy Trinity: In Scripture, History, Theology, and Worship* (New Jersey: P&P Publishing Co., 2001), 148.

content. The Christological formulation of Nicaea (325) is the basis of Basil's pneumatology. Just as the Son belongs rightly to the Godhead, so also the Spirit is placed within the same Deity, not under or outside it. Because the Spirit is indivisibly united in being and agency with the Father and the Son, he is to be equally rendered that which only God should receive: honor and worship. Basil inculcated in the Church's worship the form *with* which he regarded as rooted not only in tradition but most importantly in Scripture. He also saw this form not as contradictory, but complementary with the customary form of worship, "Glory to the Father *through* the Son *in* the Spirit." The former admits of the immanent unity and close communion of the members of the Trinity; the latter admits of the way the Triune God deals with us in the economy of salvation. Basil writes that one must believe that the Spirit belongs intrinsically to the same Godhead as the Father and Son for one's own salvation, and concomitantly for the possibility of true worship. The contemplation of the Spirit's titles, operations and gifts is the dynamic of true worship. The saving import of the Spirit's deity lies in this: the Spirit places us in Christ so that our worship, as a participation in the Son's communion with the Father, is found pleasing. The believer, "the place of the Spirit," is enabled to offer doxology to God.[4] The Church's worship is truly ours insofar as it participates in the Spirit's unitive movement through the Only-begotten to the Father. The aim of this chapter is to show how the confession of the Spirit's deity in Basil's treatise is constitutive of a theology of worship, in which not only is the Spirit the lawful object of worship, the one who receives our praise, but also the perfecting cause, the one through whom our worship through the Son finds admission into the heavenly choir of angels.

Basil's Reticence: *Homoousios*

It is historically accurate that one would not find in Basil's *On the Spirit* an explicit assertion of the deity of the Spirit as that in Gregory of Nazianzus' *Fifth Theological Oration*: "What then? Is the Spirit God? Most certainly. Well, then, is he consubstantial?

---

[4] *On the Spirit*, 26.63.

Yes, if he is God."[5] Both Richard Hanson and Gary Badcock argue that, presumably for fear of creating a scandal, Basil was not as intransigent as Athanasius, his predecessor, in predicating the term *homoousios* of the Spirit.[6] Alasdair Heron concurs with them, when he says, "Basil . . . drew back – at least in his official, public statements – from calling the Spirit 'God' because it could cause offence."[7] It was primarily his pastoral concern for Church unity that caused his reticence.[8] Basil perceived the danger of the theological controversies which might turn the Church into a battlefield. The Arian controversy, for one, beset the Church like a raging storm, creating schism, irreconcilable hatred, and party spirits. Basil described the dangerous effects: "Although we are united in our hatred of common foes, no sooner do they retreat, and we find enemies in each other."[9] Thus he stated: "Since no human voice is powerful enough to be heard in such an uproar, I reckon that silence is more profitable than words."[10]

Officially the creedal term *homoousios* was reserved for the relationship between the Father and the Son. The Nicene faith constituted what Basil called the "kerygma," the publicly proclaimed teaching heard by all, which he distinguished from "dogma," the teaching "given to us secretly through apostolic tradition."[11]

---

[5] Gregory of Nazianzen, *Orationes* 29.15; 40.43 as cited in Thomas F. Torrance, *The Christian Doctrine of God* (Edinburgh: T&T Clark, 1996), 127. See Noble, "Gregory Nazianzen's Use of Scripture in Defense of the Deity of the Spirit," 123; Frederick W. Norris, "Gregory the Theologian," *Pro Ecclesia* 2 (1993): 483. Gregory Nazianzus was a close colleague of Basil.

[6] Richard Hanson, *The Search for the Christian Doctrine of God* (Edinburgh: T&T Clark, 1988), 776; Gary Badcock, *Light of Truth and Fire of Love: a Theology of the Holy Spirit* (Grand Rapids: Eerdmans, 1997), 55. Jean Gribomont, "Intransigence and Irenicism in Saint Basil's *De Spiritu Sancto*" in *Word and Spirit: A Monastic Review. In Honor of Saint Basil the Great* (Still River, Mass.: St. Bede's Publications, 1979), 118.

[7] Alasdair Heron, *The Holy Spirit* (Philadelphia: Westminster, 1983), 81.

[8] Cyril Kalam, "Basil on the Holy Spirit – Some aspects of His Theology," in *Word and Spirit*, 143. Mark J. Larson, in his "A Re-examination of *De Spiritu Sancto*: Saint Basil's Bold Defense of the Spirit's Deity," *Scottish Bulletin of Evangelical Theology* 19 (2001): 65–84, argues that a restrained style characterized Basil's *On the Spirit*.

[9] *On the Spirit* 30.77.

[10] *On the Spirit* 30.78.

[11] *On the Spirit* 17.65–66. For a discussion of Basil's use of tradition

Here in his document, he observed the "kerygma," the Church's established teaching. He applied the Christological defense of the Nicene faith to his doctrine of the Spirit, although without using the word *homoousios*. He refrained from attributing the same term to the Spirit, for that might create the adverse effect of alienating his supporters or contraries, through a misunderstanding of the terminology. So in such a crucial moment, the unity of the orthodox position took priority over theological controversy or terminological clarification. In lieu of affirming categorically the deity of the Spirit, Basil preferred to repudiate the doctrine that held that the Spirit belongs to the creaturely order, and bears no ontological status of God. Being interested in convincing rather than crushing his opponents, Basil sought to lead them through worship to an assertion of the divinity of the Spirit. For this reason he wrote *On the Spirit*, in which, in showing that his version of the doxology, "Glory be to the Father, with the Son and with the Spirit," is justifiable, he too demonstrates that the Spirit is God, although without forthrightly calling him "God."[12] Basil did not shrink from speaking the truth about the supreme nature of the Spirit. He declared: "We place our trust in the Spirit's help, and boldly proclaim the truth."[13]

Christology as Prolegomena to Pneumatology

Historically the assertion of the Son's deity is not only the ground of a true knowledge of God, but also the presupposition of true

---

to develop his pneumatology, see Emmanuel Amand de Mendieta, "The Pair Kerygma and Dogma in the Theological Thought of St. Basil of Caeserea," *Journal of Theological Studies* 16 (1965): 129–42; his *The "Unwritten" and "Secret" Apostolic Tradition in the Theological Thought of St. Basil of Caesarea* (Edinburgh: Oliver and Boyd, 1965); Richard P.C. Hanson, "Basil's Doctrine of the Tradition in Relation to the Holy Spirit," *Vigiliae Christianae* 22 (1968): 241–55.

[12] Justo Gonzalez, *A History of Christian Thought* (Nashville: Abingdon Press, 1970), vol. 1:317. Basil explicitly used the term *homoousios* in one of his letters: "And if He is not a creature, He is consubstantial with God." See Saint Basil, *Letter 8*, in *Saint Basil: The Letters*, tr., Roy J. Deferrari (Cambridge, 1950), vol. 1, 81 as cited in Larson, "Re-examination of *De Spiritu Sancto*: Saint Basil's Bold Defense of the Spirit's Deity," 67.

[13] *On the Spirit* 30.79.

worship. The indissoluble unity of the revelation of God and piety means there is no speech about God without reverential worship. The Christological controversies of Nicaea adopted what Jaroslav Pelikan called "the standard disjunctive syllogism" as the method of argumentation: either he is God or a creature; if the former, he is the object of worship; if the latter, it is idolatry to worship him.[14] The line of absolute distinction between God and the creature in respect to the identity of the Son is determinative of orthodoxy or heresy. The Council of Nicaea affirmed that the Son belongs to the uncreated order, and is himself God as the Father is, not a created intermediary between God and the world as is the case in Arius' thought. This mode of argumentation was meant to lead Arians to believe and "confess Him to be fully God, one with God, the object of worship," although they refused to concede his oneness with God.[15]

Echoing the same method of syllogistic argumentation, Basil questioned his opponents concerning whether the Spirit be placed on God's side of the line: "Will they rank Him with God, or will they push Him to a creature's place?"[16] Does the Holy Spirit belong to the created order? Does he have his being with the Son on the divine side of that line of demarcation between the Creator and the creature? Given that the deity of the Son was the central issue at the Council of Nicaea, we encounter there only the phrase "We believe in the Holy Spirit," without elaboration. The Church recognized "such vagueness would not do, that the Church of Christ was disintegrating into a jumble of warring factions, and that . . . words adequate for God, were necessary to define the catholic faith."[17] It was only in subsequent years, between 325 and 381, that profound reflection of the personal nature of the Holy Spirit emerged, which eventually led to a mature understanding of that nature. Basil the Great, bishop of Caesarea, was instrumental

---

[14] "The 'Spiritual Sense' of Scripture: The Exegetical Basis for St. Basil's Doctrine of the Holy Spirit," in *Basil of Caesarea: Christian Humanist, Ascetic*, ed. Paul J. Fedwick (Toronto: Pontifical Institute of Medieval Studies, 1981), part I, 342.

[15] J.H. Newman, *The Arians of the Fourth Century*, 3rd ed. (London: 1871), 217.

[16] *On the Spirit* 16.37. See G.L. Prestige, *God in Patristic Thought* (London: S.P.C.K, 1952), 80–86.

[17] Anderson's Introduction *On the Holy Spirit* 7.

in helping the Church find the linguistic and conceptual models for understanding the Spirit.

Athanasius has Christology as his theological prolegomena, the starting point for his pneumatology. Statements about the Spirit are to be derived from the Christological formulation. To deny the essence of the Son with the Father is to deny the essence of the Spirit. He stated, "from our knowledge of the Son we may be able to have true knowledge of the Spirit. For we shall find that the Spirit has to the Son the same proper relationship as we have known the Son to have to the Father."[18] The language of the Spirit's relationship to the Son as the Son is to the Father occurs frequently throughout his correspondence with Serapion. To cite one:

> For as the Son, who is in the Father and the Father in him, is not a creature but pertains to the essence of the Father (for this you also profess to say); so also it is not lawful to rank with the creatures the Spirit, who is in the Son, and the Son in him, nor to divide him from the Word and reduce the Triad to imperfection.[19]

Similarly evident in Basil's treatise is the movement from the confession of the Son's deity to that of the Spirit's deity.[20] Asserting the full deity of the Son, as in the Nicene Creed, was the basis for asserting the full deity of the Spirit. Basil declared, in regard to the baptismal statements with reference to Christ: "To address Christ in this way is a complete profession of faith, because it clearly reveals that God anoints the Son (the Anointed One) with the unction of the Spirit."[21] To speak of Christ is to speak of the entire Godhead. Thus Christology is the abiding presupposition of trinitarian theology. Against those who subordinate the Spirit, Basil argued that the Spirit is united through the Son to the Father,

---

[18] Letter III.1; quotations of Athanasius' *Letters to Serapion* are from C.R.B. Shapland's translation, *The Letters of Saint Athanasius Concerning the Holy Spirit* (London: The Epworth Press, 1951).
[19] Letter I.21,
[20] Kei Yamamura, "The Development of the Doctrine of the Holy Spirit in Patristic Philosophy: St. Basil and Gregory of Nyssa," *St. Vladimir's Theological Quarterly* 18 (1974): 14–15.
[21] *On the Spirit* 12.28.

and that belief in three persons upholds the orthodox doctrine of divine unity:

> As unique Persons [i.e., the Father and the Son], they are one and one; as sharing a common nature, both are one. How does one and one not equal two Gods? Because we speak of the emperor, and the emperor's image – but not two emperors . . . and since the divine nature is not composed of parts, union of the persons is accomplished by partaking of the whole. The Holy Spirit is one, and we speak of Him as unique, since through the one Son He is joined to the Father. He completes the all-praised blessed Trinity . . . He does not share created nature. He is united to the Father and the Son.[22]

Latent in the baptismal formula of Mt. 28:19–20 is the confession of the Spirit's deity on account of Jesus' own words. "This passage," Pelikan stated, "became the cornerstone of Basil's case" for the Spirit's deity.[23] The great importance Basil attached to this passage was obvious in the way he framed his own question: "But before the great tribunal what have I prepared to say on the great day of judgment?" With reverence, he then answered with these words: "This; that I was in the first place led to the glory of the Spirit by the honor conferred by the Lord in associating Him with Himself and with His Father at baptism."[24] Jesus' command in baptism reveals his delight in his communion with the Spirit, and to be ranked with him. Thus it is impious of us not to obey Jesus' own words (Acts 5:29). The arrangement of the name of Father, Son, and Spirit in "the baptism of salvation" testifies to their union and communion within God's own life.[25] The Matthean text does not establish conumeration or subnumeration, but rather the co-ordination between the Father, Son, and Spirit – the three persons conspire together in perfecting baptism. This solves the problem of subordinationism. Hence Basil challenged his opponents: "Their names are mentioned in one and the same series, how can you speak of numbering *with* or numbering *under*?"[26] If we must count, he wrote, we do so not by arithmetic adding, implying

---

[22] *On the Spirit* 18.45.
[23] Pelikan, "The 'Spiritual Sense' of Scripture," 346.
[24] *De Spiritu Sancto* 29.75.
[25] *On the Spirit* 10.24.
[26] *On the Spirit* 17.43. See Henry B. Swete, *The Holy Spirit in the Ancient Church* (Grand Rapids: Baker House, 1912), 232–34.

three separate deities. Citing Isaiah 44:6, "I am the first, and I am the last," Basil concluded that there is one supreme God and three distinct persons of equal dignity. As unique persons (Father, Son and Spirit), they are one, one and one; as sharing a common nature, all are one.[27] This order established by the Lord is not the order of rank, but of relationship, in which the Spirit's relation to the Son "equals" that of the Son with the Father.[28]

Through the baptismal formula, we are initiated into the knowledge of the Triune God.[29] The invocation of the trinitarian formula is essential to making baptism "complete and perfect."[30] The invocation of any single person alone is never alone, but always in proximity and unity with the other two. Scripture speaks of being baptized into Christ (Gal. 3:27), yet no one would say that the invocation of Christ's name alone renders baptism efficacious. Likewise, when Scripture speaks of being baptized with the Spirit (Acts 1:5), it does not intend to say the invocation of the Spirit's name alone suffices. To speak of Christ is to speak of the Triune God, even when Scripture may omit the names of the Father and the Spirit; likewise to speak of baptism by the Spirit alone does not exclude the other two. The three persons are inseparably united in being, communion and agency, without which baptism is divested of its saving reality.

Basil's opponents refused to accept his position that baptism in the Spirit suffices for the Spirit to be ranked with God. Based on I Cor. 10:2, "They were baptized into Moses in the *cloud* and in the *sea*," they denied the Spirit's consubstantiality with God. They argued that it was common of the old to profess faith "in the Lord *and* in his servant Moses" (Ex. 14:31) without magnifying either. Thus baptism in the Spirit is no basis for ranking him with God, just as baptism in Moses is no basis for exalting him above others. As a response, Basil undertook a typological exegesis of I Cor. 10:2, conceiving of Moses' exodus event as a shadow or type of the grace which was yet to come.[31] The order in which he discussed

---

[27] *On the Spirit* 18.45. Basil Studer, *The Trinity and Incarnation of the Early Church*, tr. Matthias Westerhoff & ed. Andrew Louth (Collegeville: The Liturgical Press, 1993), 142, where he states that Basil was the first to distinguish between *hypostasis* and *ousia*.

[28] *On the Spirit* 17.43.

[29] *On the Spirit* 29.75.

[30] *On the Spirit* 12.28.

[31] *On the Spirit*, 14.31.

these two types is not the same as they actually appear in the text. Here Basil transposed the order of the text, beginning with type "sea" instead of type "cloud." This transposition parallels Basil's understanding of what happens in baptism.[32] In the sea, the enemies are swallowed up by its killing waves; in baptism, the enmity between us and God is swallowed up in victory. The old self dies in the waves, as typified by the "sea," and the new self rises from the water imbued with the Spirit, as foreshadowed by the "cloud."

> The people emerged from the sea unharmed, and we come up from the water as alive from the dead, saved by the grace of Him who has called us. The cloud is a shadow of the Spirit's gifts, for He cools the flames of our passions through the mortification of our bodies.[33]

If the separation of the Spirit from the first two persons renders baptism ineffectual, Basil reasoned, the same holds true for the confession of faith. Should the confession of the deity of the Spirit be wanting, Christ and all his redeeming benefits are devoid of any saving efficacy:

> How can we be safe if we tear the Spirit away from the Father and the Son? Faith and baptism are two inseparably united means of salvation. Faith is perfected through baptism; the foundation of baptism is faith, and both are fulfilled through the same names. First we believe in the Father, Son, and Holy Spirit; then we are baptized in the name of the Father, the Son, and the Holy Spirit. The profession of faith leads us to salvation, and then baptism follows, sealing our affirmation.[34]

All three persons work together as One God *ad extra*, achieving salvation for us. Christ, the Spirit and salvation are so closely bound that none can be viewed independently of the other. Basil thus exhorted his people to preserve the Spirit's deity in the

---

[32] Michael A.G. Haykin, "'In the Cloud and In the Sea': Basil of Caesarea and the Exegesis of I Cor. 10:2," *Vigiliae Christianae* 40 (1986): 142.
[33] *On the Spirit* 14.31.
[34] *On the Spirit* 12.28. Also cited in Michael A.G. Haykin, *The Spirit of God: The Exegesis of 1 & 2 Corinthians in the Pneumatomachian Controversy of the Fourth Century* (Leiden: E.J. Brill, 1994), 130.

profession of faith, and praise him together with the Father and the Son at baptism.

Correspondence Theory: Spirit's Titles, Operations and Gifts

Procedurally Basil moved from Christological titles, works and blessings to discern the proper nature and dignity of Christ. Titles perform the task of identifying the nature and grace of Christ. Titles such as Son, Only-begotten, Power and Wisdom of God, and Word are reflective of his supreme dignity, exalting him as "the name which is above every name" (Phil. 2:9). It is with these titles that Christ is glorified as God and Son together *with* the Father. The phrase *with him* denotes the Son's communion with his Father. Basil dealt with this Christological question: In what way does the Son come *after* the Father? Does it refer to a later in time, or in rank, or in dignity? In God, he argued, there is no before, nor after. An *after* in time is senseless, for how could the Maker of the ages hold "a second place; no interval could possibly divide the natural union of Father and Son."[35] Basil elaborated:

> Even limited human thought demonstrates that it is impossible for the Son to be younger than the Father; first, we cannot conceive of either apart from their relationship with each other, and second, the very idea of 'coming after' is applied to something separated from the present by a smaller interval of time than something else which 'came earlier' . . . In addition to being impious, is it really not the height of folly to measure the life of Him who transcends all times and ages, whose existence is incalculably remote from the present? Things subject to birth and corruption are described as prior to one another; are we therefore to compare God the Father as superior to God the Son, who exists before the ages?[36]

For Athanasius, as for Basil, the begetting of the Son is not a temporal begetting, involving procreation, separation or creation. "The supreme eminence of the Father is inconceivable; thought and reflection are utterly unable to penetrate the begetting of

---

[35] *On the Spirit* 6.14.
[36] *On the Spirit* 6.14.

the Lord."[37] Basil maintained the concept of the Son's begetting within the "tangible boundaries" of the two words of St. John: "In the *beginning was* the Word." He wrote: "No matter how far your thoughts travel backward, you cannot get beyond the *was*. No matter how hard you strain to see what is beyond the Son, you will find it impossible to pass outside the confines of the *beginning*."[38] Therefore the preposition *with* is rightly attached to the doxology of the Church, which speaks of the Son and the Father as inseparably one in name and nature, as the radiance and its source (glory) are inseparably joined.

Basil continued: an *after* in place, which relegates the Son as subordinate to the Father, also does not make sense because the Father cannot be separated from the Son spatially. There is no partition in the being of God, for God is indivisibly one. God permeates all things, and cannot be confined in defined places. Both the Father and Son are one incorporeal, divine Being who, in their own rights, cannot be conceived in the same manner as corporeal beings. The opponents' error, Basil contended, lies in their misunderstanding of biblical metaphors. They wrongly applied "in a fallen, fleshly sense" form, shape, and bodily position to a being like God, confining the absolute, the infinite, the incorporeal within prescribed boundaries of the creaturely world. This is tantamount to collapsing the distinction between the uncreated order and created order. When Hebrews 1:3 spoke of the Son as sitting at the Father's right hand, the writer did not intend a creaturely meaning, referring to "a lower place as they contend, but a relationship of equality" he has with his Father. By such expression, the writer extols "the magnificence of the Son's great dignity."[39] Basil rebutted: "How is it not reckless to rob the Son of His position of equality in the doxology as if He deserved to be ranked in a lower place?"[40] He exhorted his opponents to learn that the phrase right hand refers to Christ as "the power of God and wisdom of God, and the image of the invisible God, and the brightness of His glory, and the one whom God the Father

---

[37] *On the Spirit* 6.14.
[38] *On the Spirit* 6.14.
[39] *On the Spirit* 6.15.
[40] *On the Spirit* 6.15.

has sealed, whom the Father stamped with the image of His Person."[41]

Other titles such as Shepherd, King, Physician, Bridegroom, Way, Door, Fountain, Bread, Axe, and Rock reveal the grace of Christ, not his nature.[42] Most appropriate to these titles is the phrase *through whom*, which expresses our relationship with him, or the way in which he works grace in us. Since both the Father and the Son are involved in creation, the act of creating from the Father *through* the Son substantiates "their unity of will."[43] The "commandment" the Father gave to the Son is not one that proceeds from a superior to an inferior; nor does a "transmission of will" from the Father to the Son occur temporally in a created order, with an interval of time in between, but it is like a reflection of an object in a mirror occurs eternally within the Godhead "without passage of time."[44] Therefore the phrase "*through whom* admits of a principal [antecedent] cause, but cannot be used as an objection against the efficient cause."[45] Basil listed a treasury of blessings which reaches us from the Father *through* the Son: revelation, sanctification, illumination, guidance, healing, providence, etc. The preposition *through* reflects an order in the Godhead, which God keeps in its proper place without attributing diminutive inferiority or slavish obedience to a being like God. For the order has nothing to do with the order of importance or value, but with the relationship between the Father and the Son. Thus it is godlike glory for the Son to obey the Father who commands, as is proper to the relationship between them. From this, Basil derived his conclusion concerning the nature and work of the Son whose origin is the Father:

> [T]he Word was full of His Father's grace; He shines forth from the Father, and accomplishes everything to His parent's plan. He is not different in essence, nor is He different in power from the Father, and if their power is equal, then their works are the same. Christ is the power of God, and the wisdom of God. All things were made through Him, and all things were created through him and for him, not as if

---

[41] *On the Spirit* 6.15.
[42] *On the Spirit* 8.17.
[43] *On the Spirit* 8.21 (Italics are mine).
[44] *On the Spirit* 8.20.
[45] *On the Spirit* 8.21 (Italics are mine).

He were discharging the service of a slave, but instead He creatively fulfills the will of His Father.[46]

Consequently the Church accepted both forms of worship, on the one hand ascribing glory to the Son with the Father, and on the other hand affirming the way God's grace reaches us from the Father through the Son in a differentiated unity between them. The form (*with*) was most appropriate for adoration offered to the immanent Godhead, while the form (*through*) was best for giving thanks for the way God deals with humans in the economy of salvation.

> Whenever we reflect on the majesty of the nature of the Only-Begotten, and the excellence of His dignity, we ascribe the glory to Him *with* the Father. On the other hand, when we consider the abundant blessings He has given us, and how He has admitted us as co-heirs into God's household, we acknowledge that this grace works for us *through* him and *in* him. Therefore the best phrase when giving Him glory is *with whom* and the most appropriate for giving thanks is *through whom*.[47]

The same procedure emerges in Basil's apprehension of the Spirit's dignity. The justification of his liturgical practice is to be sought in three sets of biblical passages that deal with titles, activities and gifts. The theological implications for the nature of the Spirit, and the causal connection with worship, can be drawn from the same. Not by discursive exercise, but by contemplation, Basil proceeded from the Spirit's titles, operations and gifts to an assertion of the supreme nature of the Spirit. In so doing, he accentuated a correspondence between God's nature and God's names, God's immanent being and God's economic actions, his divine attributes and the various gifts. Arguably, he claimed, it is possible to "arrive to a certain extent at intelligent apprehension of the sublimity of His nature and of His approachable power" by pondering upon the meaning of his name, the greatness of his works, and the bountiful blessings of his.[48]

Basil asked, "First of all, who can listen to the Spirit's titles and not be lifted up in his soul? Whose thoughts would not be

---

[46] *On the Spirit* 8.19.
[47] *On the Spirit* 7.16. Also cited in Christopher A. Hall, *Learning Theology with the Church Fathers* (Illinois: InterVarsity Press, 2002), 106.
[48] *De Spiritu Sancto* 19.48.

raised to contemplate the supreme nature?"[49] He began listing the different titles for the Spirit in the Bible: "He is called the Spirit of God (Mt. 3:16), the Spirit of truth who proceeds from the Father, the right Spirit, willing Spirit. His first and most proper title is Holy Spirit, a name most especially appropriate to everything which is incorporeal, purely immaterial, and indivisible."[50] While nowhere did Basil say that the Spirit is God, he saw a correspondence between these titles and the Spirit's supreme nature. The biblical language for the Spirit reflects the very nature of the Spirit. For instance, an incorporeal being such as the Spirit "cannot be circumscribed. When we hear of the word 'spirit' it is impossible for us to conceive of something whose nature can be circumscribed or is subject to change or variation, or is like a creature in any way."[51] All his titles are his by right and nature, not by exaltation.

> The Spirit is called holy, as the Father is holy and the Son is holy. For creatures, holiness comes from without; for the Spirit, holiness fills His very nature. He is not sanctified, but sanctifies. He is called good, as the Father is good; the essence of the Spirit embraces the goodness of the Father . . . He shares the name Paraclete with the Only-Begotten, who said, "I will ask the Father, and He will give you another Paraclete." The Spirit shares these titles held in common by the Father and the Son; He receives these titles due to His natural and intimate relationship with them.[52]

As a solution of the Tropici's problem about the origin of the Spirit, Basil wrote: the Spirit is "from God," not in the way creaturely things are from him, but as "proceeding" from the Father, "not by generation, like the Son, but as breath of his mouth."[53] Constitutive of the Godhead is a relational dynamism, in which the three persons mutually relate to each other. The Spirit is called "the Spirit of Christ, since he is naturally related to Him (Rom. 8:9)"; as "the Paraclete, he reflects the goodness of the Paraclete (Father) who sent Him, and His own dignity reveals the majesty of Him from Whom He proceeded," just as the Son's dignity reveals the

---

[49] *On the Spirit* 9.22.
[50] *On the Spirit* 9.22.
[51] *On the Spirit* 9.22.
[52] *On the Spirit* 19.48.
[53] *On the Spirit* 18.46.

majesty of Him from whom he came.[54] The testimony of mutual glory of the Father, Son, and Spirit is in the Fourth Gospel, where the Son glorifies the Father (17:4), the Spirit glorifies the Son (16:14), and the Father glorifies the Son (13:28). The glory that they share is not a servile kind, offered by a creature to his superior. It is a kind of glory shared by "intimates, and it is this which the Spirit fulfills."[55] The Spirit, who is "from God," never exists outside God, but is eternally related to the Father and the Son within the Godhead, and hence is to be glorified with them.

Scripture also testifies that the Spirit is called *Lord*. Basil wrote: "Our opponents place the Holy Spirit among the ministering spirits sent forth to serve . . . Let them listen to even more testimony of the Spirit's Lordship: 'Now the Lord is the Spirit' (II Cor. 3:17), and 'this comes from the Lord who is the Spirit' (II Cor. 3:18)."[56] As proof, Basil quoted the Apostle's words at length: "To this day, when they read the Old Testament, that same veil remains uplifted, because only through Christ is it taken away . . . when a man turns to the Lord the veil is removed. Now the Lord is the Spirit" (II Cor. 3:14, 16–17).[57] Basil's identification of the Spirit as Lord is later incorporated into the Constantinopolitan Creed: "And in the Holy Spirit, the Lord and life-giver, Who proceeds from the Father, Who is worshipped and glorified together with the Father and Son, Who spoke through the prophets."[58] The creedal declaration that the Spirit is Lord, as Thomas Torrance states, possesses "the effect of affirming full belief in the unqualified Deity of the Holy Spirit along with the Father and the Son."[59] The same effect may be predicated of Basil's attribution of the Spirit as Lord, a title specifically reserved in the biblical tradition for God himself.[60]

The Spirit's operations are the ground of his being God, neither an intermediary nor a creature. By the Christological method, Basil justified a theology of worship proper to the Spirit on the basis of the works he performs. Just as "the recital of [Christ's] benefits is an appropriate argument in favor of the doxology [addressed

---

[54] *On the Spirit* 18.46.
[55] *On the Spirit* 18.46.
[56] *On the Spirit* 21.52.
[57] *On the Spirit* 21.52.
[58] John H. Leith, ed., *Creeds of the Churches: A Reader in Christian Doctrine from the Bible to the Present*, 3rd ed. (Atlanta: John Knox Press, 1982), 33.
[59] Torrance, *The Christian Doctrine of God*, 96.
[60] Larson, "A Re-examination of *De Spiritu Sancto*," 71.

to] him,"⁶¹ so also "the enumeration of the wondrous works that [the Spirit] has done" is the legitimate basis of glorifying him.⁶² Concerning the Spirit's deeds, Basil wrote: "His works are ineffable in majesty, and innumerable in quantity."⁶³ Because the Spirit performs various works which are exclusively divine, he must share the divine nature. For instance, if sanctification is exclusively a divine work, and if it is the Spirit who sanctifies (I Cor. 6:11), then the Spirit must be God. We know of the loftiness of the Spirit's nature because the Spirit works as the Father and the Son do. Basil illustrated this by considering creation. Based on Ps. 33:6, "By the Word of the Lord the heavens are made, and all their hosts by the Spirit of His mouth," Basil asserted that while three persons are named: the Lord, His Word, and His Spirit, yet David did not acknowledge more than one creator. The Lord does not act separately, nor does the Word act separately; nor does the Breath act separately. All three persons work *ad extra* in full unity with himself as one God in creation, as in salvation. Creation is a work performed exclusively by God, but because Scripture attributes the operations of creation to the Spirit, then the Spirit's deity is affirmed. The Spirit cannot be separated in being and act from the Father and the Son. He is united with them in being the cause of everything that exists. So when thinking of creation, he advised:

> [F]irst think of Him who is the first cause of everything that exists: namely, the Father, and then of the Son, who is the creator, and then the Holy Spirit, the perfector . . . The Originator of all things is One: He creates through the Son and perfects through the Spirit. The Father's work is in no way imperfect, since He accomplishes all in all, nor is the Son's work deficient if it is not completed by the Spirit. The Father creates through His will alone and does not need the Son, yet chooses to work through the Son. Like the Son works as the Father's likeness, and needs no other cooperation, but He chooses to have His work completed through the Spirit.⁶⁴

I Cor. 2:11 also adds to the support of the dignity of the Spirit. Here Basil adopted a form of argument from human personality

---

⁶¹ *De Spiritu Sancto* 8.17.
⁶² *On the Spirit* 23.54.
⁶³ *On the Spirit* 19.49.
⁶⁴ *On the Spirit* 16.38. See Thomas F. Torrance, *The Trinitarian Faith*

to divine personality. Analogously, the Spirit is to God just as the spirit of man is to man. The Spirit cannot be a creature, for he searches the deep things of God, a work which is beyond the possibility of a created being, but solely divine. Therefore the Spirit is not of a nature alien to God, just as the human person is not of a nature alien to him. The Spirit "is said to have the same relationship to God as the spirit within us has to us: 'For what person knows a man's thoughts except the spirit of the man which is in him? So no one comprehends the thoughts of God except the Spirit of God.'" That the Spirit is the revealer of the mysteries of God is "the greatest proof" of his deity.[65]

For Athanasius, Psalm 36:9, "In Thy light do we see light," was a proof for the Son's deity: "In as much as the Father is eternal, his Radiance, who is his Logos, is eternal."[66] To rephrase the words of the psalm: "In Thy light [that is, in the Radiance or the Son] we see the light [that is, the light of the Father]." The same text became instead a proof for the Spirit's deity in Basil's treatise. So the light in which the saint sees the light of God was not the light of Christ as the revealer, but "the illumination of the Spirit, the true light that enlightens every man that comes into the world."[67] It was Athanasius' position, and the consensus of the tradition that the Johannine phrase in Jn. 1:9, "the true light that enlightens every man," is exclusively a reference to the unique status of the Second Person of the Trinity. However by applying the Christological phrase to the Third Person, Basil attributed the same unique status to the Spirit. As true light, the Spirit works as the Son does in revelation, this very work that rightly belongs to God. Thus the Spirit and the Son mutually coinhere in being and in the external indivisible work of revelation. The Spirit enables the saint to behold the glory of the Only-begotten, the true

---

(Edinburgh: T & T Clark, 1988), 228; Lewis Ayres, *Nicaea and Its Legacy: An Approach to Fourth-Century Trinitarian Theology* (Oxford: Oxford University Press, 2004), 196.

[65] *On the Spirit* 16.40.

[66] Athanasius, *Contra Arians* 1.7.25 as cited in Pelikan, "The 'Spiritual Sense' of Scripture," 342.

[67] *On the Spirit* 18.47.

light. He does this not from "outside sources," but from himself "personally."[68]

Just as what is done by one person is done by all three in a differentiated unity, so conversely what is done by us to one person is done to the same Godhead. So to sin against the Spirit is to sin against God. Underlying Acts 5:3–4 is Basil's identification of the Spirit as essentially one with God.

> Let our opponents determine what place they will give to the Holy Spirit. Will they rank Him with God, or will they push him down to a creature's place? Peter said to Sapphira, 'How is it that you have agreed together to tempt the Spirit of the Lord? You have not lied to men but to God,' and this shows that to sin against the Holy Spirit is to sin against God. Understanding from this is that in every operation, the Holy Spirit is indivisibly united with the Father and the Son.[69]

The common rejection by the world of the Father, Son, and Holy Spirit adds to the evidence of their natural communion and essential unity. The world, conceived as "life enslaved by carnal passions," does not know the Spirit (14:17); nor does it know the Father (17:25); nor does it see the Son (14:19). As indicated earlier, glorification of one person is predicated of all three in the one Godhead. Likewise rejection of the Spirit alone is predicated of all three, thus of the same Godhead. This shows that the Spirit cannot be separated from the Godhead. He derives glory from his association with the Father and the Son, and Jesus' own testimony in Mt. 12:32: "Every sin and blasphemy will be forgiven men; but the blasphemy against the Holy Spirit will not be forgiven."[70]

There is an overlap between the Spirit's deeds and his gifts. The latter too forms a distinct argument for the Spirit's deity. The principal gift is salvation, along with numerous blessings including "knowledge of the future, understanding of the mysteries, apprehension of hidden things, distribution of wonderful gifts, heavenly citizenship, a place in a choir of angels [worship], endless joy in the presence, becoming like God, and, the highest of all desires, becoming God."[71] The Spirit fashions the soul into a temple for God to dwell so that it could partake of what he

---

[68] *On the Spirit* 18.47.
[69] *On the Spirit* 16.37.
[70] *On the Spirit* 18.46.
[71] *On the Spirit* 9.23.

lavishly bestows. The Spirit sanctifies the soul, the temple in which he dwells, and illuminates its eyes so that it might behold in him both the Son and Father.

> Like the sun, He will show you in Himself the image of the invisible, and with purified eyes you will see in this blessed image the unspeakable beauty of its prototype. Through Him hearts are lifted up, the infirm are held by the hand, and those who progress are brought to perfection. He shines upon those who are cleansed from every spot, and makes them spiritual men through fellowship with Himself.[72]

The Spirit is of God, the breath of his mouth; he possesses the power to sanctify; how can he be a mere creature? Being sanctified by the Spirit, the soul is enabled to fulfill the goal of its existence: deification. Basil's deification doctrine has its root in the Alexandrian theology of Athanasius, whose definition was moral and ethical, not essential.[73] Only by the Spirit is God's sanctification accomplished, and we can partake of the heavenly blessings: our ascension to the Kingdom of heaven, our adoption as God's children, our freedom to call God our Father, and sharing in eternal glory.[74] For instance, to adopt as children of God cannot be the work of any other than God. The Spirit is the causative agency of our adoption, as the Apostle says in Rom. 8. Therefore the Spirit cannot be a creature but must be God.

Based on I Corinthians 14:24–25, "But if all prophesy, and an unbeliever or outsider enters, he is convicted by all, he is called to account by all, the secrets of his heart are disclosed; and so, falling on his face, he will worship God and declare that God is really among you," Basil drew out the implications of Paul's teaching concerning the Spirit: "If God is recognized to be present among prophets because their prophesying is a gift of the Spirit, let our opponents determine what place they will give to the Holy Spirit. Will they rank Him with God, or will they push him down to

---

[72] *On the Spirit* 9.23.

[73] Athanasius, *On the Incarnation*, tr. & ed. by Sister Penelope Lawson (New York: MacMillan Publishing Co., 1946), VIII.54. Cf. Gregory of Nazianzus, *The Fifth Theological Oration: On the Spirit*, in *Christology of the Later Fathers*, ed. Edward R. Handy, vol. 3 of *The Library of Christian Classics* (Philadelphia: Westminster Press, 1954), 31.10, 199.

[74] *On the Spirit* 15.36.

a creature's place?"⁷⁵ In respect to the distribution of gifts in the Corinthian congregation, Paul offered a trinitarian interpretation: "Now there are varieties of gifts, but the same Spirit; and there are varieties of services, but the same Lord; and there are varieties of workings, but it is the same God who inspires them all in everyone . . . All these are inspired by one and the same Spirit, who apportions to each one individually just as He wills" (I Cor. 12:4–6, 11).[76] By ruminating on this passage, he deduced his conclusion that the Spirit is not separated from the Father and the Son, and that all three conspire together in the dispensation of gifts. It is the Father who originates the gifts, the Son who sends them, and the Spirit who inspires in us an appropriation of them. Priority, not superiority, is due to the Spirit, who brings into perfection the gifts of the one and same God. This passage evinces an order, not of essence (*ordo essendi*) but of experience (*ordo cognoscendi*), in which gratitude is offered, first to the Spirit, then the Son, and finally the Father.

> God works in various ways, and the Lord serves in various capacities, but the Holy Spirit is also present of His own will, dispensing gifts to everyone according to each man's worth . . . Just because the Apostle in the above passage mentions the Spirit first, and the Son second, and God the Father third, do not assume that he has reversed their rank. Notice that he [Paul] is speaking the same way we do when we receive gifts: first we thank the messenger [Spirit] who brought the gift; next we remember him [Son] who sent it, and finally we raise our thoughts to the fountain and source of all gifts [Father].[77]

Additionally, in the distribution of these gifts, the Spirit's activity was understood as that of one who "is simple in being; his powers are manifold: they are wholly present everywhere and in everything. He is distributed but does not change. He is shared, yet remains whole."[78] The divine attributes of simplicity, omnipotence, omnipresence, immutability, and indivisibility are predicated of the Spirit. Thus the being of the Spirit is consubstantial with God.

Therefore the same glory, attributed to the God and Father of our Lord Jesus Christ and the Only-begotten Son, is attributed to

---

[75] *On the Spirit* 16.37.
[76] *On the Spirit* 16.37.
[77] *On the Spirit* 16.37.
[78] *On the Spirit* 9.22.

the Spirit: "He is divine in nature, infinite in greatness, mighty in His works, good in His blessings; shall we not exalt Him; shall we not glorify Him? I reckon that this 'glorifying' is nothing else but the recounting of His own wonders."[79] Grasping, even partially, the major works of the Spirit as in creation, sanctification, revelation, illumination and adoption inevitably exalts us to praise the Spirit's unapproachable nature. Basil unequivocally declared: "Understanding all this, how can we be afraid of giving the Spirit too much honor? We should fear that even though we ascribe to Him the highest titles we can devise or our tongues pronounce, our ideas about Him might still fall short?"[80]

Prepositional Uses in Scripture And Tradition

The customary form for the Greek Christian worship was "Glory to the Father *through* (*dia*) the Son *in* (*en*) the Holy Spirit?"[81] The form, "Glory to the Father *with* (*meta*) the Son together *with* (*syn*) the Holy Spirit," is the point at which Basil was attacked for being nontraditional and innovative.[82] In his rebuttal, Basil saw the importance of the different prepositional uses in Scripture. Warning against an intellectual idleness that counts theological terminology as secondary, he wrote: "Instruction begins with the proper use of speech, and syllables and words are the elements of speech. Therefore to scrutinize syllables is not a superfluous task . . . Hunting truth is no easy task; we must look everywhere for its tracks . . . If a man spurns fundamental elements as insignificant trifles, he will never embrace the fullness of wisdom."[83] The prepositions used in doxologies contain deeper meaning than at first glance. More crucially, Basil saw behind the attack of the Pneumatomachians a greater theological opposition:

> These are the reasons for their vexation: they say that the Son is not equal with the Father, but comes after the Father. Therefore it follows that glory should be ascribed to the Father *through* Him, but

---

[79] *On the Spirit* 15.36.
[80] *On the Spirit* 19.49.
[81] Anderson's Introduction, *On the Spirit*, 11.
[82] *On the Spirit* 6.13.
[83] *On the Spirit* 7.16.

not *with* Him. *With* Him expresses equality but *through* Him indicates subordination.[84]

The immediate implication of this prepositional reticence on the part of his opponents becomes apparent in relation to the third person of the Trinity, that if the Son is subordinate to the Father, then the Spirit is placed on an even lower plane. The main feature of this heresy concerns its ontological subordination of the Spirit, according to which the Spirit cannot be "ranked with the Father or the Son, but under the Father and the Son, not in the same order of things as they are, but beneath them, not numbered with them."[85] As a result, the heretics "divide and tear away the Spirit from the Father, transforming His nature to that of a ministering spirit."[86]

The dissimilar prepositions, according to the Pneumatomachians, are "made to indicate a corresponding nature."[87] Based on I Cor. 8:6, "there is but one God, the Father, from whom all things came and from whom we live, and there is but one Lord, Jesus Christ, through whom all things came and through whom we live," they argued that *from* refers to the Father, *through* refers to the Son, *in which* would most appropriately refer to the Spirit.[88] And these prepositions were teleologically designed to describe the differences of nature between the Father, Son, and Spirit, since each corresponds to his specific nature, totally alien from the others. Contrarily Basil considered such reasoning unbiblical, but philosophically based on the four Aristotelian causes: formal, material, efficient, and final.[89] He spoke of the disastrous result of this technical discussion of prepositions: "Cause (*from*) has one nature, an instrument (*through*) has another, and place (*in*) yet another. So the Son's nature is alien to the Father's, since the tool is by nature different from the craftsman, and the nature of the Spirit is foreign to both, since place and time are different from tools or those who handle them."[90] These temporal aspects of causality, Basil argued, are inapplicable to an uncreated being

---

[84] *On the Spirit* 7.16.
[85] *On the Spirit* 6.13.
[86] *On the Spirit* 10.25.
[87] *On the Spirit* 2.4.
[88] *On the Spirit* 2.4.
[89] *On the Spirit* 3.5.
[90] *On the Spirit* 4.6.

like God. He then went on to demonstrate the wide variety of prepositional usages as descriptions of the essence and activity of the three persons. *From which* can refer to the Father as well as inanimate objects as wood and clay. Its use is not restricted to the Father, and cannot be used to support a distinction of natures. Differences in prepositions were meant to distinguish between the Persons and to describe the union of one identical nature that interpenetrates among the three Persons without confusion. His position is enhanced by resorting to Rom. 11:36, "for *from* him and *through* him and *to* him are all things." This shows up the errors of his opponents' exegesis, for these dissimilar prepositions predicated of the Son do not support a distinction, but an identity of nature. He continued: *from whom* can refer to the Son (Eph. 4:15–16; Col. 2:19; Jn. 1:16; Lk. 8:46), and also to the Spirit (Gal. 6:8; I Jn. 3:24; Lk. 1:20). The same preposition used of three persons does not support three alien natures. *Through whom* or *by whom* can refer to the Father (I Cor. 1:9; II Cor. 1:11; Rom. 6:4; Isa. 19:15), and also the Spirit (II Tim. 1:14; I Cor. 12:8). Preposition *in* are used in relation to the Father (Ps. 108:13; 89:16; II Thess. 1:1; Rom. 1:10; 2:17), and also to the Son and the Spirit, of which biblical instances are plentiful. The afore-discussed inevitably leads Basil to conclude: "But I cannot refrain from remarking that the 'wise hearer' may easily discover that if terminological differences indicate differences in nature, then our opponents must shamefully agree that identical terminology is used for identical natures."[91]

His prepositional definition lends support to the Spirit's immanental relationship with the Father and the Son within the same Godhead. The doxological language, "Glory to the Father *with* the Son, together *with* the Holy Spirit," points to the union of identical nature between the three persons. Basil knew far too well that his *with* doxology was not contained in Scripture. Even so, it cannot be established from Scripture that prepositions must be confined to a particular person of the Trinity. The various prepositions in Scripture which were used for the persons of the Trinity support Basil's specific use of *with* to accentuate the unity of the Son and the Spirit with the Father.

Basil knew of no place in Scripture where the doxology championed by the Pneumatomachians was found. The doxological phrases beginning with *through* and *in* are found in Scripture,

---

[91] *On the Spirit* 5.11.

he argued, yet not one instance that conforms precisely to their championed doxology, "Glory to the Father *through* the Son *in* the Holy Spirit," can be found in Scripture.[92] Basil's point was that his opponents also appealed to custom or tradition to justify their doxology. They, in their insistence that *with* is alien, while *through* is biblical, are themselves guilty of theological innovation. Rather the Church endorses both Christological usages, for there is no contradiction between them. As stated earlier, the phrase *with him* denotes the Son's relationship with his Father; the phrase *through him* denotes our relationship with him, in which his grace comes to us. Correspondingly the same pattern transpires in Basil's pneumatology. The phrase *with them* denotes the communion of the Spirit within the Trinity, and thus justifies a doxology proper to the Spirit, who is inseparably united with the Father and the Son; the phrase *in us* expresses our relationship with the Spirit, or the situations where the Spirit works grace in us. These two sets of theological terminology complement each other: one describes God as God – the one living Being equally shared by the Father, Son and Spirit – the proper object of our worship, and another describes God's work of salvation in us through the Son by the Spirit, the befitting cause of our gratitude.

> As far as His relationship to the Father and the Son is concerned, it is more appropriate to say that He dwells *with* them rather than *in* them . . . Whenever the union between things is intimate, natural, and inseparable, it is more appropriate to use *with* since this word suggests an indivisible union. On the other hand, in situations where the grace of the Spirit comes and goes, it is more proper to say that the Spirit exists *in* someone, even in the case of well-disposed persons with whom He abides continually. Therefore, when we consider the Spirit's rank, we think of Him as present *with* the Father and the Son, but when we consider the working of His grace on its recipients, we say that the Spirit is *in* us.[93]

There is another approach in Basil's use of the distinction between *with* and *in*.[94] He observed in certain texts that when the

---

[92] *On the Spirit* 25.58.
[93] *On the Spirit* 26.63.
[94] David Rainey, "The Argument for the Deity of the Holy Spirit according to St. Basil the Great, Bishop of Caesarea" (ThM Thesis, Vancouver School of Theology, 1991), 38.

preposition *in* is used, *with* is actually intended. This is not his innovation, but is borne out by the context which determines its definition. For instance, Ps. 65:13 reads, "I will go into thine house *in* burnt offerings," in which the preposition *in* actually signifies *with*. Similarly Ps. 104:37 reads, "He brought them out *in* silver and gold," or Ps. 43:9, "Thou wilt not go forth *in* our armies." All these verses indicate that the preposition *in* carries the force as *with*. While his enemies preferred the expression *in the Spirit*, which to them designates degrees of dignity, Basil used both *with* and *in the Spirit* as interchangeable expressions of a dignity just as lofty. This approach strengthens the theological presupposition that the Spirit is ranked equal with the Father and the Son, not under or outside them. Basil's use of the preposition *with* in his doxology spells the absolute death of any subordinationism and Sabellianism, for the preposition affirms both "eternal communion [of one essence] and unceasing cooperation [of distinct persons]."[95]

Basil's criticism of his opponents springs from his love of both Scripture and tradition. The phrase *with whom* has been preserved unchanged as the tradition of the Fathers. Basil esteemed so highly the traditions of the Fathers that he stated, "If we attacked unwritten customs, claiming them to be of little importance, we would fatally mutilate the gospel."[96] It was Basil's concession that without the unwritten tradition (liturgical or doctrinal), the true meaning of the written Scriptures might escape our grasping. He enumerated well-known fathers in the Church who have used the doxological form *"with* the Spirit." For instances, Dionysius of Alexandria, in his second letter, on *Conviction and Defence*, concluded with these words: "Since we have received a form and a rule from the presbyters who have gone before us, we offer thanksgiving in harmony with them, and following everything they have taught us, we conclude our letter to you. To God the Father, and the Son our Lord Jesus Christ, *with* the Holy Spirit be glory and dominion unto ages of ages. Amen."[97] Eusebius of Caesarea, too, invoked "the holy God of the prophets, the Giver of Light, through our Savior Jesus Christ, *with* the Holy Spirit."[98] The notable Origen, in the eighth chapter of his *Commentary on*

---

[95] *On the Spirit* 25.59.
[96] *On the Spirit* 27.66.
[97] *On the Spirit* 29.72.
[98] *On the Spirit* 29.72.

the Gospel according to John, clearly declared that the Spirit is to be worshipped: "The washing with water is a symbol of spiritual washing, when the filth of wickedness is washed away from the soul. Nevertheless, if a man submits himself to the Godhead of the adorable Trinity, this washing will become the source and fountain of graces for him, through the power of the invocation."[99] And again, Basil quoted Origen's *Commentary on the Epistle of Romans*: "The holy powers are able to reflect the Only-begotten, and the divinity of the Holy Spirit."[100] This form of doxology was not unknown even to Julius Africanus the historian, who in his *Epitome of the Times*, wrote: "We who are acquainted with the meaning of prophecy, and are not ignorant of the grace of faith, offer thanks to the Father, who gave Jesus Christ, the Savior of all and our Lord, to us, His own creatures. Glory and majesty be to Him, *with* the Holy Spirit, unto all ages."[101] These churchmen apprehended the power of the unwritten tradition in true religion. Basil held in high regard this "familiar and dear" word *with* of the saints: "From the day when the Gospel was first preached even until now, it has been welcomed by the churches, and, most importantly of all, has been defined in conformity to righteousness and true religion."[102] Both Scripture and tradition "have equal force in true religion. No one would deny either source – no one, at any rate, who is even slightly familiar with the ordinances of the Church."[103] Did Basil propound a double authority? No. His point was that the validity of the tradition hinges on whether its teaching concurs with the meaning of Scripture. Scripture is the prior norm, to which tradition is subservient. Thus he stated his task: "It remains for me to describe the origin and force of the word '*with*' and to show that its usage is in accord with Scripture."[104]

---

[99] *On the Spirit* 29.73. Basil mistakenly put "sixth" chapter. See note 359.
[100] *On the Spirit* 29.73.
[101] *On the Spirit* 29.73.
[102] *On the Spirit* 29.75.
[103] *On the Spirit* 27.66.
[104] *On the Spirit* 27.65. See Amand de Mendieta, *The 'Unwritten' and 'Secret' Apostolic Tradition in the Theological Thought of St. Basil of Caesarea*, 27: "Putting a tremendous emphasis on the moment of the 'unwritten' tradition coming from the Apostles and the Fathers, Basil seems to

The Spirit within the Godhead: Necessity for Worship

To place the Spirit outside the Godhead, as the Pneumatomachians did, is tantamount to committing an unpardonable sin of blasphemy against the Spirit, and thus suffers eternal consequences: "How can we separate the Spirit from His life-giving power and associate him with things which by nature are lifeless? Who is so perverse; who is so devoid of the heavenly gift, so unnourished by God's good words; who is so empty of sharing eternal hopes, that he would separate the Spirit from the Godhead, and number Him among creatures?"[105] The doctrine of the deity of the Spirit has to be believed for one's salvation: "The Lord has delivered to us a necessary and saving dogma: the Holy Spirit is to be ranked with the Father."[106] Basil warned that those, who deny that the Spirit rightly belongs to the Godhead as the Father and the Son, are deprived of both salvation and true worship:

> If someone rejects the Spirit, his faith in the Father and the Son is made useless; it is impossible to believe in the Father and the Son without the presence of the Spirit. He who rejects the Spirit rejects the Son, and he who rejects the Son rejects the Father. "No one can say that 'Jesus is Lord' except in the Holy Spirit" (I Cor. 12:3), and "no one has ever seen God; the only begotten God, who is in the bosom of the Father, He has made Him known" (Jn. 1:18). Such a person has no part in true worship. It is impossible to worship the Son except in the Holy Spirit; it is impossible to call upon the Father except in the Spirit of adoption.[107]

The knowledge by which Christ is known as our redeemer is the domain of the Spirit. The Spirit's deity is necessary for the

---

place it on the same level as the 'written' and canonical tradition of the Church, namely the biblical books, and in particular the New Testament. But, according to Basil himself, the genuine 'unwritten' tradition of the Apostles and Fathers ought in fact to be in harmony with the sense of Scriptures."

[105] *On the Spirit* 24.56.
[106] *On the Spirit* 10.25.
[107] *On the Spirit* 11.27. For Calvin, the twin truths – salvation and worship – truly constitute the substances of Christianity. Calvin's thought is traceable to Basil's. See John Calvin, "The Necessity of Reforming the Church," see English translation in Calvin, *Tracts Relating to the Reformation*, vol. 1, tr. Henry Beveridge (Edinburgh: Calvin Translation

confession of Christ, otherwise nothing remains of faith, salvation, and worship.

As declared in the Constantinopolitan Creed, the Holy Spirit is Lord and Giver of Life, thus is in no sense a creature, but in every sense essentially God as the first two persons. If the Spirit who unites us to Christ is no more than a creature, and not fully and perfectly God, then our participation in Christ and all that he has done and continues to do for us are devoid of divine efficacy, and saving reality.[108] The Spirit subsists in God, and his activity is not apart from nor outside God but from within God. His activity is God's immediate activity, which draws us through Christ into the presence of God. In the language of causality, Basil spoke of "the original cause of all things that are made, the Father; . . . the creative cause, the Son; . . . the perfecting cause, the Spirit."[109] Here we are distinguishing, not separating what the three persons do, for they mutually coinhere in being and act. "To say that the Spirit is the perfecting cause of creation," Gunton wrote, "is to make the Spirit the eschatological person of the Trinity: the one who directs the creatures to where the creator wishes them to go, to their destiny as creatures."[110] In other words, the Spirit constitutes us as a new creation who would freely worship God through Christ as the proper end. By the perfecting causality of the Spirit, we are drawn through the Son into the heavenly sanctuary of divine grace and the intimacy of divine communion. The Spirit communicates to our hearts the gospel about a God who summons us into being, and includes us as his beloved in his inner life in which we partake of all the riches of God's being. The

---

Society, 1844), 126–27: "a knowledge, first, of the right way to worship God; and secondly of the source from which salvation is to be sought. When these are kept out of view, though we may glory in the name of Christians, our profession is empty and vain."

[108] See Thomas F. Torrance, *The Trinitarian Faith* (Edinburgh: T. & T. Clark, 1995), 5.

[109] *De Spiritu Sancto* 16.38. Cf. Calvin's *Institutes* 1.13.18. Following Basil, Calvin noted a distinctive action attributed to each person: "To the Father is the beginning of activity, and the fountain and wellspring of all things; to the Son, wisdom, counsel, and the ordered disposition of all things; but to the Spirit is assigned the power and efficacy of that activity."

[110] See Colin Gunton, *Father, Son and Holy Spirit: Essays Toward a Fully Trinitarian Theology* (London: T&T Clark, 2003), 81–82.

Spirit is the efficacy of God's work *in nobis* so that all the benefits Christ won are ours, if only we believe:

> Through the Holy Spirit comes our restoration to Paradise, our ascension to the Kingdom of heaven, our adoption as God's sons, our freedom to call God our Father, our becoming partakers of the grace of Christ, being called children of light, sharing in eternal glory, and in a word, our inheritance of the fullness of blessing, both in this world and the world to come. Even while we wait for the full enjoyment of the good things in store for us, by the Holy Spirit we are able to rejoice through faith in the promise of the graces to come.[111]

The focal point of the doxological form, "Glory to the Father *through* the Son *in* (*by*) the Holy Spirit," is the confession of the Spirit's deity as the dynamic of true worship. In confessing this doxology, we are not describing the Spirit's proximate relationship within the Godhead, but confessing our own weaknesses, and inability to glorify God on our own. Basil's understanding resonates with the position of Hilary who stated: "God cannot be comprehended except through God himself, and likewise God accepts no worship from us except through God himself . . . it is by God that we are initiated into the worship of God."[112] Through the Spirit, we share in the incarnate Son's communion with the Father, as Paul said in Gal. 4:6, "God has sent the Spirit of His Son into our hearts, crying 'Abba! Father!'" Only *in* the Spirit is our worship and access to God made efficacious:

> In Him we are able to thank God for the blessings we have received. To the extent that we are purified from evil, each receives a smaller or a larger portion of the Spirit's help, that each may offer the sacrifice of praise to God. If we offer glory to God *in* the Spirit, we mean that the Spirit enables us to fulfill the requirements of true religion. According to this usage, then, we say that we are *in* the Spirit, but it is not objectionable for someone to testify, 'the Spirit of God is *in* me, and I offer glory because His grace has given me the wisdom to do so.' The words of Paul are appropriate: 'I think that I have the Spirit

---

[111] *On the Spirit* 15.36.
[112] Cf. Hilary, *De Trinitate* 4:20 as cited in Philip W. Butin, "Reformed Ecclesiology: Trinitarian Grace According to Calvin", in *Studies in Reformed Theology and History*, ed. David Willis-Watkins (Princeton: Princeton Theological Seminary, 1994), 26, n. 81.

of God' (I Cor. 7:40), and 'guard the truth that has been entrusted to you by the Holy Spirit who dwells within us' (II Tim.1:14).[113]

In the life of worship, John 4:24, "God is Spirit, and his worshippers must worship Him in Spirit and in Truth," was of great importance to Basil.[114] For him, the text is a reference to Christ (Truth) and the Spirit: both constitute the manner and basis of worship. Just as the Father is made known *in* the Son, so also the Son is recognized *in* the Spirit. Likewise the worship of the Father in the Son is made possible *in* (*by*) the Spirit. The Father moves toward us in Christ, whose presence is felt in worship that we might share with him his own communion with the Father. This cannot happen without the Spirit's help. To put it in another way: the Spirit reveals Christ to us in worship, and through him enables us to offer to God both our being and act in thanksgiving and praise. To worship *in* the Spirit means that

> our intelligence has been enlightened . . . If we say that worship offered *in* the Son [the Truth] is worshipped *in* the Father's Image, we can say the same about worship offered *in* the Spirit since the Spirit in Himself reveals the divinity of the Lord. The Holy Spirit cannot be divided from the Father and the Son in worship. If you remain outside the Spirit, you cannot worship, and if you are in Him you cannot separate Him from God. Light cannot be separated from what it makes visible, and it is impossible for you to recognize Christ, the Image of the invisible God, unless the Spirit enlightens you. Once you see the Image, you cannot ignore the light; you see the Light and Image simultaneously. It is fitting that when we see Christ, the Brightness of God's glory, it is always through the illumination of the Spirit.[115]

Basil found such understanding of worship *in* the Spirit in the Old Testament. Juxtaposed with the Johannine text were the Old Testament passages in which the Spirit is understood not spatially, but figuratively as a "place" in which people are sanctified to participate in the holy of holies.[116] Words that carry a physical meaning are often transposed to a spiritual plane, for the sake of clarifying the truth behind them. Thus the figurative language (place) used of the Spirit does not downgrade, but rather glorifies

---

[113] *On the Spirit* 26.63.
[114] Pelikan, "The 'Spiritual Sense' of Scripture," 345.
[115] *On the Spirit* 26.64.
[116] *On the Spirit* 26.62.

him. For instance, when God says to Moses in Exodus 33:21, "Behold, there is a place by Me: thou shalt stand upon the rock," the "place" Basil understood as a reference to the Spirit, in whom God became recognizable by Moses. "Only in this 'special' place can true worship be offered."[117] The sacrifice indicated in Deut. 12:13–14 Basil interpreted as the sacrifice of praise offered by the Church to God. As prescribed in the Law, for the sacrifice of praise to be efficacious, it must be offered *in* the Spirit, "a place which the Lord shall choose."[118] It is in the Spirit, "the place of the saints," that the Church can offer doxology to God. This teaching, Basil claimed, came from the Lord himself, who taught us to worship God *in* Spirit and in Christ (Truth). For Basil, the Spirit is the dwelling place of the saint; conversely the saint is a suitable habitation of the Spirit, as the allusion to I Cor. 3:16 shows.[119] Just as Paul speaks *in* Christ, so also Christ speaks *in* Paul (II Cor. 2:17; 3:13). The same pattern occurs in reference to the Spirit: just as Paul utters mysteries *in* the Spirit, the Spirit does the same *in* Paul (I Cor. 14.2). Only *in the Spirit* does our worship offered *in* (through) the Son reach the Fatherly sanctuary; conversely the Spirit *in* us enables us, those whom he sanctifies, to engage in the contemplation and worship of the Godhead. In any case, the Spirit's deity is the power of efficacy of the Church's worship.

The Double Movements of the Trinity: Divine Descent and Human Ascent

Athanasius summed up the double movement in a statement which became normative in the patristic church: "God became human so that human beings should be deified."[120] The first part points to divine descent (*katabasis*), while the second points to human ascent (*anabasis*). The divine descent presupposes the sending of the Son; the human ascent presupposes the homecoming of the Son to glory, but with our humanity eternally attached. The Spirit is the power of efficacy of both movements in us. Basil too talked about

---

[117] *On the Spirit* 26.62.
[118] *On the Spirit* 26.62.
[119] *On the Spirit* 26.62.
[120] Athanasius, *De Incarnatione*, chap. 54 as cited in Jürgen Moltmann, *The Spirit of Life: A Universal Affirmation* (Minneapolis: Fortress, 1993), 299.

these two movements, but with an emphasis on the second.[121] The descending movement is *from* Father *through* the Son *in* the Spirit; the ascending movement is *from* the Spirit *through* the Son *to* the Father. The economic actions of the Trinity sum up the two sides of salvation history, which proceeds "from God" and leads "to God." On the one hand, there is God's activity from above to below, concerning which Basil wrote, "[N]atural goodness, inherent holiness and royal dignity reaches from the Father through the Only-begotten to the Spirit."[122] On the other hand, there is God's activity from below to above, of which Basil wrote, "The Spirit reveals the true glory of the Only-Begotten in Himself, and He gives true worshippers the knowledge of God in himself. The way to divine knowledge ascends from one Spirit through the one Son to the one Father."[123] The implication of this double movement for worship is that on the one hand, it is God who comes to us as human, revealing himself as the object of worship in the dynamic of the Spirit who is of the same being with the first two persons; on the other hand, by the Spirit we are led to participate in the incarnate Son's ascending movement to the Father, which includes access to the holy of holies. By the Spirit, who is not numbered with any creaturely beings, but with the Father and Son, we are drawn into his intimacy with them in the same uncreated Deity. The Spirit's proximity with the first two persons enables our communion with God, in which we enjoy the benefits of the Son's ascension to the right hand of the Father.

While the Father, Son and Spirit are personally distinct, they are inseparably united in the uncompounded nature and communion of the Godhead, and in the three-fold activity toward us. The unity of the monarchy is maintained along with the indivisible operations of three persons. Without an interval of time, the grace that reaches us from the Father through the Son in the Spirit is the same which leads us home, through the Son to the Father in the Spirit. This constituted what Basil called the "true" doctrine: "Their oneness consists in the communion of the Godhead."[124] The two-way activity of God in revelation and worship does not

---

[121] Moltmann, *The Spirit of Life*, 300; Hanson, *The Christian Doctrine of God*, 777.
[122] *On the Spirit* 18.47.
[123] *On the Spirit* 18.47.
[124] *De Spiritu Sancto*, 45 as cited in Torrance, *The Christian Doctrine of God*, 127.

compromise the oneness of being, for it is the same God who acts in a differentiated unity of his economic and immanent self-communication as the undivided and ever-blessed Trinity. The double movement is a tripersonal activity *ad extra* of the one God in a differentiated unity with himself.[125] With clarity, Basil asserted: "We worship God from God, confessing the uniqueness of the persons, while maintaining the unity of the monarchy."[126] Just as God cannot be known except through God himself, so it is with our worship, that God deems no worship except through God himself. Basil's doctrine of the union of divine operations grounds worship as a trinitarian activity, originated from the Father, effected through the Son and perfected in the Spirit. There is no work of God in which the members of the Trinity are not jointly operative. This is true of creation, redemption and worship. It is by the perfecting causality of the Spirit that the Church's worship offered in the Son reaches the Father. As a perfector, the Spirit leads us to the Son, through whom our being and our act (worship) have free access to the Fatherly sanctuary in the same Godhead. Only Spirit-perfected worship is true worship. Not only the Spirit joined through the Son to the Father is the proper object, but also the causative agency of worship, the one who exalts the community in Christ to the heavenly throne of the Father. Or to put it differently, as Gunton did: "we worship the Spirit, the one through whom we worship."[127] The unitive movement of the Spirit in which we participate is the presupposition of an efficacious worship. Worship as such is a gift of grace: what God begins in us he shall complete. God is the *alpha*, and the *omega* of worship. The reverential knowledge of God in Christ by faith is the action of the Holy Spirit, the completion of the all-praised blessed Trinity.

Conclusion

It is primarily as a theologian of the Spirit that Basil stands out.[128] Despite his restraint in the usage of the word *homoousios*,

---

[125] *On the Spirit* 18.47.
[126] *On the Spirit* 18.45.
[127] *Father, Son & Holy Spirit*, 84.
[128] Cf. Anthony Meredith, *The Cappadocians* (Crestwood: Geoffrey Chapman, 1995), 30.

he contributed to what was later affirmed in the Council of Constantinople (381) concerning the Spirit. The Spirit is to be glorified with the Father and the Son because he is the same in nature and not inferior in dignity from them. Praiseworthy is his attempt to show the necessity of the Spirit's deity as the effective agency of salvation and worship. Contemplating the meaning of the Spirit's names, acts and gifts directs our thoughts on high, and thus necessarily leads to the proper conclusion that the Spirit is God. Hence doxology is proper to the Spirit, whose ineffable dignity is an ontological derivative of his eternal relationship with the Father and the Son. With his insistence on the third person, which was characteristic of all the main theologians of his time against the Pneumatomachians, Basil succeeded in turning the Arian question into a fully trinitarian one.[129] Since then, the place of the Spirit in the Trinity began to be given lawful attention. This was in no way his invention. For the Council of Nicaea had already affirmed its faith in the Spirit, and Athanasius in learning of the subordination doctrine of the opponents was intransigent in condemning it. But Basil's treatise *On the Spirit* represents a significant landmark for the definitive introduction of the Holy Spirit in the Arian controversy, and his pneumatological insights continue to shape the subsequent thinking, including that of the protestant reformers.[130] Most significantly it was with this celebrated work that communion as an ontological category gained much attention subsequently. The Spirit himself, in being consubstantial with God, is that ever-living two-way communion between the Father and the Son. God's being as communion excludes any unipersonal view of God or tritheistic conception of Holy Trinity, but magnifies an onto-relational dynamism of the Father, Son and Spirit in the one living Being of God.

---

[129] Gonzalez, *A History of Christian Thought*, 318.
[130] Cf. David F. Wright, "Basil the Great in the Protestant Reformers," *Studia Patristica* 17 (1982): 1149–55.

Chapter Two

The Necessary Reason for Worship: On Praising the Superlative Deity in St. Anselm's *Proslogion*

Introduction

Anselm's *Proslogion* must be read in context, i.e., meditation and intent.[1] He takes as his methodological starting point the Augustinian motto of "faith seeking understanding" in order to bring out the reality of who God is.[2] The ontological argument of *Proslogion* is not an apologetic tool used to convert people to faith or to relieve people of doubt, because they are already believers. Rather it intends to furnish for the believer, not the fool, a more thoroughly explicit and integrated explanation for the things

---

[1] For Anselm's writings, see *The Prayers and Meditations of St. Anselm with the Proslogion*, tr. Sister Benedicta Ward (London: Penguin Books, 1973); *Anselm of Canterbury: The Major Works*, eds. Brian Davies and Gillian R. Evans (Oxford: Oxford University Press, 1998); *Anselm of Canterbury*, ed. & tr. Jasper Hopkins and Herbert Richardson (London: SCM Press, 1974); F. S. Schmitt, *Sancti Anselmi Opera Omnia*, 6 vols. (Edinburgh: Thomas Nelson & Sons, 1939–61). Hereafter cited as Ward, Davies, Hopkins, and S respectively.

[2] For a discussion of Anselm's relation with Augustine, see Robert D. Crouse, "Anselm of Canterbury and Medieval Augustinianism," *Toronto Journal of Theology* 3 (1987): 60–68.

which we know for certain. This intent, for his work to affect the believer, is reaffirmed in the preface of Anselm's *Contra Gaunilo*: "it will be enough for me to reply to the Christian."[3] Abiding at the center of his writing is the question of fittingness: what must be because it ought to be. His endeavor is summed up at the end of Anselm's reply to *Gaunilo*:

> For the import of this proof is in itself of such force that what is spoken of is proved (as a necessary consequence of the fact that it is understood or thought of) both to exist in actual reality and to be itself whatever must be believed about the Divine Being. For we believe of the Divine Being whatever it can, absolutely speaking, be thought better to be than not to be . . . It is, then, necessary that 'that-than-which-a greater-cannot-be-thought' *should be* whatever *must be believed* about the Divine nature.[4]

Taken as a whole, *Proslogion's* content is broader than its famous ontological proof which occupies only two of the twenty-six chapters. Had we only the ontological argument of chapters 2–4, Anselm's deity would seem a very disinterested figure. In succeeding chapters, Anselm reflected on the attributes of God in a way no different from how a Platonist would have done. But this in no way means that his discussions are removed from any passionate involvement with God. The being of God and his aesthetic attributes, which he apprehended by means of meditation and reason, are the templates from which his understanding of worship is to be deduced. The more passionate discussion of God occurs in the latter chapters where he dwelt on the blessings the triune God bestows freely and extravagantly. The revelation of God and his intimate relation with Anselm looms large from chapter 23 onward. There, he went further both in the understanding of God, and in the response which necessarily follows. The latter chapters conclude with an extended doxology, praising the triune God for the revelation of his beauty, and for the innumerable benefits, which are now enjoyed by those who seek him, here in a great hope but there in full reality. In worship, God may be experienced through enjoying, for the very purpose of insight is nothing other

---

[3] Contra Gaunilo, Preface; S. 1.21.23–1.22.2.
[4] Anselm, "Reply to Gaunilo," 10, Davies, *Anselm*, 120–21, as cited in David S. Hogg, *Anselm of Canterbury* (Aldershot: Ashgate, 2004), 97. Translation and italics are Hogg's.

than "the fullness of joy" which is promised by the Son, and is communicated to our hearts by the Holy Spirit.

Our task here is to demonstrate that the import of the fiduciary utterance in *Proslogion*, "that than which nothing greater can be thought," is of such great force that God must be believed as such, and thus *worshipped* as such. God is the divine superlative because his nature demands it, and causally it creates in us a worshipping response that is rationally fitting.[5] For Anselm, the moment of understanding is precisely the moment of doxology. What must be believed about God becomes the necessary reason for worship. He began his journey with prayer and meditation, and consequently received an understanding of God which permitted him entrance into the superlative fullness, which is "the joy of the Lord," the Blessed Trinity.

Anselm's Fiduciary Formula: "That Than Which Nothing Greater Can be Conceived"

In his preface to *Proslogion*, Anselm described how he strives to find the "one argument" sufficient by itself to show "that God really exists, that He is the supreme good needing no other and is He whom all things have need of for their being and well-being, and also to prove whatever we believe about the Divine Being."[6] After a long and frustrating struggle, the "one argument" came to him in a moment of grace and caused him to burst into joy.[7] Encapsulated in this argument is Anselm's fiduciary formula, "that than which nothing greater can be thought."[8] He assumed that from this formula, God's existence and his nature could be deduced. He restated this in his reply to Gaunilo: "this idea – 'that than which nothing greater can be thought' – proves through itself about itself (*de se per se ipsum probat*)."[9] "The formula to refer to

---

[5] Cf. Oliver Johnson, "God and Anselm," *Journal of Religion* 45 (1965): 326; Katherine Rogers, "Anselm on praising a necessarily perfect being," *International Journal for Philosophy of Religion* 34 (1993): 41–52.
[6] Davies, *Anselm*, 82.
[7] Davies, *Anselm*, xii.
[8] Ward, *Prayers and Meditations*, 245.
[9] Hopkins, 130 as cited in Jos Decorte, "Saint Anselm of Canterbury on Ultimate Reality and Meaning," *Ultimate Reality and Meaning* 12 (1988): 184.

the object of the proof," Decorte claims, "is also the means of the proof: one argument needing nothing else except itself to prove itself: *De se per se ipsum probat.*"[10] Anselm's formula seemingly parallels that of Augustine who writes: "God is not really known in the sound of these two syllables (*Deus*), but this sound, when it strikes the ears of all who know Latin, moves them to think of some most excellent and immortal nature . . . For when God is thought of, our thought tries to reach something than which nothing is better or more sublime."[11] Both Southern and Davies go further to say that Anselm's formula has its connection with Seneca (c.5BC–AD65), according to whom God's "magnitude is that than which nothing greater can be thought."[12] We cannot be sure where Anselm finds it, nonetheless it surely provides him with the starting point he needs for his proof.

The contemplative approach to learning about God involves a withdrawal from the impression of bodily senses and an entrance into a quiet place within the mind. As the subject-matter of rational investigation, God is present not as a passive observer but an active agency with whom Anselm repeatedly consults for understanding.[13] As a religious treatise from start to finish, Anselm's *Proslogion* comes as a result of a long meditation and prayer, and is written in the form of a prayer. *Proslogion* opens with a long introductory invocation, pleading for divine assistance in his faith-seeking-understanding enterprise.[14] It ends with him declaring that his aim in what follows is to achieve a proper understanding of God from a faith stance: "I do not seek to understand so that I may believe. But I believe so that I may understand. And what is more,

---

[10] Decorte, "Saint Anselm of Canterbury on Ultimate Reality and Meaning," 184.

[11] Augustine, *De Doctrina Christiana* I, vii: "*Deus ... ita cogitator ut aliquid quo nihil melius sit atque sublimius illa cogitatio conetur attomgere*" (PL 34, 22) as cited in Richard Southern, *Saint Anselm: A Portrait in a Landscape* (Cambridge: Cambridge University Press, 1990), 129.

[12] *L. Annaei Senecae Naturalium Questionum libri* viii, ed. Alfred Gercke (Stuttgart, 1907) as cited in Southern, *Saint Anselm*, 29, and Davies, "Anselm and the ontological argument," 177.

[13] Gillian R. Evans, "St. Anselm and Knowing God," *Journal of Theological Studies* 28 (1977): 434.

[14] Karl Barth, *Anselm: Fides Quaerens Intellectum* (London: SCM Press, 1958), 13.

I believe that unless I do believe I shall not understand."[15] Faith is the efficient cause of the ability to gain understanding. This leads Barth to contend that understanding (*intellegere*) is Anselm's chief end, not proving (*probare*): "As *intellegere* is achieved it issues in *probare*."[16]

Proslogion 2 begins with the prayer that Anselm might be given understanding of two things: that God is *just as* we believe, and that he is *what* we believe him to be. And what we believe God to be, he says, is "that than which nothing greater can be thought." The argument, Richard Campbell observes, consists of three distinguishable stages.[17] Chapter 2 is Stage One of the overall argument. Since he is assailed by doubt, for Anselm's interlocutor, the "fool" of the Psalter, says in his heart that there is no God, he inquires whether a thing of such a nature exists. But surely, when the fool overhears Anselm praying in the language of perfection, "that thing than which nothing greater can be thought," he understands these words, and what he understands exists in his mind, even though he does not think that it exists in reality. For it is possible for a thing to exist only in the mind without a corresponding reality to it. Even the fool, then, is compelled to agree that there exists at least in his intellect the superlative thing, whatever that might be. And certainly the superlative thing cannot exist in the mind alone. For if it exists only in the mind, it can also be conceived to exist in reality, which is greater. The words "that than which nothing greater can be thought," for Anselm, signifies an "intentional object" in the mind, which functions as an intellectual mediation of some possibly objective reality. "Concepts are that by which we grasp the real," Nichols says, "not mental impressions parallel to it."[18] Chapter 2 culminates by drawing the sub-conclusion that the being than which nothing greater can be conceived, which he does not yet understand to be God, exists in reality. The First Stage of the overall argument states that this being has to exist not only intra-mentally but also extra-mentally.

---

[15] Ward, *Prayers and Meditations*, 244.
[16] Barth, *Anselm*, 14.
[17] Richard Campbell, "Anselm's Theological Method," *Scottish Journal of Theology* 6 (1979): 554.
[18] Aidan Nichols, "Anselm of Canterbury and the Language of Perfection," *Downside Review* 103 (1985): 211.

Some have argued that *Proslogion* 3 presents a totally different proof of God's existence than that *Proslogion* 2 has offered.[19] This is far from Anselm's intent.[20] While chapter 2 is primarily concerned with why something than which nothing greater can be conceived cannot just be in the mind, chapter three proceeds to add that something than which nothing greater can be conceived is, not just *in re* (in existence) but that something *in re* (in existence) cannot possibly fail to be.[21] The reasoning of *Proslogion* 2 is being carried a stage further, thus Anselm begins *Proslogion* 3 with an assertion: "That *is* so truly, that it is not possible to think of it not existing."[22] Furthermore *Proslogion* 3 consists of two distinct stages. Stage Two occupies the first half of chapter 3, which establishes his claim. In Davies' paraphrase:

1. We can think of something existing which cannot be thought not to exist.
2. Such a thing would be greater than something which can be thought not to exist.
3. So something than which nothing greater can be thought cannot be something which can be thought not to exist.
4. So something than which nothing greater can be thought cannot be thought not to exist.[23]

Here again God does not explicitly figure, nor does necessary existence enter, until Stage Three, which occupies the second half of *Proslogion* 3.

At Stage Three, Anselm addressed God in the language of fiduciary address: "This being is yourself, our Lord and God. Lord my God, you so truly are, that it is not possible to think of you as not existing. And rightly so."[24] This stage consists of two

---

[19] Norman Malcolm, "Anselm's Ontological Arguments," *Philosophical Review* 69 (1960): 45.
[20] See Richard E. La Croix, *Proslogion II and III: A Third Interpretation of Anselm's Argument* (Leiden: E.J. Brill, 1972), where he argues that these two chapters do not separately contain logically complete arguments for God's existence; rather they, taken together, constitute a complete argument.
[21] Davies, *Anselm*, "Anselm and the ontological argument," 162.
[22] Ward, *Prayers and Meditations*, 245.
[23] Davies, *Anselm*, "Anselm and the ontological argument," 163.
[24] Ward, *Prayers and Meditations*, 245.

legs, the first of which is based on a new premise that to say that anything greater than God can be thought is to imply that our understanding could rise beyond God and judge its Creator, which is manifest nonsense. The second leg, the more compelling of the two, hinges on the premise that "whatever else there is, except You alone, can be thought not to be. You alone, then, of all things most truly exist and therefore of all things possess existence to the highest degree."[25] Everything that is not identical to God can be thought not to be, and therefore it possesses less existence. God, being the greatest in a chain of being, exists to the highest degree.[26] Anselm addressed God: "But what are you save that supreme being, existing through Yourself alone, who made everything else from nothing?"[27] If God is the greatest conceivable being, there is no going beyond him, and he cannot be causally dependent upon something else. So a proper understanding of God as the greatest conceivable being should convince us that God must exist and must do so necessarily. *Proslogion* 15 argues on behalf of God's necessary existence, in terms of a reduction to absurdity of the premise – the inconceivable premise that something greater than a being "greater than can be thought" can be thought. It states: "Lord, you are then not only that than which nothing greater can be thought; you are something greater than it is possible to think about. For since it is possible to think that this could exist, if you are not this thing, then a greater than you can be thought; and that will not do."[28] This premise is a logical consequence of Anselm's formula, not to be treated as a "new" formula to approach God.[29] Contrary to the fool, Anselm's assessment in *Proslogion* 4 shows that God must be understood or believed to be, not by another but simply by an existence he himself possesses.

---

[25] Davies, *Anselm*, 88.
[26] Cf. Robert Brecher, *Anselm's Argument: The Logic of Divine Existence* (Aldershot: Gower, 1985), 11, argues that Anselm is working within the Platonic metaphysic of a hierarchy of being, which is mediated to him through Augustine. Southern, in *Saint Anselm*, 134, notes that there is no proof that Anselm has read Plato's *Timaeus*, although the book was in the library at Bec.
[27] Davies, *Anselm*, 89.
[28] Ward, *Prayers and Meditations*, 257.
[29] Decorte, "Anselm of Canterbury's Ultimate Reality and Meaning," 182.

> [N]o one, indeed, understanding what God is can think that he does not exist, even though he (the fool) may say these words in his heart either without any [objective] signification or with some peculiar signification. For God is that-than-which-nothing-greater-can-be-thought. Whoever really understands this understands clearly that this same being so exists that not even in thought can it not exist. Thus whoever understands that God exists in such a way cannot think of Him as not existing.[30]

The rational analysis raises Anselm's mind to the understanding of God as the superlative deity, for which Anselm could do nothing but offer a sacrifice of thanksgiving.[31] What began in *Proslogion* 2 with the petition for understanding that God is *just as* we believe, and that he is *what* we believe him to be has now been fulfilled in *Proslogion* 4, where Anselm closed his argument with a prayer of thanks. Schufreider writes, "such closure suggests that we have a complete and completed movement of thinking in which the demands prayed for from the start have been met."[32] Based on such construction, that the ontological argument for God's existence is enclosed by two prayers, Anselm does expect the fool to understand at least the "necessity," but not the "certainty," of God's existence.[33] Only the faithful could grasp the latter. In light of this, Barth offers his paraphrase of Anselm's approach to *Proslogion*: "While I believe, I also believe that the knowledge for which I seek, as it is demanded and rendered possible by faith, has faith as its presupposition, and that in itself it would immediately become impossible were it not the knowledge of faith."[34] "[T]he attainment of *intellegere*," says Hogg, "is [causally] dependent on the quality of *credere*."[35] Fairly speaking, the celebrated Anselmian identification of God is no definition. Rather it is a conclusion, not of a pure rationalist but of a rational mystic, whose pursuit is

---

[30] Ward, *Prayers and Meditations*, 146. See Oliver Johnson, "God and St. Anselm," *Journal of Religion* 45 (1965): 327.
[31] Davies, *Anselm*, 89.
[32] Gregory Schufreider, *Confessions of a Rational Mystic* (Indiana: Purdue University Press, 1994), 200.
[33] Hogg, *Anselm*, 101.
[34] Barth, *Anselm*, 26.
[35] Hogg, *Anselm*, 101.

to achieve a transposition from pure believing to an experiential encounter with the superlative deity affirmed by faith.[36]

The Fiduciary Utterance as the Ground of Worship

Evans notes a difference in Anselm's writings.[37] Whereas in the treatises, Anselm dealt with intellectually demanding problems with the intention of helping others to achieve a rigorous faith-seeking-understanding by reason alone, in the *Prayers and Meditations*, he expressed his own feelings in order to inspire the mind of the reader to the sublimity of God in love and reverence. Anselm wrote down long meditations with reverential fear of God as the ultimate goal. This is included as the preface of *Prayers and Meditations*, usually attributed to Anselm:

> The purpose of the prayers and meditations that follow is to stir up the mind of the reader to the love or fear of God or to self-examination. They are not to be read through in a turmoil but quietly, not skimmed or hurried through, but taken a little at a time, with deep and thoughtful meditation. The reader should not trouble about reading the whole of any of them, but only as much as, by God's help, he finds useful in stirring up his spirit to prayer.[38]

Both activities – rational reflection and meditative prayer – serve the same purpose, that is, to bring people into close communion with God, albeit by different routes. Evans also recognizes that in *Dicta Anselmi*, Anselm habitually places more emphasis on I-thou encounter with God, without undermining the I-it aspect of knowing God, or denigrating knowing about God.[39] Accordingly it is arguable that *Proslogion* contains both activities. What

---

[36] A. Stolz, "Anselm's Theology in the *Proslogion*," in *The Many-Faced Argument*, eds. John Hick and Arthur McGill (London: Macmillan, 1968), 183–208.
[37] Evans, "St. Anselm and Knowing God," 436.
[38] Ward, *Prayers and Meditations*, 89. Also cited in her "Anselm of Canterbury and His Influence," in *Christian Spirituality: Origins to the Twelfth Century*, eds. Bernard McGinn, John Meyendorff & Jean Leclercq (New York: Crossroad, 1985), 197.
[39] *Memorials*, 148.3 as cited in Evans, "St. Anselm and Knowing God," 436.

Anselm is offering is not just a logical argument, which he does not undercut, but a spiritual experience, which is his ultimate *telos*. His intent is to issue a transposition from faith seeking understanding to understanding seeking worship, the latter being his chief end. What we (a) understand by the word "God" must be (b) believed, and what God must be believed to be – "that than which nothing greater can be thought" – he ought to be (c) worshipped. *Proslogion* is a piece of affective devotion, which he intends to affect the believer to truly understand God, to fully embrace him and wholeheartedly praise him with the fiduciary language of the superlative. This is evident in chapter 5 where he immediately moved from whom God is to the praise of him, because worship is at the heart of his program:

> What then are You, Lord God, You than whom nothing greater can be thought? But what are You save that supreme being, existing through Yourself alone, who made everything else from nothing? For whatever is not this is less than that which can be thought of; but this cannot be thought about You. What goodness, then, could be wanting to the supreme good, through which every good exists? Thus you are just, truthful, happy, and whatever it is better to be than not to be – for it is better to be just rather than unjust, and happy rather than unhappy.[40]

Having seen God for himself via rational reflection, the faithful Anselm is elevated to the superlative deity, to whom thanksgiving, adoration and praises are rightly due. For what must be believed about God is indeed what he ought to be, namely the unsurpassable perfection. This unsurpassable reality demands a fiduciary response that is necessary, natural and proper to a being like God. The necessary reason for God now becomes the necessary reason for worship. As the causative agency of our worship, the divine superlative stirs our soul toward him. It is the first cause of all human activities including our joyful praises, earnest thanksgiving and reverential fear.

The Inaccessibility of the Superlative Deity: The Hidden God

Immediately after chapter 15 where he exalted the fitting nature of God – the highest nature which is peculiar to God alone – Anselm proceeded to work out his doctrine of God in relation to

---

[40] Davies, *Anselm*, 89.

worship. Chapter 16 focuses on a reflection on the inaccessibility of God, while maintaining the completeness of God's presence to us and our presence to him.[41] The oneness of the superlative deity is the dynamic for the first entrance into the theme of worship. Yet the experience from this chapter is of an inaccessible light that leaves the soul in darkness. As Anselm acknowledges, "I have no experience of *you* [God as he is]." This corresponds to *Proslogion* 1, where he describes the "inaccessible light" in which God dwells. The interaction between himself and this God is not one of friendship but of wonder.[42] God in his divine self is hidden, and is at a distance from the worshipper, even though he yearns to lay hold of God's essential being. God cannot be comprehended in his own majesty because the true God's majesty is precisely his hiddenness, not to be grasped by any but himself. This type of knowing God is impossible for us, for, says Anselm, God dwells in unapproachable light, and as such he is a hidden God. To the extent that God "hide[s]" from the soul in his "light and beauty," he is beyond reach and thus does not concern us.[43] There is no possibility of relationship between God and the soul at this point. This is the first fruit Anselm reaps from the existence of the superlative God. A theology of worship must observe the limit posed by the hiddenness of the supreme majesty. True worship does not have anything to do with the God who hides in his majesty, for he does not will that we should penetrate into his Godhead directly. Any unmediated worship of God would only dash us into pieces. "[The eye of the soul]," said Anselm, "is dazzled by its glory, mastered by its fullness, crushed by its immensity, confounded by its extent."[44] Although the hidden God is inaccessible, we can apprehend God in parts. We see, but our seeing is limited, in comparison to the immensity of God's essential being.[45] That God hides in his inaccessible light is awe-inspiring, fear-instilling, and death-causing. However the annihilating or negative knowledge of the superlative God in his unapproachable light is causally useful, as it causes Anselm to prostrate before him in silence and awe.

---

[41] Ward, *Prayers and Meditations*, 258.
[42] Ward, *Prayers and Meditations*, 240.
[43] Ward, *Prayers and Meditations*, 259.
[44] Ward, *Prayers and Meditations*, 257.
[45] Ward, *Prayers and Meditations*, 256.

The revelation of the superlative deity seizes upon the worshipper, while at the same time humbling him so that he is made known of the inability to see, taste, hear and inwardly feel the God who is his very life and the great All. To know the superlative deity is to know himself. This is the second conclusion from the existence of the divine superlative. Thus when the mind's eye widens, or expands into the vision of God, the being of the superlative God increases and the being of creatures decreases. Before the Great Reality, the God as he necessarily is, Anselm came to a realization of how far the soul strays from God, and how deep it still lives in darkness and misery. In his conversation with God, he wrote: "The truth is, I am darkened by myself and also dazzled by you. I am clouded by my own smallness and overwhelmed by your immensity; I am restricted by my own narrowness and mastered by your wideness."[46]

In Praise of the Superlative's "Abundant Sweetness" and "Sweet Abundance"

Though we know by revelation the superlative God, who yearns for us to dwell in him, we in our fallen condition cannot attain this. Thus chapter 18 expresses the frustration Anselm experiences in his effort to know God: "I tried to rise up to the light of God, and I have fallen back into the darkness of myself."[47] Yet Anselm was still motivated in faith to pray: "Let my soul gather together all its powers, and direct its whole understanding towards you, Lord."[48] Just as our knowledge of God is hindered by sin, so it is with our worship. The worshipping experience as ascent to God is rendered ineffectual, unless by the intervening grace of God the "Re-creator."[49] Already in *Proslogion* 1, Anselm lamented vehemently how sin has defaced God's beauty in his life and his created order, and consequently created a distance between God and his creatures.[50] *Proslogion* 17 bemoans again the hindrance of access to God due to the loss of the beatific vision through "the ancient sickness of sin."[51] Anselm longed for God to restore

---

[46] Ward, *Prayers and Meditations*, 256.
[47] Ward, *Prayers and Meditations*, 259.
[48] Ward, *Prayers and Meditations*, 259.
[49] Ward, *Prayers and Meditations*, 259.
[50] Davies, *Anselm*, 85.
[51] Ward, *Prayers and Meditations*, 258.

the distorted beauty, and to return to him that for which he was originally made, namely the blessedness of the vision of God. He then appealed to the incarnation and cross of Christ as a way out of wretched man's lot. This is more explicitly borne out in his *Meditation on Human Redemption*. There Anselm meditated how the estranged relationship of man and God is healed, and the debt which man must pay, but cannot, is abated, on account of the free offering of the one who is both God and man. The Son of God is "the strength of salvation," and thus is the answer to the believing soul.[52] Anselm's meditation reaches a turning point, where his mind is aroused from lethargy and now he experiences the piercing of the "first compunction of sorrow," which results in recognition of the need of man and the cost of his redemption.[53] In a dialogical form between the soul and Christ, Anselm prays: "You are in bondage, but through the cross you have been redeemed. You were a servant, but through the cross you have been set free . . . How can I be glad about my salvation when it comes only because of Your (Christ's) sorrow?"[54] Out of this experience of sorrow there emerges the "second compunction of desire" for dedication to Christ to whom he owes his entire self, and for a final consummation in the life to come at which point the entire self is made his.[55] Although not as Christocentric as in *Meditation on Human Redemption*, a turning point also occurs in *Proslogion* 9, in which his mind, having been pierced by the first compunction of sorrow, is stirred to embrace the second compunction of desire for God, which eventuates in doxological praise of God and his compassion for sinners. This is another fruit he reaped from a proper meditation on the superlative deity. The cross, which is already contained here in his meditation of God's unbounded goodness, is the remedy of our estrangement from God, and thus our ascent to God understood as worship is now restored. The more Anselm understood this deity and his relationship to him, the more the compunction breaks out into worship, raising his soul to thank God for his immeasurable generosity: "Ah, from what generous love and loving generosity compassion flows out

---

[52] Ward, *Prayers and Meditations*, 77.
[53] Ward, *Prayers and Meditations*, 79, where she uses the term "compunction" as descriptive of the third stage of the Anselmian pattern of prayer.
[54] Anselm, "A Meditation on Human Redemption," in Hopkins, *Anselm*, 141.
[55] Ward, *Prayers and Meditations*, 77.

to us! Ah, what feelings of love should we sinners have towards the unbounded goodness of God!" Understanding thus issues in gratitude and praise. *Proslogion* 9 bears this out:

> Truly the source whence flows the stream of your compassion is hidden in the deepest and most secret place of your goodness . . . So you are compassionate because you are entirely and supremely good . . . How deep is your goodness, O God! The source of your compassion is seen, but is not seen clearly; whence the stream flows is known, but it is not fully known whence it springs. It is the fullness of your goodness that makes you loving towards those who sin against you, but why this should be so is hidden in the depths of your goodness.[56]

What is known is this: the offering made by Christ is greater than the offence of the world. But what is hidden is this: why then should not the efficacy of the cross be extended to all? The fact that God moves toward sinners with extravagant goodness is known, but why this should be so remains hidden in the most secret place of his goodness. It is thus that Anselm was caught up in wonder why the tremendous reality of God, the all-just One, who wants nothing in return, should bestow blessings upon the wicked and guilty creatures, himself included. Anselm's appeal to God's goodness revives and enflames the lukewarm love in his heart. Consequently he felt so powerfully the effect of God's mercy that his soul was aroused to praise him: "How deep is your goodness, O God!"

For Augustine, greatness, a quantitative notion, is not to be predicated adjectively of God.[57] God is great, not by a greatness he derives from elsewhere, but by the very greatness he himself is substantially. If God has his greatness by participation in this other greatness, then this other greatness would be greater than God, which is manifest absurdity, for there is not anything which is greater than God. Anselm's view coincides with Augustine's in that greatness is not a quality, but a substance. Just as God's greatness cannot be conceived as a quality or quantity, so it is with God's goodness. Goodness thus is not to be predicated of God other than substantively. *Proslogion* 12 says: "Clearly, whatever you are, you are in your self; you are not derived from another.

---

[56] Ward, *Prayers and Meditations*, 250.
[57] Cf. Augustine, *De Trinitate* 5.1.2 as cited in Hopkins, *A Companion to the Study of Anselm*, 131.

You are the very life by which you live, the knowledge by which you know, the goodness by which you are good, and so on."[58] The superlative goodness is his by right and nature, not received from elsewhere. However the divine nature, which is boundless goodness, seeks to communicate. God's deity consists in the fact that it is his glory to give to, and to identify with, sinners. It is not out of a lack in the source from which the stream of God's compassion flows forth to sinners. Rather it is the fullness of God's supra-abundant goodness that moves God to be kindly disposed toward sinners.

God is merciful (compassionate) toward us, says Anselm, yet he is impassible in himself. How does he reconcile these two attributes? The former is his primary moral perfection which communicates; the latter implies a lack of compassion, because impassibility is immunity to all negative affects, including having a feeling of compassion for the wretched. These two can be reconciled, argues Brian Leftow, "because while compassion is a matter of what we feel, being merciful is an inner state manifested in what we do. While God feels no sorrow, His inner state, whatever it is in terms of feeling, issues in an effect we correctly identify as mercy, and this is reason to say that God's inner state is one of mercy."[59] It is in this light that Anselm denies any feelings of love and compassion in God himself, insisting that although we experience the effects of God's love, God's being is not affected by our experiences. Anselm's solution to the paradox of a compassionate and an impassible God is to assert that

> You are merciful in relation to us and not in relation to Yourself? In fact, you are [merciful] according to our way of looking at things and not according to your way. For when you look upon us in our misery it is we who feel the effect of your mercy, but You do not experience the feeling. Therefore You are both merciful because You save the sorrowful and pardon sinners against You; and You are not merciful because You do not experience any feeling of compassion for misery.[60]

---

[58] Ward, *Prayers and Meditations*, 254.
[59] Leftow, "Anselm's Perfect-being theology," in *Cambridge Companion to Anselm*, 152.
[60] Davies, *Anselm*, 91.

The traditional notion of divine impassibility is affirmed in Anselm insofar as God is not understood to be subject to any creaturely passions, nor is he emotionally unstable or manipulated. That God's being lacks any feelings does not entail an outright denial of any possibility of God–world relation, as if God is completely uninvolved in our lives but exists in his transcendent bliss and solitariness. Impassibility is predicated of God, as it is interpreted as an affirmation of divine freedom and constancy, which constitutes the basis for God's relation with the world. For Anselm, there is an infinite surplus of goodness in this superlative being that intimately embraces the world, not from divine deficiency, but from the supra-abundance of love. What a great deficiency of benevolence that would be if God should reserve for himself the abundance of his fullness! A God that does not communicate his goodness is a defective one, not worthy to be recognized, much less worshipped. The God who exists in a flux also is not worthy of worship, but the God whose constancy is his beauty or his inner state is. Here lies the paradoxical nature of God: *God as he is* is impassible, although we feel the "abundant sweetness" flowing forth from his "sweet abundance." The latter, to which Anselm appealed, is the dynamic of praise proper to him, who is one of a kind: "O mercy, from what abundant sweetness and sweet abundance do you flow forth for us! O boundless goodness of God, with what feeling should You be loved [adored or worshipped] by sinners."[61]

On Praising the Inherent Attributes of the Divine Superlative

The fiduciary utterance continues to raise Anselm's mind to think of some most excellent and immortal nature of God. He reverted to the eternity and scope of God in *Proslogion* 18–22, which is no different from the first examination in *Monologion*. The aesthetic attributes of the superlative deity, which he appealed by means of meditation and reason, is the template from which the essence of worship is to be found. If God is the superlative thing and the necessary being, it ought to be characterized by sheer ontological independence. This is intrinsically connected with a belief in divine aseity, a part of the traditional notion of God's transcendence. Only God is *agenetos*, unoriginated. Every creaturely being has

---

[61] Davies, *Anselm*, 92.

its being from and through God, except God who has his own being from and through himself. God as such is *a se* or *ex se*, from himself, and *per se*, through himself.[62] The Platonic metaphysic of being is operative in Anselm's framework in which degrees of existence come into place. Not all things that exist are of equal value, and of the same distinction of degrees. There are degrees of gradation in the natures of things. As an example, the nature of a horse is better than that of a tree, but the nature of a human is by far more excellent than that of a horse. Nonetheless reason demands that there is some nature which is superior to others in such a way that it is inferior to none. As a result, we know that just as all things that exist are what they are through the supreme nature, "the one and only one nature which is superior to others and inferior to none," for that reason this nature, "the greatest and best of all existing natures," has its very being through itself.[63] All things that are exist from the same highest nature, this one nature is that than which there is nothing greater, and for that reason that nature has its existence from itself, while other things have theirs from another. Anselm describes God as the highest nature, which always is because it is the "Ultimate Reality" that grounds the existence of all limited, spatial and contingent things.[64]

For Anselm, *esse ex se* and *esse per se* are notions of causality. The matter by which an artifact is made is the material cause of the object, and the craftsman who fashions it is its efficient cause. But how does one think of God as causing himself? The difficulty lies in conceiving divine aseity as a property God possesses in virtue of being *causa sui*, causing itself, as opposed to causing something other than itself. Anselm was keenly aware of the difficulty when one applies the creaturely understanding of causality to a being such as God. "What is said to exist through something," he argued, "seems to be through it either as an efficient cause or as its matter, or as some other aid, as through an instrument."[65] Anselm refuted on good grounds any of these three kinds of causality as the way in which God is through himself.

---

[62] See *Monol.* 5 as cited in John Morreall, "The Aseity of God in St. Anselm," *Sophia* 23 (1984): 35.
[63] *Monol.* 4, Davies, *Anselm*, 14–16.
[64] Decorte, "Saint Anselm of Canterbury on Ultimate Reality and Meaning," 182.
[65] *Monol.* 6, Hopkins, *Companion*, 11–12.

> But something that exists in any of these three ways – maker, material and tool – exists through something other than itself, and so is posterior to, and somehow less than, this other thing. The supreme nature, however, definitively does not exist through something other than itself, nor is it posterior to, or less than itself or any other thing.[66]

The language of causality is inapplicable for a being like God because it involves the undesirable elements of temporal succession and inferiority. God does not exist through another, nor is he later than or less than anything, himself included.

Anselm also rejected a notion of God existing through himself understood merely negatively, that he exists through nothing. For God does not exist through merely a lack of dependence on something else and a lack of dependence on God himself. In *Monologion* 3, he writes: "Everything that exists, exists either through something or through nothing. But nothing exists through nothing. For it is impossible even to conceive of something existing through nothing. Whatever exists, then, exists only through something."[67] Anselm then repeated this argument in *Monologion* 6 that God does not exist through nothing, since it is inconceivable that something as the supreme nature, namely God, exists through nothing.

> If then it is out of nothing, then either through itself or through something else. But nothing can exist out of nothing through itself, since necessarily, what comes to exist (from nothing and through something) is posterior to that through which it comes to exist. But since the supreme essence is not prior to itself, it does not come to exist out of nothing through itself.[68]

Anselm explained the doctrine of divine aseity by an imperfect analogy of light:

> [I]n the same way as we talk of brightness. Brightness through and from itself is bright and through and from itself brightens. For 'brightness', 'to brighten', and 'something that is bright' are related to each other, in the same way as are 'existence' and 'to exist' and 'something that exists' (i.e., something that has being or reality). Therefore supreme existence, supremely to exist, and the supreme existing thing (or

---

[66] *Monol.* 6, Davies, *Anselm*, 17.
[67] Davies, *Anselm*, 13.
[68] Davies, *Anselm*, 17–18.

supreme reality) go together rather like 'brightness', 'to brighten', and 'to be bright'.[69]

The aseity of God may also be understood by way of negation, i.e., denying God the characteristics of creatures. Unlike creatures who depend for their existence on other things and ultimately on God, God himself depends on nothing at all. God exists strictly in a unique way, absolutely not subsisting in any other things or state of affairs. God's aseity consists in the fact that there is no causal dependence on things outside of God, nor is there causal dependence within God. God is simple, and is without parts, one of which is contingent upon another for its existence.[70] In God, there is no before or after, no becoming or ceasing to be, as there is in creatures.[71] God exists in an absolute way, i.e., most fully and truly, causally independent of everything else, utterly simply, without beginning or end or mutability of any kind. As such God's existence is of a different order, namely that he himself depends on nothing at all. He exists strictly, not because anything else exists or because certain conditions or causes for God's existence are met. Precisely, there are no causes or conditions for God to be, nothing could prevent him to be, and nothing could cause him not to be. Put positively, God is self-existent, and self-sufficient – these phrases may be predicated of God only insofar as they do not imply God having some kind of dependence on himself. God is *a se* and *per se*, not in the sense that he causes himself, for causality belongs to the creaturely order, or in the sense that he exists from nothing, as if there is a lack of dependence on himself, but in the sense that he, of a different ontological order, is eternally complete and sufficient unto himself.[72]

There is in Anselm's program a causal linkage between belief in the superlative deity and the necessary response of the faithful as the outcome of it. Contemplation of the aforementioned aesthetic attributes reaches the compunction, which ultimately causes that longing and seeking for God to break out into worship. This is evident in *Proslogion* 22, where Anselm reached a turning point in which he now prayed, addressing the most high in an elevated

---

[69] Davies, *Anselm*, 18.
[70] Ward, *Prayers and Meditations*, 258–59; *Monol.* 16 and 17, Davies, *Anselm*, 28–30.
[71] Davies, *Anselm*, 97–99.
[72] Morreall, "The Aseity of God," 43.

doxological language proper to him: "Lord, you alone are what you are and who you are."[73] God – the "singularly unique and uniquely singular" being – is so ontologically different from all else that he in no way has anything in common with, nor does he share his nature with, other beings.[74] God is, first and foremost, "one of a kind" – a way of expressing that he is completely unique, that "there cannot be more than one of this kind."[75] Being of a different order, he does not just possess distinctive features of his own kind, but is himself a distinctive kind of his own. This understanding of God generates from Anselm a response that is rationally fitting. To rephrase Anselm: Lord, there is none like you, for you alone are that than which no greater can be *worshipped*. Yet we do not worship him as though he has needs or lacks or contingencies, but extol him for what he is and who he is – the one and highest good, entirely self-sufficient, eternally complete, the ultimate ground of every contingent thing that exists, and the one to whom we wholly owe our being and well-being. A rational clarification of this superlative being and its inherent attributes allows the eye of the mind to participate in the inner vision of God. Yet this seeing God does not mean the worshipper has direct contact with the essence of God as he is. The "true being" proper to God alone remains inscrutably hidden from the one who praises him for who he is – "life, light, beauty, wisdom, blessedness, eternity and many other good things."[76]

The Trinity as the Dynamic of Worship

The initial result of the search for Anselm was an awareness of God's distance, which is finally overcome by an apprehension of the dynamic and diffusive nature of the superlative fullness. There is no greater delight than to possess by faith the superabundant joy, which is the Triune God. Chapters 23–26 enact the progressive diffusion of God's goodness within the Trinity and the response of the believer to the God Anselm has presented. The Triune God is the inspiration that enables the faithful to break through to the

---

[73] Ward, *Prayers and Meditations*, 261–62.
[74] *Monol.* 65; S I. 45.
[75] *Monol.* 65; S I, 45.
[76] *Monol.* 65; S I. 45; Ward, *Prayers and Meditations*, 262.

inaccessible light, and participate through the Spirit in the 'fullness of joy' promised by the Lord.

A Brief Summary of the Trinity

Chapter 23 marks a significant point at which Anselm shifts his meditation from the one divine essence to the Trinity and its internal relation. Whereas chapter 22 identifies the superlative deity as the one supreme good, chapter 23 identifies the one supreme good as the Trinity: "That this good is equally Father, Son, and Holy Spirit; and that this is the one Being necessary, which is entirely good, wholly good, and solely good."[77] *Proslogion* 23 is the only chapter that elucidates the Trinity in God and the relationships between the three persons. Surely *Proslogion* does have a lot to say on his concept of God, but less on what may be called the nature of God as Trinity. An overview of Anselm's work shows that *Monologion* does the job of clarification on his concept of God, particularly God in Trinity.[78] Thus Anselm sees no need to repeat here what has been amply written on the Trinity. In a doxological form, he describes densely the procession of the Persons from the "highest unity."[79]

> You are this good, O God the Father; this is Your Word, that is to say, Your Son. For there cannot be any other than what You are, or any thing greater or lesser than You, in the Word by which You utter Yourself. For Your Word is as true as You are truthful and is therefore the very truth that You are and that is not other than You. And You are so simple that there cannot be born of You any other than what You are. This itself is the Love, one and common to You and to Your Son, that is the Holy Spirit proceeding from both. For this same Love is not unequal to You or to Your Son since Your love for Yourself and Him, and His love for You and Himself, are as great as You and He are. Nor is that other than You and than Him which is not different from You and Him; nor can there proceed from Your supreme simplicity what is other than from which it proceeds. Thus, whatever each is singly, that the whole Trinity is altogether, Father, Son, and Holy Spirit; since each singly is not other than the supremely simple unity

---

[77] Hopkins, *Companion*, 108.
[78] Evans, *Anselm*, 99.
[79] Ward, *Prayers and Meditations*, 262–63.

and the supremely unified simplicity which can be neither multiplied nor differentiated.[80]

As processions, the Father is without beginning, and is the principle of the Son and the Spirit. The Son comes from the Father as begotten, but is himself, together with the Father, the principle of the Holy Spirit. The Spirit proceeds from both the Father and the Son, but is not the principle of another. This is what is known as the *filioque* doctrine. God has nothing in common with anything else: this superlative being "neither divides itself among many substances" as a universal does, nor "unites with any other by virtue of a common essence" as all individual things are.[81] Against Sabellianism, Anselm asserts that God exists in a differentiated unity as Father, Son and Spirit. The highest good must necessarily be wholly one, not many. Father, Son and Holy Spirit do not differ as God, for they are co-eternal, co-equal, and co-exist in a con-substantial triad. Each singly is God, and all three altogether are God, yet only One God. They differ in the way each person is God in relation to the others. Anselm's thinking is traceable to Augustine who asserts: "God is everything that he has except for the relations through which each person is referred to the other."[82] What is crucial for Anselm is this: the origin of the Holy Spirit is not rooted in the mutual love between the Father and the Son, but in love as the divine essence shared by both – viz., their one Godness of love. *Filioque* is thus sought in the ontologically fundamental unity of the Father with the Son, rather than in their differentiation. As clarification, let me cite *Monologion* 54: "This is based on the fact that the Love [Spirit] does not proceed from the Father and the Son being two separate things. Rather it proceeds from their being one . . . It is from essence not relatedness that Father and Son give out this great good."[83]

The "not other" (*non aliud*) language in *Proslogion* 12 contributes to Anselm's understanding of the Trinity. The language of God's self-existence in chapter 5 is framed as a rhetorical question: "But what are you, but that which, highest of all things alone existing through itself (*per seiptum*), made all other things out of

---

[80] Davies, *Anselm*, 100.
[81] *Monol.* 65; S I. 45.
[82] Augustine, *The City of God*, 2.10.1; *de trinitate* 5.5–6 as cited in my *Apologetic for Filioque*, 26.
[83] *Monol.* 54, Davies, *Anselm*, 62.

nothing?" The same recurs in chapter 12 but as a direct assertion: "But certainly whatever you are, you are not through another but through yourself?" (*non per aliud es quam per teipsum*). The uniqueness of Anselm's pattern of ascent lies in his method of addressing God: from "through itself" (chapter 5) to "through yourself" (chapter 12), proceeding from indirect to direct, from impersonal to personal. Then he further augments his personal address "through yourself" with a negative qualification "not through another." This addition is already implied in his positive assertion "through itself," and may seem superfluous. Nevertheless, it foreshadows future insights, and thus prepares the way for chapter 22, where he understands God's existence *non per aliud* as existence that is "proper and absolute."[84] Finally he adapts this *non aliud* language in his description of the Trinity in chapter 23, where the Son is *non aliud*, "not other" than the Father, and the Spirit is "not other" than the first two persons. He asserted the language three times as he speaks of God's threefold unity: "for each [Person] is not other than [*non est aliud quam*] most highly simple unity and most highly one simplicity, which cannot be multiplied and cannot be other and other [*nec aliud et aliud*]."[85] "In the unfolding of the *Proslogion*, then, Anselm the narrator's discovery of *non aliud* language in chapter 12," argues McMahon, "is not negligible, for it prepares him to treat the Persons of the Trinity in a way that God's 'existing through himself,' alone, does not enable."[86]

The *filioque* doctrine, which is affirmed in *Proslogion* 23, is worthy of assertion and attention, especially as it relates to the enjoyment of God in worship. The Spirit, who proceeds from Father and Son, is "the one love" that flows between the Father and the Son. This means that there already abides in God's life a relational dynamism between the three persons: the Father loves the Son and the Son loves the Father, with the Spirit of love binding them. In respect to the life of faith, *filioque* ties closely the Spirit to Christ. The work of the "marvelous Counselor" is to communicate to us the gospel: in Christ's cross and resurrection, our friendship with God is now restored, and together with it the goods we now enjoy

---

[84] Robert McMahon, *Understanding the Medieval Meditative Ascent* (Washington: The Catholic University of America Press, 2006), 176.
[85] *Prosl.* 23; S 117.
[86] McMahon, *Understanding the Medieval Meditative Ascent*, 176.

by participation. The work of redemption is completed, and the benefits Christ has acquired for us by his death and resurrection belong to us in faith. The benefits remain hidden and are of no use to us unless God causes us to perceive and receive them. Unless the Spirit comes to counsel us and applies to us this treasury of goods, all the goods promised by God would have been kept at a distance, not enjoyed by the faithful. The "fullness of joy" Christ promises would be of no avail. In this case, the work of Christ would have been in vain. When considering the work of inculcating the benefits of Christ's cross and sufferings for our salvation, which is precisely the Spirit's, we must think of *filioque* in which the work of the Son and the work of the Spirit are closely related. The foundation of their reality consists in a single essence (love) which all three share in a differentiated unity verified distinguishably as relations. In saying this, the Spirit participates fully and equally in the oneness of love between the Father and the Son, which he also conveys to the believer. God has revealed himself and opened to us the profundity of his sheer, boundless love. Moreover, none could come to recognize the Father's love were it not for the Lord Christ. But neither could we know of Christ's heart had it not been revealed by the love of Holy Spirit. The love that flows between the Father and the Son is the love of the atoning sacrifice of Calvary. In it, God's forgiveness and God's self-offering coincide. Thus a denial of the *filioque*, says Gerald Bray, implies a denial of the Son's atoning love in the life of the believer, although Anselm does not explicitly draw such conclusion.[87]

The Dynamic and Self-diffusive Nature of the Superlative Good

The Triune God is "the one and highest Good" (*unum et summum bonum*), in whom all goodness, all beings and all well-being consist. Yet supreme Goodness without communication is not worthy of the dignity of the highest Good. Anselm endorses the medieval conception of the Good as self-diffusive (*bonum diffusum sui*), which is already foreshadowed in *Proslogion* 9, where he discusses the dynamic nature of the fullness of goodness. Diffusion of the good reaches its climax from chapter 23 onward, where praise is rendered to the Triune God who does not reserve goodness for

---

[87] "*Filioque* in History and Theology," *Tyndale Bulletin* 34 (1983): 127–28.

himself, but resolves to communicate. Perfect goodness is not static, but dynamic; it is not self-contained, but self-communicative. Truly, the Triune God is the source from which flows toward believers the stream of superabundant goodness. Abiding here is the compunction which bursts into praise, as it does in chapter 9: "How deep is your goodness, O God!" God's being as Triune is constituted by the dynamic fullness of goodness, and thus is the catalyst for the believer's full experience of God and the benefits that proceed from this relationship.

The superlative greatness possesses so powerful a force that whenever a believer hears it, he is necessarily aroused to long for him. Immediately after praising the Trinity, Anselm mustered up his energies to consider the nature and extent of so great an uncreated Good, which is God, by comparing it to that of the created goods. Just as good things are enjoyable, so joy must arise from intellectually dwelling upon divine goodness. For if particular goods issue forth so much delight, he considered intently, how much more delightful it is to possess that Good which holds within it the delight of every good? And the kind of joy gained from created things is not the same as that which is given by the Creator, as the Creator is different in kind from the creature. If created life is good, how good must be that life which creates? He reasons: "In short, if there are many great joys in enjoyable things, how rich and how great must be the joy [to be found] in Him who made all these delightful things!"[88] Interlaced with Scriptures, Anselm enumerated a long list of the kinds of goods for those who are capable of enjoying the highest Good. He praised God for these goods which are to be enjoyed by the faithful. To cite a few:

> If *beauty* delights you, "the just will shine as the sun" [Mt. 13:43]. If the *swiftness* or *strength* or *freedom* of the body that nothing can withstand [delights you], "they will be like the angels of God" [Mt. 22:30]; for it is "sown as a natural body and shall rise as a spiritual body" [I Cor. 15: 44] by a supernatural power . . . If it is *satisfaction*, they will be satisfied "when the glory of God will appear" [Ps. 16:15] . . . If it is *melody*, there the choirs of angels play unceasingly to God. If it is *pleasure* of any kind, not impure but pure, God "will make them drink from the torrent of His pleasure" [Ps. 35:9] . . . If it is *friendship*, they will love God more than themselves and one another

---

[88] Hopkins, *Companion*, 109.

as themselves, and God will love them more than they love themselves and one another, and He loves Himself and them through Himself . . . If it is *honors and riches*, God will set His good and faithful servants over many things [Mt. 25: 21, 23] and will in fact be so; and where the Son will be there also they will be, *"heirs indeed of God and co-heirs of Christ"* [Rom. 8: 17].[89]

As co-heir with Christ, we are given a participation in Christ's sonly communion with the Father, and in the heavenly choir of angels. This good wrought by Christ is communicated to us by the Holy Spirit. The trinitarian experience is God's gift, which we embrace by faith.

The End of Insight: "Joy" – that God is

The beauty of the superlative deity and the goods that proceed from this sole Beauty is the dynamic of worship, as it delights the believing soul. The reasoning Anselm applied to that which he holds dear surely leads him to the vision of the superlative greatness, whom he not only accepts as the object of faith, but now receives as the object of adoration or delight. Such vision issues in him a greater enjoyment of God – "that than which nothing greater can be thought." The participation in the superabundant Goodness is of such quality and of such enormity that it necessitates a corresponding superabundant joy in the hearts of those who lay hold of it. This insuperable joy is given to those who ask of it, for it is promised by the Son of God who speaks to us in John 16:24, "Ask and you shall receive that your joy may be full". But this promise is confirmed in the hearts of the elect ones by the Holy Spirit that the fullness of joy is indeed theirs by faith. God through the Holy Spirit, the "marvelous Counselor,"[90] assures them that this abundant joy in which they rejoice is indeed the joy of their Lord. Yet this "joy" is not to be understood as "an adjective genitive – the joy that the Lord has – but a subjective one: the joy that the Lord is."[91] Just as goodness is not that God possesses, but that he is, so also joy, God's final name in *Proslogion*, is a predicate

---

[89] Davies, *Anselm*, 101–02 (Italics are mine).
[90] Hopkins, *Companion*, 112.
[91] McMahon, *Understanding the Medieval Meditative Ascent*, 207.

of God's being substantially. God is the superlative fullness, and in Anselm's own words: "fullness of joy that is more than full."[92]

As stated earlier in chapters 1 and 18, and now in 24–26, the very purpose of insight is joy, or rather joyous entrance into the superlative fullness. Anselm asked that we follow this proper order in achieving the goal of understanding God: to know God is to love him; to love him is to enjoy him. The more he knows God the more he loves him; the more he loves him the more he rejoices in him – all of these are made possible through the counsel of the Holy Spirit. The goodness of the Trinity surpasses all temporal goods, and diffuses so enormous and so rich a joy that all the blessed together for eternity will not be capable of containing its fullness. In that perfect heavenly bliss, the just shall so love God that his being will not be able to "exhaust God's worthiness to be loved." Similarly, this joy is so great that "the whole" of it cannot enter us, but we, rather, will enter "wholly" into the joy of the Lord.[93] Faith allows the faithful to see for himself such a multiplication of joy in that great blessedness that his heart could only praise the bliss of heaven where God is all in all. The seeking leads to a finding which leads to worship understood as a participation in the beatific vision of the superlative fullness.

In worship, the superlative fullness can only be enjoyed in part, but there in full. Anselm delighted in God for offering him a foretaste of the future full joy, and for enabling him to make some progress into it. "[T]his joy beyond measure still remains" to be experienced proleptically until the point of fullness.[94] That is why the whole concludes, as this chapter does, in the way it has begun: with a moving prayer, asking God for more of the proleptic enjoyment of the beatific vision where the beauty of the superlative fullness is fully enjoyed.

> O God, I pray, let me know and love You, so that I may rejoice in You. And if I cannot in this life [know, love, and rejoice in You] fully, let me advance day by day until the point of fullness comes. Let knowledge of You progress in me here and be made full [in me] there. Let love for You grow in me here and be made full [in me] there, so that my joy may be great with expectancy while there being full in realization. O Lord, through Your Son You command – or rather, You counsel – us to

---

[92] Ward, *Prayers and Meditations*, 266.
[93] Hopkins, *Companion*, 112.
[94] Ward, *Prayers and Meditations*, 266.

ask; and through Him You promise that we shall receive, so that our joy may be made full. O Lord, I ask for what You counsel through our marvelous Counselor; may I receive what You promise through your Truth, so that my joy may be full. God of truth, I ask to receive it, so that my joy may be made full. Until then, let my mind meditate upon [what you promised], let my tongue speak of it. Let my heart love it; let my mouth proclaim it. Let my soul hunger for it; let my flesh thirst for it; let my whole being desire it until such time as I enter into the joy of my Lord, the triune God, blessed forever. Amen.[95]

---

[95] Hopkins, *Companion*, 112.

Chapter Three

Participation in the Constitutive Kiss: Worship in Bernard of Clairvaux's *Song of Songs*

Introduction

The importance of Bernard's sermons on the *Song of Songs* for worship is clearly discernible.[1] A theology of praise is passionately illustrated in the "kiss," the chief metaphor of love, which Bernard employs to speak of the doxological experience the bride enjoys with her groom. The kiss is the main template from which worship as a participation in the *constitutive kiss* of the Trinity is found.[2] Worship originates in the eternal drama of love in which the Father and the Son mutually kiss each other, with the Spirit binding them

---

[1] See Hughes O. Old, *The Reading and Preaching of the Scriptures in the Worship of the Christian Church*, vol. 3: *The Medieval Church* (Grand Rapids: Eerdmans, 1999), 274. The *Song of Songs*, Old writes, is Bernard's *summa theologica*, a summary of his theology. Quotations will be taken from Bernard of Clairvaux, *On the Song of Songs*, 4 vols. (Kalamazoo: Cistercian Publications, 1989). Hereafter abbreviated as *Song* in the text, and SS in the footnote.

[2] Kilian McDonnell, in "Spirit and Experience in Bernard of Clairvaux," *Theological Studies* 58 (1997): 11, writes: "In a constitutive sense this kiss [of the mouth] is restricted to the inner trinitarian life." The phrase *constitutive kiss* is my own creation.

in the unitive kiss. This drama is made visible in God's descending movement toward us: God condescends in Jesus Christ, kissing a sinful world in order to redeem it. The Father's heart is made manifest in the drama of salvation as the Word is made flesh, the Bridegroom, in the power of the Spirit. It is the groom who by his life and passion wins the love of the Church, making her his bride. The Holy Spirit completes the drama by inculcating in the bride the gifts that the groom has provided for her. Thus the bride also knows the love of the Father who with extravagance gives her the name of daughter and constitutes her as his daughter-in-law, the beneficiary of the sweet caresses of his Son. Conversely, there is an ascending movement of the bride toward God: the Spirit transforms her and unites her to the groom, allowing her a lawful participation in the immanent kiss the Son has with the Father. Like Augustine before him, Bernard sees this participation in the life of the Trinity as the domain of the Spirit, since he is the very kiss (love) of the Father and the Son. As the kiss, the Spirit is the object of the bride's desire and the dynamic of worship, arousing in the bride an upward movement of her heart to sing and give glory to her beloved who is one with the Father. The kiss that the groom offers is the gift of the Holy Spirit, by which the bride is taken up into the infinite sweetness or embrace of the Father and the Son. The kiss of the Spirit is so efficacious that it issues in the bride a reverential attitude, for the object of her heartfelt desire is no human being but the Lord her God, who is to be worshipped with the Father and the Spirit from eternity.

The true worshipper must follow the God-ordained order, moving from below to above, from the groom's humanity or back to an apprehension of the mystery of the divine being that is love. A Christological focus on Jesus' humanity, especially his passion, has a vital bearing on Bernard's understanding of worship. Contemplation of the wounds of Christ, where God invests his dignity, virtue and glory, is a gift of the Spirit, and thus not to be despised. Through the groom's passion, the bride is led to see God as he is hidden beneath his humanity. Thus in worship, her gaze must be on the lowliness and humility of the cross, in which the groom is most himself. The bride is to turn her eyes away from God as he is, for she has no share in the majesty of God. To meditate on the cross aright is to be drawn by the groom's lovableness and to receive his embrace or kiss, by which the bride comes to recognize him as her lover before he is her beloved. The groom's passion fills the bride with God's steadfast love, by which she is loved and learns to love. The primacy of God's love as demonstrated in the groom's wounds is the condition of, and the dynamic behind, her reciprocal love and ardent praise of him. By virtue of the union with the groom, which is an action of the Spirit, the bride enjoys and secures all that the groom is and possesses, which includes an entrance into the heavenly sanctuary and an ontological participation in the fullness of the kiss. This chapter focuses primarily on those materials from Bernard's eighty-six sermons on *Song* that have a direct bearing on worship.

Brief Description of the *Song of Songs*

Unlike other songs, the *Song* was composed by the artistry of the Holy Spirit, inspiring its author, Solomon, to write a joyful song that excels all others. It is a poetic interaction between the bride and the groom, the two characters representing a powerful enactment of the drama of salvation history. The upward movement of the bride in praise and worship is borne out of an experience of exulting in the Spirit: "Only the touch of the Spirit can inspire a song like this, and only personal experience can unfold its meaning."

> Let those who are versed in the mystery revel in it; let all others burn with desire rather to attain to this experience than merely to learn about it. For it is not a melody that resounds abroad but the very music of the heart, not a trilling on the lips but an inward impulse of delight, a harmony not of voices but of wills. It is a tune you will not hear in the streets, these notes do not sound where crowds assemble; only the singer hears it and the one to whom he sings – the lover and the beloved. It is pre-eminently a marriage song telling of chaste souls in loving embrace, of their wills in sweet concord, of the mutual exchange of the heart's affections.[3]

Just as there is no theology without moral life, so there is no theology without doxology. True worship consists of both a desire for the kiss of love and fulfillment of this desire. Both are the outcome of God's prior love which necessarily precedes and exceeds us.

---

[3] SS 1.6–7.

Incarnation: The Kiss as God's Descent to Us

Bernard devoted the first eight sermons on the *Song* to uncover the meaning of the kiss in the first verse: "Let him kiss me with the kiss of his mouth." He asked: "How shall I explain so abrupt a beginning?"[4] From whose mouth comes the kiss? He proceeded to identify the kiss as Christ's living active word. The kiss of his mouth signifies the complete embrace by which the Son of God has assumed our humanity. In the incarnation, the mouth which kisses is the eternal Word; humanity is the receiver of this kiss, and the kiss itself "takes its being both from the giver and the receiver, is a person that is formed by both, none other than 'the one mediator between God and man,' himself a man, Christ Jesus."[5] Since God has become man, there is no cause for fear or distrust, but only assurance that comes from this kiss of his mouth. Bernard explained this in *Song* 2:

> When I came to recognize that he is truly mine, then I shall feel secure in welcoming the Son of God as mediator. Not even a shadow of mistrust can then exist, for after all he is my brother, and my own flesh. It is impossible that I should be spurned by him who is bone from my bones, and flesh from my flesh.[6]

The dual nature of Christology, signified by the touch of divinity on humanity, this kiss, is the abiding basis for God's mighty works in reconciling "to himself all things, whether on earth or in heaven" (Col. 1:20). Christ is the kiss (peace) between God and us, the very kiss which the saints under the old dispensation longed to taste, anticipating that in him they would "find happiness and a crown of rejoicing" (Sir 15:6).[7] Obviously, true worship springs from the kiss of the Bridegroom in whom the heart of the Father for the bride is revealed. The salvific necessity of this "holy kiss" is spelt out in the summary of *Song* 2:

---

[4] SS 1.3.
[5] SS 1.10. See Dennis E. Tamburello, *Bernard of Clairvaux: Essential Writings* (NY: The Crossroad Publishing Company, 2000), 107.
[6] SS 1.12.
[7] SS 1.12.

It would seem that this holy kiss was of necessity bestowed on the world for two reasons. Without it the faith of those who wavered would not have been strengthened, nor the desires of the fervent appeased. Moreover, this kiss is no other than the Mediator between God and man, himself a man, Christ Jesus, who with the Father and the Holy Spirit lives and reigns as God for ever and ever. Amen.[8]

The Three Kisses: Feet, Hand and Mouth

The Kiss of the Feet

Who can be so privileged that they can say, "Let him kiss me with the kiss of his mouth"? Those who can utter these words recognize that they are given to them. But a soul burdened with sins, subject to carnal passions and devoid of spiritual insights may not presume to make such a request. Bernard admitted that few people actually experience this. But this should in no way lead to sheer despair, but indicate that they are on their way to salvation. In order to ascend to God, we should not begin with a kiss on the mouth, as we only arrive there after we have first approached Jesus for forgiveness, repented of our sins and persevered in the works of justice, all of which are the outcome of God's operative grace in us. For every victory that is won, God is to be credited; for every gift conferred, God is to be praised; for every touch of love, God is to be glorified; for every advance toward God, we rise in a loving contemplation of him who empowers. Therefore, grace is the causative agency of our praise of God.

Bernard espoused a theology of accommodation in which God, who dwells in inaccessible light, for the sake of us imaginative people, has taken recourse to anthropological analogy. He thus spoke of three stages of union, using the metaphor of kissing first the feet, then the hands and finally the mouth of Jesus: "There is first the forgiveness of sin [kissing the feet of Jesus], then grace that follows on good deeds [kissing the hand of Jesus], and finally that contemplative gift by which a kind and beneficent Lord shows himself to the soul with as much as clarity as bodily frailty can endure [kissing the mouth of Jesus]."[9] In metaphorical language,

---

[8] SS 1.15.
[9] SS 1.22.

these members are not God's by nature, but are the modes of our encounter with God. Bernard wrote:

> The heartfelt desire to admit one's guilt brings a man down in lowliness before God, as it were to his feet; the heartfelt devotion of a worshipper finds in God renewal and refreshment, the touch, as it were, of his hand; and the delights of contemplation lead on to that ecstatic repose that is the fruit of the kiss of his mouth.[10]

The order by which the bride encounters the groom is where Bernard's theology of praise may be gleaned. We do not immediately leap to the intimate union or, in Bernard's words, "a holier intimacy" of the kiss of the mouth. He advised that we must begin with the bottom and move to the top: "They may not rashly aspire to the lips of the most benign Bridegroom, but let them prostrate themselves with me in fear at the feet of the most severe Lord . . . All you who are conscious of sin, do not regard as unworthy and despicable that position where the holy sinner laid down their sins."[11] When sinners repent and turn from the evil that inflames their passions, the "heavenly physician" will come to their aid swiftly and issue "a genuine conversion of life."[12] This is the beginning of worship: "Prostrate yourself on the ground, take hold of his feet, soothe them with kisses, sprinkle them with your tears and so wash not them but yourself."[13] The kiss of the feet is the kiss of peace, by which the intervening gulf between God and us that is caused by sin is bridged. This is a sign of God's grace, which abolishes the distance between God and us, thereby creating for us a sweet friendship with him. As such, the doctrine of reconciliation constitutes the theological basis of true efficacious worship.

In *Song* 6, Bernard ascribed the feet to Christ's humanity, while noting that Paul ascribed the head to his divinity. The two feet occur together: one refers to mercy, the other judgment.

> That God assumed the foot of mercy in the flesh to which he united himself, is taught in the Epistle of Hebrews, which speaks of Christ as one who has been tempted in every way that we are, though he is

---

[10] SS 1.23
[11] SS 1.16.
[12] SS 1.17; 21.
[13] SS 1.17.

without sin, that he might become merciful. And the other foot that is called judgment? Does not God made man plainly point out that this also belongs to the assumed humanity where he declares: 'Because he is the Son of Man the Father has appointed him supreme judge.'[14]

With these two feet, united and controlled by the divine head, Christ appears on earth, moving among living souls, "tirelessly enlightening and searching the hearts and loins of the faithful."[15] The two feet represent the two dispositions proper to the soul starting out on the way toward God: fear and hope. While the soul ponders upon divine judgment and justice, which causes repentance and fear in him, he must also ponder the other foot, the foot of mercy, lest the knowledge of his sins and the fear of God might lead him to despair. Conversely, just as he must consider divine mercy, which creates hope and pardon in him, he must also look at the other foot, the foot of divine judgment, lest the knowledge of God's mercy might give rise to a false sense of security: "It is clearly inexpedient to kiss one without the other; a man who thinks only of the judgment will fall into the pit of despair, another who deceitfully flatters God's mercy gives birth to a pernicious security."[16] Mercy and judgment, though mutually contradictory, are so closely joined in doxological experience that they constitute the theme of our songs. Henceforth, the soul will never cease to sing about both until the time when divine mercy triumphs over divine judgment. The balance between these contrary themes must be observed.

> But you know what a teacher experience is; no longer of judgment alone or mercy alone, but of mercy and judgment I will sing to you, O Lord. I shall never forget your precepts, mercy and judgment will be the theme of my songs in the house of my pilgrimage, until one day when mercy triumphs over judgment, my wretchedness will cease to smart, and my heart, silent no longer, will sing to you. It will be the end of sorrow.[17]

---

[14] SS 1.35–36.
[15] SS 1.36.
[16] SS 1.37.
[17] SS 1.37.

The Kiss of the Hand

By the same grace that is endowed, we raise our heads from the dust with a greater confidence with the purpose of kissing the hand of God. Bernard elaborated:

> Though you have made a beginning by kissing the feet, you may not presume to rise at once by impulse to the kiss of the mouth; there is a step to be surmounted in between, an intervening kiss on the hand . . . It is a long and formidable leap from the foot to the mouth . . . Consider for a moment: still tarnished as you are with the dust of sin, would you dare touch those sacred lips? Yesterday you were lifted from the mud, today you wish to encounter the glory of his face? No, his hand must be your guide to that end.[18]

When God sees the broken soul at his feet, he seizes him by reaching down with his hands to lift him up, causing him to aspire to the glory of his face. With brevity, Bernard spoke of God's two hands to which the second kiss is given: "I shall treat not only of one hand but of two, each under a particular name. One I shall call liberality because it gives generously; the other fortitude because it powerfully defends whatever it gives."[19] He who imparts the grace to repent also imparts the power to persevere, lest we end up in a condition worse than before, should he withdraw his supporting hand. This is the second in the order of worship: we, with gratitude to our benefactor, kiss his hand, and with his hand we perform virtuous deeds. In order not to be found ungrateful, we must kiss each of these hands, acknowledging and praising God as the supplier and conserver of all good things.[20] Thus it is of utmost importance that we should not make this favor an occasion of self-glorification. All our deeds are not our doing, but come from the hands of God, to whom glory is rightly ascribed. "First of all you must glorify him because he has forgiven your

---

[18] SS 1.18–19. Cited in Franz Posset, *Pater Bernhardus: Martin Luther and Bernard of Clairvaux* (Kalamazoo: Cistercian Publications, 1999), 200; William O. Paulsell, "Virtue in St. Bernard's Sermons on the *The Song of Songs*," in *Saint Bernard of Clairvaux: Studies in Commemorating the Eighth Centenary of His Canonization*, ed. M. Basil Pennington (Kalamazoo: Cistercian Publications, 1977), 101.
[19] SS 1.37.
[20] SS 1.38.

sins [the hand of liberality], secondly because he has adorned you with virtues [the hand of fortitude]."[21] For if we, steadfast now in good works, glory in them rather than in the Lord, it is our own hand that we kiss, not God's. Kissing God's hand is seeking God's glory; to do otherwise is idolatry, and that, for Bernard, "is the greatest evil and a denial of God."[22] In *Song* 10, Bernard stressed that contrition, thanksgiving and pious deeds are the "three ointments" of worship by which the bride is anointed, which please the groom.[23]

The Kiss of the Mouth

Once we have reached the twofold experience of divine benevolence in these two kisses, we need no longer hold back. Growth in this grace expands our confidence. Now we will love with greater ardor as we, by his grace, aspire to holier intimacy. To the one who is divinely disposed, God will not deny "the most intimate kiss of all, a mystery of supreme generosity and ineffable sweetness."[24] Bernard traced out the three stages:

> You have seen the way we must follow, the order of procedure. First we cast ourselves at his feet, we 'kneel before our Lord, our maker,' deploring the evil we have done. Then we reach out for the hand that will lift us up, that will steady our trembling knees. And finally, when we shall have obtained these favors through many prayers and tears, we humbly dare to raise our eyes to his mouth, so divinely beautiful, not merely to gaze upon it, but – I say with fear and trembling – to *receive his kiss*; for "Christ the Lord is the Spirit before our face."[25] And he who is joined to him in a holy kiss becomes, at his good pleasure, one spirit with him.[26]

---

[21] SS 1.19.
[22] SS 1.22–23.
[23] SS 1.63.
[24] SS 1.19–20.
[25] It is worth noting that Bernard's allusion to Lamentations 4:20 here is filtered through a tradition of Christian interpretation that sees the "Messiah" of the text (Judah's king) as "Christ the Lord", and connects "the breath of our nostrils" with the Holy Spirit.
[26] SS 1.19–20. Also cited in M. Basil Pennington, *The Last of the Fathers: The Cistercian Fathers of the Twelfth Century. A Collection of Essays* (Still

The kiss that the Bridegroom offers is the gift of the Holy Spirit, by which the bride is drawn into the infinite sweetness or embrace between the Father and the Son. Bernard did not compose a separate treatise on the Holy Spirit. However, his characterization of the Spirit as the kiss in *Song* 8 has its roots in Augustine, according to whom the Spirit is the mutual love of the Father and the Son.[27] A brief description of this historical antecedent will help shed light on Bernard's understanding of the Spirit as the bond of love.

Augustine: The Holy Spirit as the Bond of Love

In his notable work *De Trinitate*, Augustine developed a theology of the Spirit that corresponds to the doctrine of dual procession: "The Holy Spirit is communicated by the Father and the Son. He is their mutual Gift."[28] Biblically, the word most commonly linked to the Spirit is "gift" (cf. Acts 2:38; 8:20; 10:45; 11:17). He is "gift" because he is given to us, the recipients of the benefits of the cross, as a gift from both Father and Son. However, Augustine did not confine the meaning of gift to the temporal realm, as a gift bestowed only in time. There is a congruence of the economic and immanent rendering of gift so that the Spirit may be called Gift

---

River, Massachusetts: St. Bede's Publications, 1983), 83–84.

[27] The following scholars concur that Bernard's position on the Holy Spirit is traceable to Augustine: Elizabeth A. Dreyer, "An Advent of the Spirit: Medieval Mystics and Saints," in *Advents of Spirit*, eds. Braford E. Hinz & D. Lyk Dabney (Milwaukee: Marquette University, 2001), 137; Veli-Matti Kärkkäinen, *Pneumatology. The Holy Spirit in Ecumenical, International, and Contextual Perspective* (Grand Rapids: Baker Academic, 2002), 52; Anne Morris, "The Trinity in Bernard's Sermons on the Song of Songs," *Cistercian* 30 (1995): 46; Howard Watkin-Jones, *The Holy Spirit in the Medieval Church* (London: The Epworth Press, 1922), 128–29.

[28] *De Trinitate* VI.11, in *A Select Library of the Nicene and Post-Nicene Fathers of the Christian Church. St. Augustine: On the Holy Trinity, Doctrinal Treatises, Moral Treatises*, ed. Philip Schaff (Grand Rapids: Eerdmans, 1953), 3:84. NPNF translation is used unless otherwise indicated. *The Later Christian Fathers*, ed. & tr. Henry Bettenson (Oxford: Oxford University Press, 1970). The reference will be followed by Bettenson. *Augustine: Later Works, Library of Christian Classics*, vol. 8, ed. John Burnaby (London: SCM, 1955). The reference will be followed by LCC.

(*donum*) eternally prior to his being given (*donatum*). Augustine wrote:

> A further question has been raised; whether, just as the Son derives from his begetting not merely his sonship but his actual existence, so also the Holy Spirit derives his being from his being given, not only his character as a gift, but his actual existence; whether he existed before he was given, but was not yet a gift, or whether he was a gift even before he was given, in that God was to give him. But if he does not proceed except when he is given, he clearly could not proceed until there was someone to whom he might be given . . . Does the Holy Spirit always proceed, not in time only; but from eternity? But because he proceeded in order to be potentially a gift, he was already a gift before there was any recipient . . . For a gift can exist before it is given . . . The Spirit is eternally a gift, but the gift is bestowed in time.[29]

This question of the relation of the *opera ad extra Trinitatis* to the *opera ad intra Trinitatis* Augustine resolved by reasoning *a posteriori* from the temporal mission in time to an affirmation of an immanent procession in eternity. The Spirit is beforehand in eternity the one that he reveals himself to be, namely Gift. Immanently, and not just economically, the Spirit is to be referred to both the Father and the Son. The Spirit is the common gift of the Father and the Son in the immanent Trinity. The reciprocity of gift exchange, which is the Holy Spirit, is to be understood as, "a certain unutterable communion of the Father and the Son . . . [B]oth the Father is a spirit and the Son a spirit, both the Father is holy, and the Son holy. In order, therefore, that the communion of both may be signified from a name which is suitable to both, the Holy Spirit is called the gift of both."[30] Yet this inexpressible communion can best be described as "love": "Therefore, the Holy Spirit, whatever it is, is something common both to the Father and the Son. But that communion itself is consubstantial and coeternal; and if it may fitly be called friendship, let it be called; but it is more aptly called love."[31] As regards this point, Augustine began with our experience of the Spirit in the economy of salvation, as the love of God poured out in our hearts (Rom. 5:5), to conceive love as the

---

[29] *De Trinitate* 5.16 (Bettenson, 230).
[30] *De Trinitate* V.11; XV.17.
[31] *De Trinitate* VI.5.

most appropriate term for the Spirit as a divine person. He was aware that Scripture does not explicitly say that the Spirit is love. However, he argued that if God's being is defined in I John 4:8 as love, and the Spirit is God, it follows naturally that the Spirit is love. He spoke of the Spirit as proceeding from the mutual love of the first two persons for each other. The love that God is is bestowed first on the Son, who in turn returns the received love to the Father, with the Spirit binding them as mutual love. The love which proceeds from the Father and the Son is the fruit of and reality of their mutual love. "The divine act of love," O'Collins explains, "gives rise to its eternal, immanent fruit (*impressio amati in amato*), the Holy Spirit."[32] The Spirit, the gift of both the Father and the Son, is love, and thus he reveals to us the "common love" by which the first two persons mutually love each other. Toward the end of his *De Trinitate*, Augustine argued from mutual love to ontological communion between the first two persons, showing that both ideas are practically interchangeable: "And if the love by which the Father loves the Son and the Son loves the Father ineffably demonstrates the communion of both, what is more suitable than that He should properly be called love who is Spirit, common to both."[33] Related to the Spirit as "the bond of love" (*vinculum caritatis*) is the idea of relation within the Godhead, in which the persons of the Trinity are defined by their relations to one another.[34] The Spirit is thus the relation of love and communion between the first two persons, a relation which Augustine saw as foundational to the Apostle John's emphasis on the unity of will and purpose of the Father and the Son.

For Augustine, temporal mission corresponds to eternal procession; the former reveals a divine person in his eternal origin. From this, he argued that the Spirit has to be thought of as proceeding from the Son. One of the main proof texts for this is John 20:22, wherein the risen Christ is reported as "breathing upon his disciples" and saying, "receive the Holy Spirit." Augustine understood this to correspond to the eternal procession of the Spirit from the Son.

---

[32] Gerald O'Collins, *The Tripersonal God: Understanding and Interpreting the Trinity* (New York: Paulist Press, 1999), 136.
[33] *De Trinitate* XV.19.
[34] *De Trinitate* XV.17.

> For as to be born, in respect to the Son, means to be from the Father; so to be sent, in respect to the Son, means to be known to be from the Father. And as to be the gift of God in respect to the Holy Spirit, means to proceed from the Father; so to be sent, is to be known to proceed from the Father. Neither can we say that the Holy Spirit does not also proceed from the Son, for the same Spirit is not without reason said to be the Spirit both of the Father and of the Son. Nor do I see what else He intended to signify, when He breathed on the face of the disciples, and said, "receive ye the Holy Spirit." For the bodily breathing, proceeding from the body with the feeling of bodily touching, was not the substance of the Holy Spirit, but a declaration by a fitting sign, that the Holy Spirit proceeds not only from the Father, but also from the Son.[35]

Subsequently Augustine wrote of the manner in which the *filioque* doctrine can be affirmed. The Father endows the Son with the capacity to spirate the Spirit. It is in a "primordial" sense (*principaliter*) that the Spirit proceeds from the Father (*de Patre principaliter*), but only in a derivative sense that he proceeds from the Son. Augustine draws on Tertullian's term *principaliter* to defend the distinctive role of the Father within the Godhead. Commenting on John 15:26, where the Lord says, "whom (Holy Spirit) I send unto you from the Father," he writes: "The original source (*principium*) of the entire divinity (*divinitatis*) – or to put it better, of the being of God (*deitatis*) – is the Father."[36]

> God the Father alone is He from whom the Word is born, and from whom the Holy Spirit principally proceeds. And therefore I have added the word principally (corresponds to the Greek saying, "by way of the first principle"), because we find that the Holy Spirit proceeds from the Son also. But the Father gave him this too, not as to one already existing, and not yet having it; but whatever he gave to the only-begotten Word, he gave by begetting him. Therefore he so begat him as that the common Gift should proceed from him also, and the Holy Spirit should be the Spirit of both.[37]

---

[35] *De Trinitate* V.6 (LCC, 188); *De Trinitate* 5.5–6.
[36] *De Trintate* IV.20 as cited in Brian E. Daley, "Revisiting the '*Filioque*': Roots and Branches of An Old Debate, Part One," *Pro Ecclesia* X (2001): 41.
[37] *De Trinitate* XV.17, 29.

The Holy Spirit as Kiss/Love in Bernard

Bernard treated the Holy Spirit more in connection with his operation than with his being. However, this does not mean that he says nothing of the relationship that the Son has with the Spirit in the immanent Trinity. His *Sermons on the Feast of Pentecost* supports his *filioque* doctrine:

> The Holy Spirit is God himself . . . And therefore, with regard to the Holy Spirit, if I allow that it is not procession by which he proceeds from the Father and the Son, nevertheless I know that it is something, namely inspiration. For there are two from whom and by whom he may proceed . . . Understand that the Father is the principal Spirit, not because he is greater, but because he alone is from nothing, while the Son is from him, and the Holy Spirit is from both.[38]

Concerning the double procession of the Spirit, he wrote in his *Epistola* 107: "Concerning the Holy Spirit Scripture bears witness in that He proceeds, breathes forth, indwells, fills, glorifies. He is said to proceed in two ways; whence and whither? Whence? From the Father and the Son. Whither? To the creatures . . . by breathing forth He calls whom He has predestined; by indwelling He justifies whom He has called."[39] The eternal procession of the Spirit is logically prior to, and the presupposition of, the temporal procession of the Spirit. Bernard began with the experience of the Spirit in the economy of salvation to speak of Love as the most suitable name for the Spirit. This is evident in his little book *On Love*: "God is love. The Holy Spirit is denoted especially by the name of love. He himself is the Love of the Father and the Son . . . also whatever can be common to Both . . . For the Spirit is he who imparts life to the spirit of man, and teaches and trains him to love God."[40]

In *Song* 8, Bernard employed the metaphor of the kiss to speak of the twofold procession of the Spirit in God's being. This is most

---

[38] *Festo Pentenostes, Sermo* 1 as cited in Watkin-Jones, *The Holy Spirit in the Mediaeval Church*, 128.

[39] *Epistola* 107 (*Ad Thomam Praepositum de Beverla*) as cited in Watkin-Jones, *The Holy Spirit in the Mediaeval Church*, 128.

[40] *Tractatus de Charitate*, cap. 10 as cited in Watkin-Jones, *The Holy Spirit in the Mediaeval Church*, 129.

evident in his exposition of John 20:22, where Jesus, after breathing upon the disciples, said: "Receive the Holy Spirit."

> That favor, given to the newly-chosen Church, was indeed a kiss . . . [T]he invisible Spirit, who is so bestowed in that breath of the Lord that he is understood to proceed from him equally as from the Father, [is] truly the *kiss* that is common both to him who kisses and to him who is kissed. Properly understood, the Father is he who kisses, the Son is he who is kissed, then it is not wrong to see in the kiss the Holy Spirit, for he is the imperturbable peace of the Father and the Son, their unshakable bond, their undivided love, their indivisible unity . . . The Holy Spirit indeed is nothing else but the love and the benign goodness of them both.[41]

The Father is the source of the mystery of divine being that is love. "Thus, the Father, when he kisses the Son, pours forth into him the plentitude of the mysteries of his divine being, breathing forth love's deep delight."[42] The Son, who is begotten from eternity, receives all he is (including the kiss) from the Father and who returns his embrace (kiss) as his equal. "Because he was joined to him as an equal and embraced him as an equal – he does not beg for a kiss from an inferior position; rather on equally sublime heights mouth is joined to mouth, and by a prerogative that is unique he receives the kiss from the mouth."[43] In *Song* 42, Bernard asserted that there is no attenuation of being in the procession of the Son, who "receives all that he is from the Father."[44] They mutually coinhere in being and in glory; thus for the Son to receive glory from the Father in order to give it back to the Father does not entail a lack of it, for they are one.[45]

The kiss, which emanates from the one who kisses and the one who is kissed, is the Holy Spirit who proceeds equally from the Father and the Son as their mutual love, and is also their common gift to the bride. Bernard thus links the temporal mission of the Holy Spirit, revealing and communicating the knowledge of the kiss of the Father and the Son to us, with his immanent procession, speaking of the Holy Spirit as their undivided bond and love.

---

[41] SS 1.46–47.
[42] SS 1.50.
[43] SS 1.51–52.
[44] SS 2.218.
[45] SS 4.112–13.

Thus love, the very being of the Trinity, is ascribed in a special way to the Holy Spirit. All three persons exist from eternity in a differentiated unity, but without a distinction of will and purpose. Each in his proper mode and with one will and power, they participate as one God in the economy of salvation. The trinitarian act of mission consists of "the Father lovingly sending his Son and of the Son freely obeying the Father," with the Spirit of reciprocity between them.[46]

The kiss of the Father is incarnate in the Son, but is mediated to us in the power of the Spirit. Sent by both the Father and the Son, the Spirit conveys to us "the light of knowledge" and "the fire of love."[47] He renders possible the knowledge of the Godhead and represents the intimacy of love both within God's triune life and between God and us. The Holy Spirit is thus the bond of love within the Godhead and openness of love for us. The communion of love that is the Triune God is the spring of that same love poured out in the drama of salvation history, bestowing upon us the gift of a "kiss [from] the kiss of the mouth." As Morris puts it, "The kiss of the mouth, the gift of love and knowledge, which is the ineffable union of the Father and the Son, is the Holy Spirit, who is also, as the kiss from the kiss of the mouth, gift for us."[48] Furthermore, the same love that embraces the Father and the Son overflows as gift into the world in the mission of the Spirit. Bernard wrote in his *Song* 18:

> And so, he who is the primal Fountain of life full in himself and filled with himself, gushed forth and danced into the secret places of the heavens about him to fill them all with his favors. And having endowed these remotest heights and recesses, he burst forth our earth, saving men and beasts through his munificence, multiplying his mercies everywhere.[49]

---

[46] SS 1.47.

[47] SS 1.48. See James W. Zona, "'Set Love in Order in Me': *Eros*-Knowing in Origen and *Desiderium*-Knowing in Saint Bernard," *Cistercian Studies* 34 (1999): 158, where he argues that the metaphor of "fire" is traceable to Origen.

[48] Morris, "The Trinity in Bernard's Sermons on the Song of Songs," 47.

[49] SS 1.136.

The Kiss of the Kiss as the Dynamic of Worship: Participation in the Kiss of the Mouth

In *Song* 8, Bernard made a sharp distinction between "the kiss of the mouth" and "the kiss of the kiss." The former is the prerogative of the Father alone, while the latter refers to the Spirit, that unique bond between the Father and the Son. Bernard moved very quickly to develop the implications of this distinction for worship, our ascent to God. No matter how high we aim in making the offer of our mouths, we would necessarily find ourselves remote from the lips of the Most High, for the direct kiss of the mouth of the groom belongs to the Father alone, who loves his Son and embraces him with a kiss that is supremely unique. This embrace, or *perichoresis*, that is spoken of here is between equals: the eternal Father embraces the co-eternal Son, the infinite his equal. It is also mutual: the Father and the Son embrace each other with the very same love. Thus the kiss from the mouth is the kiss between the Father and the Son, not between the Son and humanity, as it is in *Song* 2. The "supreme kiss" signifies the infinite mutual embrace of love and knowledge of the Father and the Son: "What can it be if not a kiss that is utterly sweet, but utterly a mystery as well?"[50] This eternal, ineffable kiss, not offered to any creatures, occurs within the immanent Godhead:

> This is a kiss from mouth to mouth, beyond the claim of any creature . . . That the Son is in the Father and the Father in the Son signifies the kiss of the mouth. But the kiss of the kiss we discover when we read: "Instead of the spirit of the world, we have received the Spirit that comes from God, to teach us to understand the gifts that he has given us."[51]

Knowledge of the kiss of the mouth is given in revelation by the only Son, who is in the bosom of the Father. But to apprehend the sweet mystery of the kiss is to receive "the kiss [from] the kiss of the mouth," which is the gift of the Spirit. "No creature has been privileged to comprehend the secret of this eternal, blessed

---

[50] SS 1.45. See Edith Scholl, "The Sweetness of the Lord: *Dulcis* and *Suavis*," *Cistercian Studies* 27 (1992): 361, where she observes that the metaphor of "sweetness" is rooted in the patristic authors, especially in Augustine and Gregory the Great.
[51] SS 1.51.

and unique embrace; the Holy Spirit alone is the sole witness and confidant of their mutual knowledge and love."[52] By virtue of the Spirit being sent by Christ, he provides us with that divine kiss. The Spirit reveals Christ to us in worship, and through him enables us to offer to God both our being and activities (thanksgiving and praise).

The Son is united to the Father as an equal and embraces him as an equal. This equality does not collapse their personal distinctions, however, for they are not one person, but two. Only the Son, who is the Father's equal, his co-eternal and his only-begotten, receives the Father's kiss directly and totally. "For Christ therefore, the kiss meant a totality, for Paul only a participation; Christ rejoiced in the kiss of the mouth. Paul only in that he was kissed by the kiss."[53] The Son received the fullness of the kiss; the bride received only a participation in that kiss. Thus the bride cannot plead, "Let him kiss me with his mouth," but "Let him kiss me with the kiss of his mouth." Theological discourse must observe this distinction between the former, which speaks of the immediate kiss between equals, and the latter, which is the Song's unique way of articulating that true worship or the experience of union with God is mediated, just as relationship with him is never immediate.[54] Constitutively, the kiss of the mouth is restricted to the intra-trinitarian life. And yet, by participation it is communicated to the bride. She is given the "participated kiss," which Bernard called "the kiss of the kiss,"[55] namely the Spirit. The bride dares not ask for the *constitutive kiss*, which belongs to God's divine life, but for the kiss itself, for the Holy Spirit in whom both the Father and the Son are revealed to her. She cannot reach that glorious countenance on her own, but grasps it only when the Most High condescends to her level, to be kissed by her. When the bride begs for the kiss, it is the Son whom she approaches, since it is by him that it is made manifest. Yet this revelation is fulfilled in us through the kiss, that is, through the Holy Spirit, a fact to which St. Paul bears witness: "These are the very things that God has revealed to us through the Spirit" (I Cor. 2:10). Bernard commented: "It is by giving the Spirit, through whom he reveals, that he shows

---

[52] SS 1.50.
[53] SS 1.51–52.
[54] Tamburello, *Bernard of Clairvaux*, 110.
[55] Cf. McDonnell, "Spirit and Experience in Bernard of Clarivaux," 11, where the term "participated kiss" is coined.

us himself; he reveals in the gift, his gift is in the revealing."[56] Only those who have experienced the kiss (Spirit), which itself is revelation, can grasp the mystery of the constitutive kiss of the Godhead.

The kiss of the Spirit is the very object of the bride's desire when she asks to be kissed. It is also the dynamic of the bride's outrageous boldness with God by asking what she desires.[57] Not only is the Spirit the unitive kiss between the Father and the Son, he is also the very openness of their mutual kiss, since it is through his kiss that the Father and the Son indwell the bride. In receiving this kiss, the unitive love constitutive of the Trinity is shared with the bride. The Spirit is the power of efficacy, enabling us to share in the kiss of love (intimate communion) between the Father and the Son. The kiss of the mouth, which is reserved for the equals, the Father and the Son, is extended to the bride as a participation, not as a totality. This participation in the constitutive kiss between the Father and the Son is a gift of the Spirit, by which the bride has a share in the holier intimacy of God's glorious countenance:

> Felicitous, however, is this kiss of participation that enables us not only to know God but to love the Father, who is never fully known until he is perfectly loved . . . Let that man who feels he is moved by the same Spirit as the Son, let him know that he too is loved by the Father . . . For if marriage according to the flesh constitutes two in one body, why should not a spiritual union be even more efficacious in joining two in one spirit? And hence everyone who is joined to the Lord is one spirit with him.[58]

In the participated kiss, the bride has "witness too from the Father, how lovingly and courteously he gives her the name of daughter, and nevertheless invites her as his daughter-in-law to the sweet caresses of his Son."[59] The Spirit of the Son is the fulfillment of the bride's desire, that she is given an ontological participation in the sweetness of the groom's kiss that is identical to the Father's. The bride is given the kiss (Spirit), whose kiss gains for her a legitimate

---

[56] SS 1.48.
[57] Dreyer, "An Advent of the Spirit: Medieval Mystics and Saints," 138; Stanley Burgess, *The Holy Spirit: Medieval, Roman Catholic and Reformation Traditions* (Peabody: Hendrickson Publishers, Inc., 1997), 57.
[58] SS 1.52.
[59] SS 1.52.

entrance through the Son into divine life. Thus to worship God aright is to worship him only through participating in the Son's communion with the Father in the dynamic of the Spirit.

The union of divine operations, which Bernard affirmed along with the unity of the Godhead, grounds worship as a trinitarian activity, originated from the Father, effected through the Son, and perfected in the Spirit. There is no work of God in which the persons of the Trinity are not jointly operative. Just as this is true of creation and redemption, so it is with worship. As the initiatory descent of worship, the Father moves freely toward us in Christ, whose kiss is felt that we might share with him his sweet communion with the Father. This cannot occur without the Spirit's help. The ineffable sweetness that God is flows to us from "the sweet name of Father,"[60] through "the unutterable sweetness of the Word,"[61] in the Holy Spirit, "the very sweetness of God," who "with all the skill and sweetness of his [divine] artistry" accomplishes his work in our inmost being.[62] As the corresponding ascent of worship, the Spirit leads us to the Son, through whom our being and act (worship) have free access to the Fatherly sanctuary in the same Godhead. The unitive movement of the Spirit in which we participate is the condition of the possibility of true worship, which is through the Son to the Father. In the perfecting causality of the Spirit, all our corresponding activities – prayer, piety, obedience, service, praise – reach the Father, the proper object of our worship, through his Son, the mediator of our worship. We approach God with the sacrifice of praise, thanksgiving, prayers and service – these enacted responses of faith have the indwelling Spirit as the source. The spiritual union the bride enjoys with her groom is so efficacious that it yields in the bride a reverential attitude toward the Lord her God, the king who falls in love with her beauty (cf. Ps. 44:11ff): "See then, from whom this bride demands a kiss. O Soul called to holiness, make sure that your attitude is respectful [reverential], for he is the Lord your God, who perhaps ought not to be kissed, but rather adored [worshipped] with the Father and the Holy Spirit for ever and ever."[63] The reverential knowledge of God in Christ by faith is the action of the kiss (Spirit). By the

---

[60] SS 1.106.
[61] SS 4.209.
[62] SS 1.127.
[63] SS 1.52.

kiss of the kiss, the bride can attain to the kiss of the groom's mouth, by which the sweetness of the Fatherly kiss is hers. As the perfector of worship, the Spirit exalts the community in Christ to the heavenly throne of the Father. The soul enjoys the fruit of the kiss, and is stirred to praise him: "What sweetness! What grace! What mighty love! Can it be that the Highest of all is made one with all?"[64]

Nature of Mystical Union

Only by the kiss (Spirit), the unitive principle, is the bride drawn into the union, not of identity or essence, but of the love that the Son shares with the Father. The mystical union is not that of pantheism, in which the abolition of the distinction between divinity and humanity is the goal.[65] The union with Christ, to which the pious soul attains, is radically distinguished from a consubstantiality that occurs between Father and Son in the Trinity. *Song* 71 draws a sharp contrast between divine unity and creaturely unity. The groom and the Father are truly and perfectly one; they mutually indwell each other. This unity is one of a kind, totally distinct from that of the bride and the groom, even though they are able to mutually abide as one spirit. The unity of the Father and the Son is of an immanent ineffability, "capable equally of containing and being contained but capable of containing each other without being divisible and of being contained without being divided."[66] Bernard elaborated on this through a distinction between the words one substance (*unum*) and one subject (*unus*). The Father and the Son are not one subject, *unus*, because the Father is one subject and the Son is another. But they are one substance, inseparably one, *unum*. As pure spirit, God's essence is utterly simple, without partition. On the contrary, God and the soul are not one substance, and thus cannot be said to be *unum*. The soul is not to be understood pantheistically, as an extension of God's being. Yet they are united as one spirit in the bond of love: "But that unity is caused not so much by the identity of essences

---

[64] SS 3.177.
[65] See Ernest Heinrich Klotsche, *The History of Christian Doctrine* (Grand Rapids: Baker, 1979), 133, where he said that Bernard's mysticism is "pure, spiritual and free from pantheistic ideas."
[66] SS 4.55.

as by the concurrence of wills . . . [N]ot only the difference in kind but also the difference of degree in these unities is clear enough; for the one exists in the one mode of being [and the same essence] and the other between different modes [existing essences]."[67] While God is one, *unum*, in being and essence, God and the soul are one, *unus*, in spirit. Whereas the former unity, by which the Father and the Son are *unum*, exists as uncaused from eternity, the latter unity, by which God and the soul are one, is brought about by the action of the Spirit. The soul's union with God, as Stiegman pointed out, "is not a fusion of natures, but a conformity of wills . . . Bernard's mystical aspiration is not the loss of self, but a holding of all in common as with spouses, particularly the common will."[68] It is a happy union, but pales in comparison with the union of the holy Godhead. This is borne out in Bernard's *Song* 71:

> Thus the soul which finds its good in cleaving to God will not consider itself perfectly united with him until it perceives that he abides in her and she in him. Not even then may she be said to be one with God as the Father and the Son are one, although "he who cleaves to God is one spirit with him . . ." Surely no one in his senses, either on earth or in heaven, would appropriate to himself that utterance of the Only-begotten Son: "I and the Father are one."[69]

The mystical union is neither vacuous of content, nor is it irrational. It requires spiritual knowledge and love for the union to be complete – this is wrought by the Spirit.[70] Bernard repudiated two types of people who have no part in the divine kiss: those who know the truth without loving it, and those who love it without understanding it. Just as the Word indwells us to instruct us in wisdom, so the Spirit draws us to the love of wisdom. Those whom the Spirit kisses love with understanding and understand

---

[67] SS 4.55. See Arie de Reuver, *Sweet Communion. Trajectories of Spirituality from the Middle Ages through the Further Reformation*, tr. James A. De Jong (Grand Rapids: Baker Academic, 2007), 54.

[68] Emero S. Stiegman, "Humanism in Bernard of Clairvaux: Beyond Literary Culture," *The Chimarea of His Age: Studies on St. Bernard of Clairvaux*, ed. Ellen Rozanne Elder and John Sommerfeldt (Kalamazoo: Cistercian, 1980), 36; Gillian R. Evans, *The Mind of St. Bernard of Clairvaux* (Oxford: Clarendon Press, 1983), 122.

[69] SS 4.53.

[70] Etienne Gilson, *The Mystical Theology of St. Bernard* (London/New York: Sheed and Ward, 1940), 152.

with loving. The kiss (Spirit) is the completion of the union of the bride and her groom, in which ignorance and lukewarmness are excluded. *Song* 8 reads:

> For the Spirit teaches not by sharpening curiosity but by inspiring charity. And hence the bride . . . She asks rather for a kiss; that is, she calls upon the Holy Spirit by whom she is simultaneously awarded with the choice repast of knowledge and the seasoning of grace. How true it is that the knowledge imparted in the kiss is lovingly received, since the kiss is love's own token . . . He is in truth the Spirit of wisdom and insight . . . is fully equipped with the power of kindling the light of knowledge and infusing the delicious nurture of grace.[71]

Bernard's conviction that God is not really known until he is loved finds support in Romans 1:21, where Paul bemoaned about people who possessed knowledge but refused to love and honor God. Knowledge devoid of the fervor of devotion is not the fruit of the kiss (Spirit). By the experience of the Spirit, "the principle of insertion,"[72] the bride is inserted into Christ who becomes a spring inside her, welling up to eternal life. She cannot rest content with the knowledge she possesses, but aspires to the worship of the Most High.[73] Of the bride's desire, Bernard wrote in *Song* 9:

> 'I cannot rest,' she said, 'unless he kisses me with the kiss of his mouth. I thank him for the kiss of the feet. I thank him too for the kiss of the hand; but if he has genuine regard for me, let him kiss me with the kiss of his mouth. There is no reason of ingratitude on my part; it is simply that I am in love. The favors I have received are far above what I deserve, but they are less than what I long for. It is desire that drives me on, not reason. Please do not accuse me of presumption if I yield to this impulse of love.'[74]

The kiss of the kiss that she experiences sets her soul aflame for the groom. By that kiss, she perceives the desire of the lover and

---

[71] SS 1.49.

[72] McDonnell, "Spirit and Experience in Bernard of Clairvaux," 10.

[73] Cf. Marsha L. Dutton, "Intimacy and Imitation: The Humanity of Christ in Cistercian Spirituality," in *Erudition at God's Service: Studies in Medieval Cistercian History, XI*, ed. John R. Sommerfeldt (Kalamazoo: Cistercian Publications, 1987), 57.

[74] SS 1.54. For a detailed study of desire, see Michael Casey, *Athirst For God: Spiritual Desire in Bernard of Clairvaux's Sermons on the Song of Songs* (Kalamazoo: Cistercian Publications, 1988).

will know that the groom is nigh. "She will detect with happy eyes the eye that gazes on her like a sun-ray piercing wall, and at last she will hear the voices of jubilation and in love will call out: 'my love, my dove, my beautiful one'" (Sg. 2:9).[75] In that union, the bride secures and enjoys everything that the groom is: "Christ became for us the wisdom of God, and justice, and sanctification and redemption" (I Cor. 1:30). The kiss (Spirit) is the dynamic of the bride's vehement love for the groom.

> This is loving God with the whole soul . . . If, with the help of the Spirit, the soul attains such strength that it remains steadfast no matter what the effort or difficulty, if the fear of death itself cannot make it act unjustly, but even then it loves with the whole strength, this then is spiritual love. I think the name is very fitting for this special love because of the fullness of the Spirit in which it excels. This is enough for those words of the bride: "Therefore the young maidens love you so much." In those things that to follow may he open to us the treasure of his mercy, the one who guards them, Jesus Christ, our Lord, who lives and reigns in the unity of the Holy Spirit, God, for ever and ever. Amen.[76]

Bernard stressed the role that the Spirit plays in enabling Christians to cry, "Abba, Father" (Gal. 4:6). However, we are told to be sensitive to the movements of the Spirit so that we can act in accordance with his will. The bride must render an obedience that is proper to God, the one who is worthy of worship. In his *Song* 46, Bernard deemed that obedience was essential to the preparation for mystical union and contemplation:

> Therefore you must take care to surround yours with the flowers of good works, with the practice of virtues that precede holy contemplation as the flower precedes the fruit . . . The Bridegroom will not sleep in the same bed with you, especially if, instead of the flowers of obedience, you have bestrewn it with the hemlock and nettles of disobedience. Because of this he will not listen to your prayers. When you call he will not come. Nor will this great lover of obedience who preferred to die rather than disobey, put himself into the power of one who will not obey.[77]

---

[75] SS 3.99.
[76] SS. 1.154–55
[77] SS 2.244.

To the soul that has been prepared by the Father for the ways of the Lord, God will not withhold the blessing of his presence, "even though he who visits in the Spirit comes secretly and stealthily like a shy lover."[78] The one who feels loved will sense the fire of divine love, which indeed consumes, but does not debase: "It is a coal of desolating fire, but a fire that rages against vices only to produce a healing unction in the soul."[79] God's love burns vehemently hot in the face of unrighteousness as proof that he cares. Yet this anger is not a vindictive kind; nor is it a frustrated love turned sour. Rather, it is an expression of the groom's passionate love that "burns pleasantly and devastates felicitously."[80] The groom pours out his wrathful opposition against anything that might hinder the sweetness of the intimacy with the bride. Thus the groom performs a work of cleansing to arouse and prepare the bride, to make her aware of her fallen state, that afterward she might the more sweetly relish what God's action makes of her. Accordingly the presence of the groom, which the bride feels within, is two-fold in its effects, in the power that transforms her and the love that inflames her.[81] This too is bound up with the idea of compunction, the piercing effect of God in the bride, inflaming the soul with love for heavenly goods. Breaking forth in praise and awe is accomplished through a sequential order, from the recognition of personal sinfulness to a positive apprehension of divine mercy. Bernard here is indebted to Gregory the Great, according to whom compunction entails an acknowledgment of one's inadequacy and a fervent desire for the coming of the groom.[82] "[W]hen the compunction of fear has become complete,"

---

[78] SS 3.99.
[79] SS 3.102.
[80] SS3.102.
[81] SS 3.102.
[82] Gregory the Great, *Dial* 3.34 (PL. 77:300a): "First the soul thirsting for God is pierced (*compungitur*) by fear and afterwards by love. In the beginning, the soul is moved to tears at the remembrance of its evil deeds, and it fears the prospect of eternal punishment. But when, after a long and anxious experience of pain, this fear works itself out, then is born in the soul a calmness coming from the assurance of forgiveness and the soul is inflamed with love for heavenly joys. He who previously wept at the prospect of being led to punishment, now begins to weep most bitterly because he is far from the Kingdom. For the mind contemplates the choirs of angels, the community of the blessed spirits

Gregory wrote, "then it draws the soul into the compunction of love."[83] Being moved or pierced by a realization of God's fervent love despite her sinfulness, the bride's entire orientation changes from fear to the love of God. The soul that calls on the groom to return, as the bride does in *Song* 2, truly enjoys the intimacy of his sweet presence so that it could be said of her: "My heart became hot within me, as I mused the fire burned (Ps. 38:4)."

Bernard felt the effects of the Word's visit on his soul, although he did not always perceive the "different times" of his coming. In *Song* 74, he recounted: "I perceived his presence, I remembered afterwards that he had been there with me; sometimes I had a presentiment that he would come, but I was not conscious of his coming or his going. And where he comes from when he visits my soul, and where he goes, and by what means he enters and goes out, I admit that I don't know even now."[84] The Word is not localized, not in any place, and thus is not perceptible to the exterior senses. By ourselves, we cannot perceive the Word. But his presence can be sensed, perceived or felt only by the happy soul "who has his being from him, lives for him, and is moved by him."[85] Hence the ability to enter into the embrace of the groom lies not in our own power, but in God's Word which moves the heart through the kindling of vehement love to understand and delight in his presence. God's prior love must meet the fallen creature so that the first dawn of light occurs and the desire for him, which he creates in us, might be fulfilled. God alone is the efficient and final cause of love. In *On Loving God*, Bernard wrote:

> God offers the opportunity, he creates the affection, and consummates the desire. He makes, or rather is made himself lovable. He hopes to be so happily loved that he will not be loved in vain. His love prepares and rewards ours . . . O Lord, you are so good to the soul

---

and the splendor of the unending vision of God and it becomes still more downcast at being separated from these eternal goods than it was when it wept out of fear of unending evils. For it is a fact that when the compunction of fear has become complete, then it draws the soul into the compunction of love." As cited in Casey, *Athirst for God*, 122. See also Jean Leclercq, *The Love of Learning and the Desire for God* (New York: Fordham University Press, 1982), pp. 25–36.

[83] Gregory the Great, *Dial* 3.34 as cited in Casey, *Athirst for God*, 122.
[84] SS 4.90.
[85] SS 4.90.

who seeks you, what must you be to the one who finds you? More wonderful still, no one can seek you unless he has already found you. You wish to be found so that you may be sought for, but sought for to be found. You may be sought and found, but nobody can forestall you.[86]

Therefore to be drawn by the groom is "to receive from him the desire by which she is enticed, the desire of good actions, the desire to bring forth fruit for the Bridegroom, for to her the Bridegroom is life, and death gain."[87] To the one driven by an impulse to worship God and thus to resort to him in thought, reading, prayer and in obedience, God reveals himself gradually by means of this familiarity and thus becomes sweet to her in the Spirit of his Son.

The ascent to God is not a self-willed initiative, as it were, apart from grace, but it is a gift of God, which impels the believer toward final glory or completion. The deep void within the human soul can only be filled by an intimacy with God, the fruit of God's kiss. The spiritual desire, which necessarily leads to divine union, is nothing but a mirroring of the divine desire, which constitutes humanity with no other purpose than union with him. *Song* 57 states:

> And if the discourse sounds sweet and agreeable, if antipathy is banished by eagerness to listen, then not only is the Bridegroom believed to be on the way but to be speeding, that is, coming in one's desire. His desire gives rise to yours; and because you are eager to receive his word he is hastening to enter your heart; for he first loved us, not we him.[88]

The journey back to God is of reason by the Word of God, the immediate cause of spiritual desire in us, and by the will through the effective agency of the Holy Spirit. Not by works, but purely by grace is that mystical union initiated and enjoyed. Its essence is an inward relationship, not an outward performance. The union is not a creaturely kind, but an ineffably spiritual kind. When the

---

[86] Bernard, *On Loving God* (Kalamazoo: Cistercian Publications, 1995), 24, as quoted in Bernard McGinn, *The Growth of Mysticism: Gregory the Great through the 12th Century* (New York: The Crossroad Publishing Company, 1999), 195.
[87] SC 3.108.
[88] SS 3.101.

Word speaks, Bernard wrote, it is actually "the Spirit who speaks," and thus the conversation between the Word and the soul must be spiritually understood.

> So whenever you hear or read that the Word and the soul converse together, and contemplate each other, do not imagine them speaking with human voices nor appearing in bodily form. Listen, the Word is a spirit, the soul is a spirit; and they possess their own mode of speech and mode of presence in accord with their natures. The speech of the Word is loving kindness, that of the soul, the fervor of devotion . . . The speech of the Word is an infusion of grace; the soul's response is wonder and thanksgiving.[89]

The Word infuses in the soul "the power to love, and to know it is loved in return."[90] Love then fulfills the lover, which fulfillment is the gift of God, the indwelling of the Holy Spirit. The grace-filled character of the bride's desire will grow stronger insofar as the relationship with the groom is prolonged. Abiding in desire is an indication of at least a partial possession of God, the very object of the love. Hidden in desire is the seed of its own fulfillment. Thus God is to be extolled for never ceasing to work through grace, bringing into fruition the desire he implants in the bride. All human activities, including cleansing from sin, growth in holiness and praise of him, are the results of the impartation of God's efficacious grace. The Spirit works in the soul, transforms it and eventually creates the worship of the groom who fills the bride with awe and wonder. Happy is the bride who is united by the Spirit to the groom, to receive the sweetness of his kiss or embrace, which is one with his Father!

Worship from Below, the Wounds of Christ: A Great Gift of the Spirit

Union with Christ, though it is fulfilled in the spiritual realm, begins through the love of creaturely humanity, which is assumed by the groom and signified by the kiss of his mouth. Bernard's emphasis is not so much on who Christ is in essence, i.e., God and Man in unity, but what that person does for us (*pro nobis*).

---

[89] SS 2.238; 3.35–36
[90] SS 2.238.

The *pro nobis* aspect of Christ's person is typical of Bernard's Christology. Essential to this is the Bernardine concept of "Christ's double right to the kingdom of heaven," as found in what was called the *Bernard Legend*.[91] Underlying this concept are Christ's two important rights: one inherited by him on account of his being the Son of God; and the other earned by the merit of his passion, which he communicated to the believers. Bernard reportedly acknowledged:

> I know very well that I am unworthy to possess the kingdom of heaven through my own merit. However, my Lord Jesus Christ has won heaven by a twofold right, namely, by inheritance from His Father, and by merit of His Passion; whereof He is content with the one, and gives me the other. Therefore, I claim heaven as my own right, and shall not be confounded.[92]

Driven by the soteriological significance of the person of Christ, Bernard insisted on cleaving to Christ's lowly humanity as a means through which the contemplative gains an inward vision, not so much of who God is in himself, as of what he has done for us, namely God's steadfast love as manifested in the wounds of Christ. "His greatest achievement," Workman commented, "was to recall devout and loving contemplation to the image of the crucified Christ, and to found that worship of our Savior as the 'Bridegroom of the Soul'."[93] The purpose of incarnation includes a

---

[91] Cf. J. de Voragine, *Legenda aurea,* 4th ed. (Heidelberg: Verlag Lambert Schneider, 1963), ch. 120. The Bernard Legend is found there on 658–72. Bernard's concept of Christ's double right is picked up by Martin Luther. See LW 30, 230; WA 20, 624, 3 as cited in my Luther monograph, *Luther as a Spiritual Adviser: The Interface of Theology and Piety in Luther's Devotional* Writings (Milton Keynes: Paternoster, 2007), 20.

[92] Voragine, *Legenda Aurea*, 665.

[93] H.B. Workman, "Bernard of Clairvaux," *Encyclopedia of Religion and Ethics*, ed. James Hastings (New York: Scribner's Sons, 1917), 1.532. Reinhold Seeberg, in *The History of Doctrines* (Grand Rapids: Baker, 1977), 53, wrote: "The strongest feature of Bernard is the energy with which he leads the souls of his hearers and readers to immerse themselves in the contemplation of the humanity of Jesus, particularly his passion." Cf. Bent Hagglund, *History of Theology* (St. Louis, MO: Concordia Publishing House, 1966), 203: "Meditation on Christ's earthly life, and particularly on His sufferings, were at the center of Bernard's mysticism. Above all he was motivated by the concept of Jesus as the soul's bridegroom which

revelation of God's lovableness, which attracts human adoration of him. In a strikingly lyrical fashion, Bernard expressed: "Even clad in my form, how beautiful you are, Lord Jesus!"[94] God's attractiveness looms large, and is ever before us in the memory of Christ (*memoria Christi*). In the cross, the groom is most himself, that is, in his opposites: majesty in humility; glory in shame; power in weakness. Thus, in worship, the bride's gaze must be on the lowliness, shame and weakness of the cross, in which the groom "makes, or rather is himself made lovable."[95] The groom leads the bride to see God as he is hidden beneath his humanity, working out her salvation in the hidden way. She is to turn her eyes away from God as he is, for she has no share in the majesty of God. To meditate on the cross aright is to be drawn by the groom's lovableness and to receive his embrace or kiss, by which the bride comes to recognize him as her lover before he is her beloved. This is the fruit of Christ's passion: to be apprehended by the groom as his beloved in the Spirit.

To meditate on the cross is to reap the rewards of what Christ's passion has achieved for us. Undeniably, meditation rightly acquaints us with the knowledge of sin, by which we are crushed. But contrition should not be our endless preoccupation, lest we end up in deeper guilt and despair.[96] We should move beyond the kiss of the feet to the kiss of hand; we are to dwell on the glad remembrance of God's bountifulness, by which our confidence and faith are immovably certain. To combat a burdened soul and guilty conscience, Bernard recommended placing before us, as he did, "Jesus and him crucified":

> The world rages, the body presses, the devil lays his snares: I do not fall because I am founded on the rock. I have sinned gravely, my conscience is disturbed, but not perturbed, because in my heart *I remember the wounds of the Lord* . . . What sin is so 'deadly' that it cannot be forgiven in the death of Christ. If therefore a medication so powerful and efficacious finds entrance into my mind, no disease, however virulent, can frighten me . . . Whatever is lacking in my

---

he derived from the Song of Solomon."

[94] SS 2.57. Also cited in Emero Stiegman, "Bernard of Clairvaux, William of St. Thierry, the Victorines," in *The Medieval Theologians*, ed. G.R. Evans (Oxford: Blackwell Publishers, 2001), 133.
[95] Bernard, *On Loving God*, 24,
[96] SS 1.70.

own resources I usurp for myself from the heart of the Lord, which overflows with mercy. And there is no lack of clefts by which they are poured out. They pierced his hands and his feet, they gored his side with a lance, and through these fissures I can suck honey from the rock.[97]

We must lay hold of the merit of Christ's passion, whereby we claim heaven as our own and shall not be confounded. We learn to accustom ourselves with the gift of redemption and praise God, through the merit of the cross, for making possible all intimacy with him. For this is accomplished in the crucified Son, in whom God has invested his dignity, honor and worship. The work of redemption which the incarnate Son achieves is strong enough to excite love and praise in the redeemed. In *On Loving God*, Bernard wrote: "For it behooves us, if we would have Christ as a frequent visitor, to fill our hearts with faithful meditations . . . in the mercy that Christ showed us in dying for us."[98] Bernard deemed the incarnation and passion of the Son causative of our upward movement toward God in praise and holy living. This is evident in his *Song* 20:

> Notice that the love of the heart is, in a certain sense, carnal, because our hearts are attracted most toward the humanity of Christ and the things he did or commanded while in the flesh . . . The soul at prayer should have before it a sacred image of the God-man, in his birth or infancy or as he was teaching, or dying, or rising, or ascending. Whatever form it takes, this image must bind the soul with the love of virtue and expel carnal vices, eliminate temptations and quiet desires. I think this is the principal reason why the invisible God willed to be seen in the flesh and to converse with men as man. He wanted to recapture the affections of carnal men who were unable to love in any other way, by first drawing them to the salutary love of his own humanity and then gradually raise them to spiritual love.[99]

The "carnal love," Bernard said, "becomes better when it is rational, and becomes perfect when it is spiritual."[100] This movement is made possible through the agency of the Spirit. Thus, "this devotion to

---

[97] SS 3.143 (Italics).
[98] Bernard, *On Loving God*, 139–40; 142.
[99] SS 1.152.
[100] SS 1.152.

the humanity is a gift," Bernard emphasized, "a great gift of the Spirit."[101]

In *Song* 11, Bernard stressed the efficacy of meditation on Christ's humanity and the salutary fruits one reaps from this. The work of redemption should by no means be allowed to disappear from the memory of the redeemed. We could recount the countless benefits that the Lord, so merciful and tender-hearted, bestows on sinners, for which praise and glory are rightly due. Concerning this work, Bernard mentioned two important points for consideration: manner and fruit.

> The manner involved the self-emptying of God; the fruit was that we should be filled with him. Meditation on the former is the seed-bed of holy hope; meditation on the latter is an incentive to the highest love. Both of them are essential for our progress because hope without love is the lot of the time-server and love without hope grows cold.[102]

The manner of our redemption consists of a movement of God toward us, that by a community of will with the Father, the Son "emptied himself even to the assuming [kissing] of human nature, even to accepting death, death on a cross."[103] Christ's humanity is the window into the unfathomable mystery of divine being that is love. This is borne out succinctly in *Song* 61, where Bernard argued that the suffering love demonstrated in Christ's humanity is the love of the Father who desires our salvation.

> The nail that pierced him has become for me a key unlocking the sight of the Lord's will . . . The nail cries out, the wound cries out that God is truly in Christ, reconciling the world to himself. "The iron pierced his soul" (Ps. 104:8), and his heart has drawn near, so that he is no longer one who cannot sympathize with my weaknesses. The secret of his heart, so that through the clefts of his body; that mighty mystery of loving is laid open, laid open to the tender mercies of our God in which the morning sun from on high has risen upon us. Surely his heart is laid open through his wounds![104]

---

[101] SS 1.154. Brian Patrick McGuire, *The Difficult Saint: Bernard of Clairvaux and His Tradition* (Kalamazoo: Cistercian Publications, 1991), 228.
[102] SS 1.71–72. See John R. Sommerfeldt, *The Spiritual Teachings of Bernard of Clairvaux* (Kalamazoo: Cistercian Publications, 1991), 74.
[103] SS 1.75.
[104] SS 3.143–44. See Oluf Schonbeck, "Saint Bernard, Peter Damian, and the Wounds of Christ," *Cistercian Studies* 35 (1995): 276–78.

Meditation on Christ's wounds is thus no small favor, for it fills the bride with the love of the groom, Jesus Christ, the mediator between God and man, who is of one being with the Father and the Spirit. Since both the Father and the Son mutually coinhere in being and agency, the Sonly activity is also the "fatherly activity."[105] What the Son does corresponds to what the Father does, and the Spirit is the openness of their mutual activity. The nail, the suffering and death of Christ, is the key to unlock the heart of the Father. The groom lays down his own life for his bride – this he does in response to the love of the Father who sends. We should begin with the heart of the groom and ascend to the heart of the Father, and know for sure that they are one identical heart, which yearns for us. The heart of the groom, which is laid open by his wounds, is also the heart of the Father. Everything the groom does for the bride on the cross manifests the tender mercy of the Father, whose nature it is "always to have mercy and pardon."[106] Thus no text from the whole of the Bible meant more to Bernard than I John 4:8, "God is love," for this conveys all that we need to know about him: love is not that which God possesses, but that which he is. "God loves too, though not through a gift distinct from himself: he is himself the source of loving. And therefore it is all the more vehement, for he does not possess love, he is love."[107] God's being as love is thus relational, but this is in no way understood in any creaturely sense as meaning that a soul must go outside itself to overcome its lack and seek perfection. Rather, the utterly transcendent mystery of the Trinity is fullness of love. The eternal relationship of love in the Godhead consists in the Father's self-giving to the Son, who receives all that he is from the Father, and the Son's return of all that he is to the Father in love, for God does not love with a gift distinct from himself. The Holy Spirit is the bond of love between the Father and the Son and also the openness of their embrace, which is shared with the bride in the gift of salvation. As love in essence, God cannot do other than love. The mystery of God's being as love is laid open through the suffering of the groom, who loves from complete and spontaneous freedom, not out of any deficiency of his infinite being. This pure abundance of love that suffers incites friendship

---

[105] SS 4.33.
[106] SS 4.33.
[107] SS 3.121.

and worship from the bride, the complete opposite of what a pure impassible deity might be expected to produce. Like most Christian theologians, Bernard rejected the conception of a God who could be changed from without or be affected by what lay outside his own being. But he affirmed that God could be moved from within by the freedom of his love for his creatures. "God cannot suffer, but he can suffer with, he whose nature it is always to have mercy and to spare."[108] In doxology, we thank the giver (God) not merely for his inestimable good gifts but for himself who is essentially goodness.

God's desire for a partnership of love with us is not a sign of imperfection, but of a fullness of love that communicates. This partnership implies mutuality, not equality: "'My beloved is mine and I am his.' There is no doubt that in this passage a shared love blazes up, but a love in which one of them experiences the highest felicity, while the other shows marvelous condescension. There is no betrothal or union of equals."[109] No one can appropriate to oneself the union of equals, for that is tantamount to collapsing the distinction between the divine unity and creaturely unity, between God's intra-trinitarian love and human love for him. As an unequal, we cannot love God to the extent of the supreme love that occurs only between the Father and the Son. Nevertheless, by the Love that the groom is,[110] the bride is able to respond to him and repay his favor in some measure, even if "not as an equal."[111] This is befitting the nature of love: "Love is a great reality, and if it returns to its beginning and goes back to its origin, seeking its source again, it will always draw afresh from it, and thereby flows freely."[112] To love Love without hope of external profit is pure love; to do otherwise is total disorder. No creature could attain such identification, except the bride who comes closest in her total self-giving without thought of self or return. Her relationship with the Triune God who is love is sweet, prudent and vehement.[113] What pleases the groom is not that the bride loves less, being a lesser being, but that she loves him with her whole heart, in which case nothing is lacking, for she has given all. To devote to the groom's

---

[108] SS 2.63 as cited in McGinn, *The Growth of Mysticism*, 194.
[109] SS 3.12.
[110] SS 4.184.
[111] SS 4.184.
[112] SS 4.184.
[113] SS 4.83.

passion is to be grasped by a love that precedes and exceeds the bride. Abiding in that intimacy is a genuine exchange of love, in which the bride's love is always anticipated and surpassed by the groom. Yet the more the bride feels the dynamism of the groom's devotion, the more she is awestruck, aroused to worship and praise him by a repetition of the romantic words: "Behold, how beautiful you are, my Love, how beautiful." The bride dances at the vision and words of the crucified Christ, her groom, and her love spills over in song to him to celebrate their betrothal: "Our bed is covered with flowers; the beams of our houses are of cedar, the paneling of cypress" (Sg. 1:15–16). The primacy of God's love revealed in Christ's passion in the Spirit is the power behind the bride's deepest love and repetitive praise of the groom:

> [W]hen the soul addresses him as beloved and praises his beauty, she is filled with admiration for his goodness and attributes to him without subterfuge or deceit the grace by which she loves and is loved. The Bridegroom's beauty is his love of the bride, all the greater in that it existed before hers. Realizing then that he was her lover before he was her beloved, she cries out with strength and ardor that she must love him with her whole heart and with words expressing deepest affection . . . The more she feels surpassed in her loving the more she gives in love; and her wonder grows when he still exceeds her. Hence, not satisfied to tell him once that he is beautiful, she repeats the word, to signify by that repetition the preeminence of his beauty.[114]

In his sixth *Parable*, *"The Story of the Ethiopian Woman Whom the King's Son Took as His Wife,"* Bernard wrote: "Christ's humanity was like a wall which yet allowed divinity to shine forth within that humanity."[115] Thus a proper consideration of Christ's humanity leads one to an apprehension of the divinity hidden in it. Begotten of the Father and being identical with him, Jesus is the revelation of God; beloved of the Father and being his equal, he is the incarnation of a love that is identical with the Father's from eternity; the kiss he offers to the bride is thus the very embrace he has with his Father. The drama of eternal love is revealed in the incarnation, with the mouth of the Son kissing the assumed humanity, dying for the bride. The eternal love of the groom who

---

[114] SS 2.238–39.
[115] *Parable* 6 as cited in Sommerfeldt, *The Spiritual Teachings of Bernard of Clairvaux*, 75.

gives himself as a ransom for the bride is revealed and poured out through the shame and wounds of the cross. It was not out of necessity, but purely out of a great love that the Son's *kenosis* was sent by the Father, that he chose the way of the cross and died as a payment for sin. In *Song* 64, Bernard exclaimed on behalf of the bride: "For he emptied himself that you might know that it was the fullness of love that was outpoured, that his loftiness was laid low and his unique nature was made to be your fellow. With whom, O Wonderful Bridegroom, have you such familiar fellowship?"[116] As an outcome, every fiber of the bride's being mounts up to praise the vehemence of the Divine Lover: "Who is there that can adequately gauge the greatness of humility, gentleness, self-surrender, revealed by the Lord of majesty in human nature, in accepting the punishment of death, the shame of the cross? O Lord. How you have multiplied your mercy, O God."[117] With rhetorical paradoxes, Bernard elaborated:

> [God] delights in companionship. What sweetness! What grace! What mighty love! Can it be that the Highest of all is made one with all? Who has brought this about? Love has brought this about, without regard for its own dignity, strong in affection and efficacious in persuasion. What could be more violent? Love prevails even with God. What could be so non-violent? It is love. What force is there, I ask, which advances so violently towards victory, yet is so unresisting to violence?[118]

Devotion to the humanity of Christ refreshes our hearts with this knowledge: "the immense sacrifice he has made for you, O man; he who was made Lord became a slave, and he who was rich became a pauper, the Word was made flesh, and the Son of God did not disdain to become the son of man. So may it please you to remember that, even if made out of nothing, you have not been redeemed out of nothing."[119] In *Song* 43, Bernard claimed that the memory of all the bitter things that the groom endured for the bride will enable her to say: "My beloved is to me a little bunch of myrrh that lies between my breasts."[120] The groom, who suffers

---

[116] SS 3.177.
[117] SS 1.74–75.
[118] SS 3.177.
[119] SS 1.75.
[120] SS 2.220.

the ignominy of the cross, is not just a beloved, but her beloved who now "lies between the breasts of [the bride]" (Sg. 1:12) who loves him.[121] The one who was king is now her beloved; the one who was on his royal couch now lies between her breasts.[122] Based on Paul's words in I Cor. 2:2, Bernard proclaimed a Christocentric philosophy:

> This is my philosophy, one more refined and interior, to know Jesus and him crucified. I do not ask, as the bride did, where he takes his rest at noon, because my joy is to hold him fast where he lies between the breasts. I do not ask where he rests at noon for I see him on the cross as my Savior.[123]

In *Song* 61, following Gregory the Great, Bernard interpreted Moses' words, "the clefts of the rock," as referring to "the wounds of Christ."[124] From this, he derived a meditation on the wounds of Christ as the ground of the bride's confidence and security. Stored in the wounds of Christ is a treasury of fruit: an abundance of goodness, fullness of grace, and perfection of righteousness. The knowledge of this treasury is hidden from those who are perishing, but revealed to the elect bride by the groom's Spirit, who leads her by the open clefts into the holy of holies.[125] The bride enjoys the fruits which she reaps from the vivifying memory of the groom's sacrificial death in the efficacy of the Spirit.

The distinction between the hidden God and the revealed man has a direct bearing on a theology of worship. This is brought out in *Song* 56, in which the groom is spoken of as "standing hidden behind the wall."[126] Bernard explained the meaning of this: "prostrate weakness was revealed in the flesh, while that which stood erect in him was hidden [behind] in the flesh: the man revealed and the hidden God are one and the same."[127] To

---

[121] SS 2.222.
[122] SS 2.222.
[123] SS 2.223.
[124] Gregory the Great, *In Cantica*, II, 15; PL 79: 499D as cited in SS 3.142. See Sheryl Frances Chen, "Bernard's Prayer Before the Crucified that Embraced Him: Cistercians and Devotion to the Wounds of Christ," *Cistercian Studies* 29 (1994): 40.
[125] SS 3.145.
[126] Posset, *Pater Bernhardus*, 249.
[127] SS 3.89.

apprehend God is not to grasp him from above but from below, the crucified Christ who, though broken in body, stands erect as God by the power of his divinity. To worship God aright is to worship him not in his glory and majesty, but in the shame and lowliness of the cross. An efficacious worship has nothing to do with the hidden God (God as he is), for none can see the "face" of God without being consumed.[128] Rather it is bound up with the face of God in Christ's humanity, "the back of the Lord," through whom the bride enters the heavenly sanctuary. She is forbidden sight of the hidden God, from whom she must flee and nest herself, as the dove does in the cleft, yet can see the God hidden beneath the crucified Christ. What can we do with the inscrutability of the hidden God, which incites death and terror? Nothing except persevere in meditation on the wounds of Christ, who ushers us into the holy of holies. Hence Christ's wounds or back forms the theological basis of the bride's entrance into the communion the groom enjoys with his Father. Bernard has the bride say:

> I will go then to these storerooms [Christ's wounds] so richly endowed; taking the prophet's advice I shall leave the cities and dwell on the rock [Christ]. I shall be like the dove nesting in the highest point of the cleft, so that like Moses in his cleft of the rock I may be able to see at least the back of the Lord as he passes by. For who can look on his face as he stands, on the glory of the unchangeable God, but he who is introduced not only to the holy place but to the holy of holies.[129]

Further, while the kenotic movement of the Son sent by the Father to die constitutes the motive of worship, the ascending movement of Christ's resurrection and ascension is the completion of worship, as the bride reaches "that holy hiding place, that hidden sanctuary, to look upon the Son in the Father and the Father in the Son."[130] Christ is the first fruits in these two respects: Resurrection and Ascension. Christ's humanity has been raised by the Resurrection and rid of every weakness. Christ's home-going to the Father is the Ascension with a glorified humanity, which is the fulfillment of his saving work.[131] This is preached in *Song* 75: "For his flesh,

---

[128] Posset, *Pater Bernhardus*, 249.
[129] SS 1.75.
[130] SS 4.114.
[131] Cf. Casey, *Athirst for God*, 239, note 204, where he refers to Bernard McGinn's descent-ascent motif: the descent of Christ is the condition

which was not of the Father, rid itself of every infirmity by the glory of resurrection before it went to the Father. It girded itself with strength, it put on light as a garment, that it might present itself to the Father in the splendor and beauty which was its own."[132] In the heavenly realm where Christ resides with the Father, the radiance of the Son shines through his exalted humanity in the splendor which is inherently his, and the beauty which was hidden by the likeness of sinful flesh is seen. The Father glorifies the Son by exalting him and the Son in turn glorifies the Father with the glory he has from eternity with the Father. Not only is the Ascension Christ's own crowning, but also ours, that we may be glorified with him and share his life with the Father. Those whom the Spirit unites to the Son are incorporated into the eternal doxology of the Father and the Son, the very glory of the Godness of God. Doxology and salvation are one: we glorify and glory in God not only for the economic act of salvation but for himself as the immanent One who saves and is to be worshipped in and for himself. Thus economic doxology is predicated of the immanent Trinity.

In union with Christ, our "head," the soul rises with Christ, ascends with him and sits with him at the Father's right hand.[133] Thus the bride sought the groom "through the streets and squares" (Sg. 3.2) in vain since he had ascended to heaven. Where the groom is, in heaven, there her faith is. Bernard commented: "Let his seat then be beside his Father, not below, so that all men may honor the Son as he honors the Father; thus it shall be seen that he is equal to the Father in majesty."[134] Faith flees from the unapproachable brightness and glory of God's majesty, and clings to the incarnate Son, whose Ascension guarantees the believer admission into the heavenly sanctuary. "[S]ince [Christ] had passed by in his Resurrection and had passed on in his Ascension, [the bride] too could not rest content with passing by [in his Resurrection] but had to pass on [in his Ascension] in faith and devotion and follow him even to heaven . . . after the resurrection he also ascended, and she likewise ascended. In fact, she passed on and she found

---

of salvation, but our ascension with Christ is the fulfillment of his work.
[132] SS 4.104–05. It must be noted that only two sermons on Christ's ascension appear in the *Song*, i.e., *Song* 75 and 76.
[133] SS 4.140.
[134] SS 4.114.

him."[135] Not only does the Ascension prefect Christ's saving work, it also perfects our worship, in which case our praises and songs that are done in faith are gathered up into the holy of holies. Faith "reaches what is unreachable," encompassing even the eternal mystery of the Trinity.[136] With a humble gratitude for this gift, Bernard wrote:

> Thank you, Lord Jesus, . . . not merely that we may be endowed with the gift of faith, but that like brides we may be one with you in an embrace that is sweet, chaste and eternal, beholding with unveiled faces that glory which is yours in union with the Father and the Holy Spirit for ever and ever. Amen.[137]

The effects of the bride's participation in the fruit of the wounds of Christ are then communicated to her soul: "The Heavenly Bridegroom . . . enters willing and often the chamber of the heart he finds decked with these flowers and fruits. Where he sees a mind occupied with the grace of His passion and the glory of His resurrection, He is willingly and zealously present there."[138] Thus to immerse in a contemplation of Jesus' passion is to be acquainted with God's kiss by which the bride arrives at true self-knowledge, that she is truly his beloved and thus is moved to adore him with reciprocal love. She willingly welcomes the groom "down from heaven into her inmost heart; into her deepest love; she wants the one she desires present to her not in bodily form but by inward infusion, not by appearing externally but by laying hold of her within. It is beyond question that the vision is all the more delightful the more inward it is, and not external."[139] The zealous descent of the groom from heaven to lay hold of the bride inwardly by his kiss is the origin of worship, and the earnest welcome of the bride in receiving his kiss is a response to the grace of his passion. The union and intimacy the

---

[135] SS 4.139. See Jean Leclercg, "The Mystery of the Ascension in the Sermons of Saint Bernard," *Cistercian Studies* 25 (1990): 9–16.
[136] SS 4.114.
[137] SS 1.86.
[138] Bernard, *On Loving God*, 138–39. See Patrick W.H. Eastman, "The Christology in Bernard's *De diligengo Deo*," *Cistercian Studies* 23 (1988): 123.
[139] SS 2.129.

bride enjoys with the groom is "a special privilege,"[140] a gift of the Spirit. In that mystical union, the groom is received intimately and inwardly, and is ultimately experienced as the all-embracing reality that arouses in the bride supreme awe and intense love. The bride is also drawn into the inner chamber of the groom's heart, just as the groom finds welcome in the bride's inmost heart. The mingling of the two hearts is the consummation of their mutual desire. The bride receives what she pleads for, the groom's kiss, the very object of her heartfelt devotion, which simultaneously is the very dynamic of her worship. Here Bernard spoke eloquently of the soul's delight of God in terms of a friend:

> And just as Moses once spoke to God as a friend to a friend and God answered him, so now the Word and the soul converse with mutual enjoyment, like two friends. And no wonder. The two streams of their love have but a single source from which they are equally sustained. Winged words honey-sweet fly to and fro between them, and their eyes like heralds of holy love, betray to each other their fullness of delight.[141]

Conclusion

Worship is thus comprehended in the groom's kiss, which is shared with the bride in the efficacy of the Spirit, the kiss of the kiss that flows between the Father and the Son. The Spirit inculcates in us the vivifying memory of Christ, in whom the groom's heart, reflective of the Father's, is made known. Not only are the groom's wounds the very object of a heartfelt devotion, but also the ground of an efficacious worship, causing in us an upward movement toward the sweetness of the kiss in the Godhead. The ontological participation in the constitutive embrace of the hidden sanctuary rightly belongs to faith, the fruit of the kiss (Spirit). The bride in a spiritual union with the Son as her groom in the Spirit is the basis of her entrance into the holy of holies. Hence the Spirit is the power of efficacy in this double movement, and also in the church's worship: only in the kiss is worship offered in the groom able to reach the Fatherly sanctuary; conversely, the Spirit enables us, those whom he transforms, to engage in the

---

[140] SS 2.129.
[141] SS 2.232.

loving contemplation of the groom's wounds through which our being and activities (our praise and thanksgiving) reach the holier intimacy of God's divine life. Worship as such is a gift of God: the grace or sweetness that reaches us from the Father through the Son in the Spirit is the same that leads us home, through the Son to the Father in the Spirit.

Chapter Four

Worship as Radical Reversal in Martin Luther's *Theologia Crucis*

Introduction

> That person does not deserve to be called a theologian who looks upon the invisible things of God as if they were perceptible in those things which have actually happened . . . He deserves to be a theologian, however, who comprehends the visible and manifest things of God seen through suffering and the cross.[1]

The theses of Luther's *Heidelberg Disputation* just quoted are indicative of his theological method – the way he did theology from the ground up and in its entirety. He did not see the cross as one doctrine (such as the atonement) set alongside the others but as the hub to which all the other doctrines connected. His was a theology of the cross (*theologia crucis*). The cross is "not only the subject of theology; it is the distinctive mark of all theology."[2]

---

[1] LW 31, 52. References from the original language will be cited where helpful. Abbreviations used in this chapter: LW = *Luther's Works* (American Editions, 55 vols.: ed. Jaroslav Pelikan and Helmut T. Lehman; St. Louis: Concordia Publishing House; Philadelphia: Fortress Press, 1955–67). WA = *D. Martin Luthers Werke: Kristische Gesamtausgabe* (100 vols.; Weimar: Hermann Bohlau Nachfolger, 1883–).

[2] W. von Loewenich, *Luther's Theology of the Cross*, tr. Herbert Bouman

A true theologian, for Luther, is concerned with God as he has chosen to reveal himself. He knows about God as he is hidden in the humanity of Christ, rests on his mother's arms and finally dies on the cross. Thus Luther averred: "Now it is not sufficient for anyone, and it does him no good to recognize God in his glory and majesty, unless he recognizes him in the humility and shame of the cross."³

Constitutive of Luther's theological method – *theologia crucis* (theology of the cross) – is, in Gerhard Forde's rendering, "a reversal in direction: God comes to us; we do not mount up to him."⁴ In order to deal with God and receive anything from him, we must observe the position in which he places us, that we are always the recipients, not the givers. Already in his lectures on Psalms, 1513–1515, Luther stressed that God is the active partner, we are the passive ones. For example, commenting on Psalm 14, he wrote that we are unable to "give anything to God that was not previously his own."⁵ Creatures do not possess any soteriological resources by which they condition God into being gracious toward them. We, of our own reason and strength, cannot ascend to heaven, "anticipating God and moving him to be gracious."⁶ Contrarily, our relation to God is determined by God himself who comes to us and through faith dwells in us. Abiding here is a theology of radical reversal in which God anticipates our works and thoughts, not the reverse. The proper order is this: God initiates his movement toward us, and makes a specific promise clearly expressed in words, which we keep in a firm faith. Our relation to God, which he establishes, is thus not one of active offering, but of passive receiving what he promises to give with extravagance and generosity. In worship, as in prayer, we do not begin and lay "the first stone, but that God alone – without any entreaty or

---

(Phildelphia: Ausburg Publishing House, 1982), 13.

³ LW 31, 52.

⁴ Gerhard O. Forde, "Luther's Theology of the Cross," in *Christian Dogmatics*, 2 vols., eds. Carl Braaten & Robert Jenson (Philadelphia: Fortress Press, 1984), vol. 2, 47. Forde regards Luther's atonement theology as "the reversal of direction." This author contends that the same applies to Luther's understanding of worship, in which God gives, we merely receive.

⁵ LW 14, 106 as cited in my *The Suffering of God According to Martin Luther's Theologia Crucis* (Bern: Peter Lang, 1995), 110.

⁶ LW 35, 81–82; WA 6, 355, 13–20.

desire of man – must first come and give him a promise."⁷ God is the causative agency of our responsive worship of him. Worship is a performative action in which God is both subject and object. As subject, God initiates the encounter, by graciously revealing himself and his will so as to draw us into communion with him; as object, he is the recipient of our praise. Just as God hides in Jesus' humanity to bestow his saving presence, we too hide in his humanity, whose priestly role we appeal to, and by which our worship reaches God in heaven. It is Christ who responds on our behalf, even as we respond with love, thanks, praise and service, but our response comes only through Jesus and his mediation. Worship as such is the gift of participating through the Spirit in the incarnate Son's priestly worship of the Father. Worship, understood under the rubrics of the Word and Sacrament, is a saving event by which God is known and Christ is communicated through the Spirit. This is not of our own making, but solely by God's efficacious grace. The task before us is to offer not a liturgical but theological, not a historical but systematic presentation, of Luther's understanding of worship from the center of his theology.⁸

Worship and the First Commandment

The First Commandment is basic for Luther's theology of worship. "The words 'I am thy God' are the standard and measure of everything that can be said about worship."⁹ God and worship are inseparably one. Our conception of God determines our idea of worship. Who is this God of whom the First Commandment speaks? For Luther, this God is the one who wills to be "our God," to be in communion with us and to act for us (*pro nobis*). God proves himself to be such by the very deeds he performs for us. The God we worship is known via the cognition of his acts. God's

---

⁷ LW 35, 81–82; WA 6, 355, 13–20. See my "The Theology and Practice of Prayer in Luther's Devotional and Catechetical Writings," *Luther-Bulletin* 14 (2005): 44–67, where it is argued that the key motive to prayer is God, since it is God who draws us unto himself.

⁸ For a study of Luther's theological understanding of music, see Robin A. Leaver, *Luther's Liturgical Music: Principles and Implications* (Grand Rapids: Eerdmans, 2007).

⁹ WA 18, 69; cf. 7, 595 and 10, I, 1, 533 as cited in Vilmos Vajta, *Luther on Worship* (Philadelphia: Fortress Press, 1958), 3 (Translation is Vajta's).

being corresponds to God's acts. The identity of God is revealed in his redemptive works, beginning with the exodus account of Israel and other mighty signs, and culminating in the sending of his Son into the world. He continues to act for us in the present through the Word, baptism and the Lord's Supper, the instruments of divine power. Worship is grounded not in the subjective condition of the worshipper, but in the God who condescends to the human realm and says to us, "I am thy God" – not an impassive Deity, but an active One who is involved in our lives. The subject of worship is God, who graciously reveals himself, and his will that he wants to be our God. This fills our hearts with praise and worship. The motive to worship is God himself, since he is the One who initiates to draw us into fellowship with him. Since creatures cannot reach God, God must lower himself to reach us. Abiding in this reversal of direction – from God to us, not vice versa – is the theology of divine accommodation. Divine revelation takes place in a form which is adjusted to human capabilities and abilities. This Luther expressly wrote in his *Lectures on Genesis*:

> It is for this reason that God lowers himself to the level of our weak comprehension and presents himself to us in images, in coverings, as it were, in simplicity adapted to a child, that in some measure it may be possible for him to be known by us . . . Therefore he puts before us an image of himself because he shows himself to us in such a manner that we can grasp him. In the New Testament we have baptism, the Lord's Supper, absolution, and the ministry of the Word . . . These are the divine images and "the will of the sign." Through them, God deals with us within the range of our comprehension. Therefore these alone must engage our attention.[10]

The foundation of worship lies in the command to have him as our true God, and receive his manifold blessings by faith. "This faith, based on God's words, is also the true worship; without it all other worship is sheer deception and error."[11] Just as God and worship belong together, so too do God and faith. Faith is the condition of efficacy, without which we could not serve God nor render worship proper to him. Apart from faith, the First Commandment could not be fulfilled. The entire treasury of gifts or benefits remains at a distance, and is of no use to us, should

---

[10] LW 2, 45–47; WA 42, 294–95.
[11] LW 42, 77.

the condition of efficacy be wanting. Conversely, idolatry is the result of the contrary of faith, and thus is nothing but unbelief.[12] This Luther elaborated in his *Large Catechism*, where he equated the question "What is it to have a god?" with "What is God?" As an answer, Luther explained:

> To have a god is to trust and believe him from the whole heart, as I have often said that the confidence and faith of the heart alone make both God and idol (*Gott und Abgott*). If your faith and trust are right, then is your God also true. On the other hand, if your trust is false and wrong, then you have not the true God; for these two belong together, viz. faith and God. That now, I say, upon which you set your heart and put your trust, is properly your god.[13]

Faith is ontologically constitutive of our creaturely status. We are so created that we cannot help but believe, and concomitantly cannot help but worship. Faith – right or wrong – orients itself to one of two directions, either toward God the creator, the One from whom proceeds all good, in which case true worship is found, or toward the created things, in which case idolatry is the outcome. Luther insisted that the creature must come to this decision as he directs his faith either to God who says to him: "I am thy God," or to an idol, a non-god. The direction of our heart alone makes both God and idol. By this, Luther did not have in mind Ludwig Feuerbach's understanding of theology as anthropology, that thus the idea of God is a projection of the human onto the transcendent screen.[14] For him, the reality of God is prior to and independent of the human experience of him; the truth of faith remains intact apart from faith. "Obviously despite his exaggerations," Bernhard Lohse comments, "Luther intended to say that in clinging to something by faith it is not enough to hold the truth of faith to be true; that which is needed is a truly saving faith, that the divine truth also applies *pro me*."[15] For this reason, Luther insisted in his

---

[12] WA 6, 212; 10, I, 1, 684; WA 6, 210 as in Vajta, *Luther on Worship*, 3.
[13] WA 30, I, 133. For English translation, see Henry E. Jacobs, *The Book of Concord* (Philadelphia: United Lutheran Publication House, 1911), 391.
[14] Cf. Ludwig Feuerbach, *The Essence of Faith According to Luther*, tr. Melvin Cherno (New York: Harper & Row, 1957).
[15] Bernhard Lohse, *Martin Luther's Theology: Its Historical and Systematic Development*, tr. Roy A. Harrisville (Minneapolis: Fortress Press, 1999), 202. See also Gerhard Ebeling, *An Introduction to His Thought*, tr. R.A.

Lectures on Galatians: "Faith is the creator of the Deity, not in the substance of God, but in us. For without faith God loses His glory, wisdom, righteousness, truthfulness, mercy, etc., in us; in short God has none of His majesty or divinity where faith is absent."[16] His emphasis is the personal, not the philosophical, aspect of faith. This Luther picked up from Bernard of Clairvaux, whom he highly esteemed as the "only" one worthy of the name "Father."[17] He never wearied of repeating the sweet two words *pro me*, which sums up the essence of the gospel. The crux of the matter is that the God with whom we have to do is not just a God who is – this is of no soteriological profit to us – but is *pro me*, that he is "my God" – this is sweet sound to our ears. The good news, that in Jesus Christ God is for us, not against us, is Bernard's emphasis as it is Luther's. "This good news cannot be known in *abstract*," Timothy George explains, "but only as one grasped it by faith in the depths of experience."[18] Not until we realize that Christ was given *pro me* do we really discern the saving significance of Christ's work. Thus Luther declared:

> Read with great emphasis these words, "me", "for me", and accustom yourself to accept and to apply to yourself this "me" with certain faith . . . The words "our", "us", "for us", ought to be written in golden letters – the man who does not believe them is not a Christian.[19]

We must choose between worship and idolatry, faith and unbelief, God and the devil.[20] We are confronted with no other choice than this: either God is "our God," the one with whom we have to do, or else by unbelief deny him as totally irrelevant. The former is true

---

Wilson (Philadelphia: Fortress Press, 1970), 250–51. Barth and Luther concur on this that the reality of God is prior to faith. See Karl Barth, *Protestant Theology in the Nineteenth Century: Its Background and History* (Valley Forge: Judson, 1973), 537–38.

[16] LW 26, 277; WA 40, I, 360.

[17] See Bernard of Clairvaux, *Sermones in Cantica*, Sermon XX, Patrologia, Series latina, CLXXXIII, 867 as quoted in LW 22, 52; WA 46, 580, 24–32, and LW 21, 283, n. 49; LW 26, 5, n.2; WA 50, 41–42.

[18] Timothy George, *Theology of the Reformers* (Nashville: Broadman Press, 1988), 60.

[19] LW 26, 176; WA 40, I, 299.

[20] Luther is described by Heiko Oberman as the man between God and the Devil. See his *Luther: Man Between God and the Devil*, tr. E. Walliser-Schwarzbart (New York: Image Books, 1992).

worship; the latter is pure idolatry. In worship, we make known the significance of his place and standing as God in our lives. If God is God in our lives, we worship as the proper outcome. Whoever considers the First Commandment considers God alone as God, worthy of our trust and worship. To do otherwise is idolatry, and is an assault on the character of God. James Moffat wrote:

> To understand this commandment and to live by it, [Luther] would say, is worship itself. His controlling belief in the divine will led him to insist that from the first God had thus laid down specific regulations about the nature of the worship which was due to Him. Ours is to obey, not to argue, much less to modify or abrogate them. The first Divine Word on worship is therefore 'thou shalt.' The human instinct of worship must obey Him who says 'I am.'[21]

Hence worship, which flows from the First Commandment, ultimately takes us back to it, and is rendered effectual by faith. God is the causative factor, faith the responsive factor. This perspective runs contrary to the works–righteousness theology of the Pelagians, which sees worship as primarily what we do.[22] The theme of worship too is intrinsically linked with major theological concepts: faith alone, grace alone, Christ alone, and Scripture alone. This Luther wrote succinctly in his 1520 treatises:

> This is the very highest worship of God, that we ascribe to Him truthfulness, righteousness and whatever else should be ascribed to one who is trusted . . . But this obedience is not rendered by works, but by faith alone. For what worse idolatry can there be than to abuse God's promises with perverse opinions and to extinguish faith in them? For God does not deal, nor has He ever dealt, with man otherwise than through a word of promise . . . But He has need of this – that we regard Him as true to His promises, wait patiently for Him, and thus worship Him with faith, hope and love.[23]

---

[21] James Moffatt, "Luther," in *Christian Worship: Studies in Its History and Meaning*, ed. Nathaniel Micklem (Oxford: Oxford University Press, 1936), 127.
[22] LW 35, 402, n. 69.
[23] Martin Luther, "A Treatise on Christian Liberty," tr., W.A. Lambert, in *Works of Martin Luther*, 6 vols., ed. C.M. Jacobs (Philadelphia: Muhlenberg Press, 1930–1943), vol. 2, 319, and "Babylonian Captivity of the Church," tr. A.T.W. Steinhaeuser, in *Works of Martin Luther*, vol. 3, 210 as cited in Elsie A. McKee, "Context, Contours, Contents: Towards a Description

The "Chief Thing" in Worship Service: "Spare Everything but the Word"

In his *Treatise on the New Testament, That is, The Holy Mass*, 1520, Luther wrote of the need to determine what constitutes a "real" Mass, and how one could truly experience it, without being void of efficacy:

> And indeed, the greatest and most useful art is to know what really and essentially belongs to the Mass, and what is added and foreign to it. For where there is no clear distinction, the eyes and heart are easily misled by such sham into a false impression and delusion. Then what men have contrived is considered the Mass; and what the Mass (really) is, is never experienced, to say nothing of deriving benefit from it. Thus alas! It is happening in our times. For I fear every day more than a thousand Masses are said, of which perhaps not one is a real Mass. O dear Christians, to have many Masses is not to have *the* Mass. There is more to it than that.[24]

For him, the real Mass is Christologically linked: "Now the nearer our Masses are to the first Mass of Christ, the better they undoubtedly are; and the further from Christ's Mass, the more dangerous."[25] He wanted continuity with the Mass first held by Christ, together with the same simplicity that was seen in the earliest Christian celebrations of the Lord's Supper. "And where the Mass is used, there is true worship; even though there be no other form, with singing, organ playing, bell ringing, vestments, ornaments, and gestures. For everything of this sort is an addition invented by men."[26] His major criticism of the Roman Mass or that of the Russians or Greeks is that they put so much emphasis on the external additions or differences of people that "the chief thing (the Word) in the Mass is forgotten."[27] They were led away from the simple institution of Christ and its proper use. Not that

---

of the Classical Reformed Teaching on Worship," *The Princeton Seminary Bulletin* XVI (1995): 174 (Translation slightly modified by McKee).

[24] LW 35, 82; WA 6, 355, 13–20. Also cited in Hans Jünghans, "Luther on the Reform of Worship," in *Harvesting Martin Luther's Reflections on Theology, Ethics, and the Church*, ed. Timothy J. Wengert (Grand Rapids: Wm. B. Eerdmans, 2004), 210.

[25] LW 35, 81.

[26] LW 35, 81.

[27] LW 35, 81.

Luther wished to discard or displace what the eyes behold and the senses suggest – be it vestments, bells, songs, ornaments, prayers, processions, elevations, prostrations, but in order that these human accretions should not become valid substitutes for "the chief thing," i.e., the words of Christ's institution, by which he performed the Mass and commanded us to do likewise with efficacy. "Without the words nothing is derived from the Mass."[28] The words of Christ's institution constitute the whole Mass – its nature, work, profit and benefits. All unchristian elements, all the festivals of saints, except those Luther interpreted as the festivals of Christ (e.g., Marian festivals of candlemas, the Annunciation, Assumption, Nativity, etc.), and any echo of the Mass as a sacrifice are excised from the service.[29] Despite the perversion, Luther had no intention of dismantling the liturgical tradition already in place, but rather aimed to purify it from later corruption, and restore it again to its evangelical use. He assured Nicholas Hausmann: "It is not now nor ever has been our intention to abolish the liturgical service of God completely, but rather to purify the one that is now in use from the wretched accretions which corrupt it and to point out an evangelical use."[30] Unlike Karlstadt's hasty and violent reformation of the cultus, Luther was more concerned about God's Word working faith in the heart inwardly than the expression of faith outwardly in new forms of worship.[31] He promulgated a reversal of direction, proceeding not from the outside to the inside, but the opposite. External reform of worship does not create true faith or godliness, but the Word does. "For the Word created heaven and earth and all things (Ps. 33:6); the Word must do this thing, and not we poor sinners. In short, I will preach it, teach it, write it, but I will constrain no man by force, for faith

---

[28] Ibid. See also Lohse, *Martin Luther's Theology*, 133.

[29] Martin Brecht, *Martin Luther. Vol. 2: Shaping and Defining the Reformation 1521–1532*, tr. James L. Schaaf (Minneapolis: Fortress, 1990), 122–23.

[30] LW 53, 20. Cited in Bodo Spinks, "Evaluating liturgical continuity and change at the reformation: A Case Study of Thomas Muntzer, Martin Luther, and Thomas Cranmer," in *Continuity and Change in Christian Worship*, ed. Robert N. Swanson (Suffolk: Boydell Press, 1999), 153. See William D. Maxwell, *A History of Christian Worship* (Grand Rapids: Baker, 1982), 75.

[31] For a study of Luther's response to Karlstadt's iconoclasm, see Carlos M.N. Eire, *War Against the Idols: The Reformation of Worship from Erasmus to Calvin* (Cambridge: Cambridge University Press, 1986), 65–73.

must come freely without compulsion."[32] Speaking of the order of the worship, Luther stated: "And this is the sum of the matter": "We can spare everything except the Word."[33] The Word must be extolled as the principal element, or else worship is vitiated.

> This word of God is the beginning, the foundation, the rock, upon which afterward all works, words, and thoughts of man must build. This word man must gratefully accept. He must faithfully believe the divine promise and by no means doubt that it is and comes to pass just as God promises. This trust and faith is the beginning, middle, and end of all works and righteousness. For because man does God the honor of regarding and confessing him as true, he becomes to man a gracious God, who in turn honors him and regards him as true.[34]

Sermon as Central in Worship Service

It was Luther's conviction that God's Word, on which the Mass stands or falls, must be preached and heard. These words must be made intelligible, thus he insisted that they be spoken loud, and in a language known to people, i.e., German, not Latin.[35] More than that, the contents of the institution require explication. Thus proclamation becomes a central piece in the worship service. "And had there been no preaching, Christ would never have instituted the Mass. He is more concerned about the word than about the sign."[36] The sermon serves the purpose of an exposition of Christ's words: "Christ has gathered up the whole gospel in a short summary with the words of this testament or sacrament."[37] Luther's definition of the sermon as an exposition of the Mass accounts for the tighter bond between sacrament and sermon. The "remembrance" aspect of the Mass Luther understood as part of

---

[32] LW 51, 77; WA 10, III, 18, 8–12.

[33] See LW 53, 14; WA 12, 37 as cited in *Ad Fontes Lutheri: Toward the Recovery of the Real Luther. Essays in Honour of Kenneth Hagen's Sixty-fifth Birthday*, eds. Timothy Maschke, Franz Posset & Joan Sckocir (Milwaukee: Marquette University Press, 2001), viii.

[34] LW 35, 82. See Jaroslav Pelikan, *Luther's Works. Companion Volume: Introduction to Exegetical Writings* (St. Louis: Concordia, 1959), 48–70, for his description of Luther's doctrine of the Word of God.

[35] LW 35, 90; WA 6, 362, 26–35.

[36] LW 35, 106; WA 6, 374, 3–4.

[37] LW 35, 106; WA 6, 374, 3–4.

God's redemptive act, not an inner attempt on our part to ascend to God. It is primarily God's causative deed, which he performs via the oral preaching of God's word: "God causes his wonderful works to be remembered."[38] This is borne out in his exposition of Psalm 111:5, "He will ever be mindful of his covenant":

> Furthermore, in the Sacrament we keep the remembrance of his covenant according to Christ's institution. For it is not our own institution or work but his. He performs it through us and in us; for he is speaking not of the inward remembering in the heart, but of the outward, public, and oral remembering to which Christ referred when he said: This do in remembrance of me – which is done through the sermon and the Word of God.[39]

The priority of preaching is the presupposition of his criticism of the structure of liturgical regulations and customs that have human accretions as their focus. Where there is no preaching, there is no worship. When God's Word is silenced, which, for Luther, is the "worst abuse" in the service, one had better neither sing nor read, nor even gather together.[40] The efficacy of God's Word means that all human additions or external adornments occupy no significant place in the worship service. Contrary to many liturgical practices of the late medieval Mass, Luther wrote, "When Christ himself first instituted this sacrament and held the first mass, there was no tonsure, no chasuble, no singing, no pageantry, but only thanksgiving to God and the use of the sacrament."[41] Originally, the gospel was not a book, but a sermon.[42] The church is not a *Federhaus* (pen house), but a *Mundhaus* (mouth house).[43]

> For since the advent of Christ, the gospel, which used to be hidden in the Scriptures, has become an oral preaching. And thus it is the manner of the New Testament and of the gospel that it must be preached and

---

[38] WA 31, I, 417 as quoted in Vajta, *Luther on Worship*, 83.
[39] WA 31, I, 417 as quoted in Vajta, *Luther on Worship*, 83.
[40] LW 53, 11. See Bodo Nischan, "Becoming Protestants: Lutheran Altars or Reformed Communion Tables," in *Worship in Medieval and Early Modern Europe. Change and Continuity in Religious Practice*, eds. Karin Maag & John D. Witvliet (Notre Dame: University of Notre Dame Press, 2004), 86.
[41] LW 35, 81; WA 6, 354, 28–31.
[42] WA 10, I, 1, 17; 10, I, 1, 626 as cited Vajta, *Luther on Worship*, 77.
[43] WA 10, I, 2, 48 as quoted in Vajta, *Luther on Worship*, 77.

performed by word of mouth and a living voice. Christ himself has not written anything, nor has he ordered anything to be written, but rather to be preached by word of mouth.[44]

Likewise Christ's apostles were not scribes, but messengers. He elaborated on this in his *Operationes in Psalmos*:

> The apostles wrote very little, but they spoke a lot . . . Notice it says let their voice be heard, not let their books be read. The minority of the New Testament is not engraved on dead tablets of stone; rather it sounds in a living voice . . . Through a living word God accomplishes and fulfills his gospel.[45]

So oral preaching was, as it still is, the proper form of God's Word. The Word of God spoken is itself the word of God speaking through human agency. "One must see the word of the preacher as God's Word."[46] Essentially preaching is God's own speech, which Luther identified as God's own deed. "The basic category for Luther's doctrine of the Word of God," wrote Pelikan, "was not the category of 'being' but the category of 'deed'."[47] This understanding has its root in Luther's study of Genesis and Psalms. God's Word is causative, efficaciously speaking reality into existence. So the prophets accomplished the work of God by what they spoke. This is evident in Luther's exposition of Psalm 2: "In the case of God to speak is to do, and the word is the deed."[48] In his *Lectures on Genesis*, the phrase "God said" Luther understood as the instrument of divine power which God employs to accomplish his work of creation. Not only does it mean the utterance of God, but also the deed of God. "The words of God are embodied realities (*res*)," Robert Jenson writes, "and not mere language."[49]

---

[44] WA 10, I, 48 as quoted in George, *Theology of the Reformers*, 91.

[45] WA 5, 537 as quoted in A. Skevington Wood, *Captive to the Word: Martin Luther, Doctor of Sacred Scripture* (Grand Rapids: Eerdmans, 1969), 50.

[46] LW 22, 526: WA 47, 227. See Gustav Wingren, *The Living Word: A Theological Study of Preaching and the Church*, tr. V.C. Pogue (Philadelphia: Fortress Press, 1960), 19.

[47] Pelikan, *Companion Volume*, 50.

[48] LW 12, 33; WA 40, II, 231. See my *Luther as a Spiritual Adviser: The Interface of Theology and Piety in Luther's Devotional Writings* (Bletchley: Paternoster, 2007), 155–59.

[49] See Robert Jenson, *Systematic Theology*, Vol 2: *The Works of God* (Oxford:

In speaking through the created order, God uses the words of a finite creature to communicate with us. "Just as a man uses his tongue as a tool with which he produces and forms words, so God uses our words, whether gospel or prophetic books, as tools with which he himself writes living words in our hearts."[50] Although the spoken word is "the word of a human being," Luther argued, "it has been instituted by divine authority for salvation."[51] It is part of the divine scheme that God assumes human form to speak with us and meet us in it, thus he can be apprehended in human speech. As such preaching is constituted as an ordained means of God's efficacious grace, irrespective of "who is speaking," because the Word of God remains free to be heard even if it comes from the mouth of the anti-thesis of his Word.[52]

Unlike the Aristotelian God, Luther's God is "never-speechless": "It was in the very nature of God to want to speak and to be able to speak."[53] He wrote: "Hear, brother: God, the creator of heaven and earth, speaks with you through his preachers . . . Those words of God are not of Plato or Aristotle but God himself is speaking."[54] Luther's deity is not an impassive deity of the Greeks, but an ever-present deity, who hides in human speech, and who is active in preaching through human voice. The God who speaks to us works causatively through the agency of preaching, wherein there remains for us only hearing, heeding and appropriating. "To hear Mass means nothing else but to hear God's Word, and thereby serve God."[55] The faithful hearers will respond: "Pay attention, we are hearing God's speech."[56] Faith grasps the words done upon us, with no works or merits of our own. The majesty of Word-Act thus must reign supreme in the worship service. When his confessor Johann Staupitz assigned him to the task of preaching in the monastery, Luther protested, "It will kill me. I won't last three months." Staupitz's remarkable reply, "When the preacher speaks, God speaks!" emboldened Luther to preach with the same boldness with which Paul spoke of his preaching office in II

Oxford University Press, 1999), 159–60.
[50] LW 10, 212; WA 3, 256.
[51] LW 10, 220; WA 3, 262.
[52] LW 3, 220: WA 43, 32.
[53] Pelikan, *The Companion Volume*, 50.
[54] WA TR 4, 531, no. 4812.
[55] LW 51, 262; WA 36, 354.
[56] LW 51, 76; WA 10, III, 15.

Corinthians 3 and 4.[57] His confidence in God's Word cemented his calling as a preacher. Inherent in such confidence is the promise of God that assures him, "Just go on preaching; don't worry about who will listen . . . You preach and let me manage."[58] Preachers could only assume the "right to speak," though not the "power to accomplish."[59] It is God's good pleasure to shine his Word in the heart, but not without the external, spoken form. Preaching is not preliminary to the sacraments, a lower stage of God's grace that we apprehend through sacramental action. Rather, like the sacraments, the apostolic proclamation brings God and all his gifts. Preaching is not a discursive reflection on God, as is the custom of the university; nor is it a rehashing of the old story, as is done in theatrical dramas. It is a saving event, wherein God attaches the promise of his saving presence. Proclamation of the Word, for Luther, is sacramental because it communicates Christ himself. This he wrote in his 1526 treatise on *The Sacrament of the Body and Blood of Christ – Against the Fanatics*:

> Again I preach the gospel of Christ into your heart, so that you may form him within yourself. If now you truly believe, so that your heart lays hold of the Word and holds fast within it that voice, tell me, what you have in your heart? You must answer that you have the true Christ, not that he sits there, as one sits on the chair, but as he is at the right hand of the Father. How that comes about you cannot know, but your heart truly feels his presence, and through the experience of faith you know for a certainty that he is there.[60]

Preaching inculcates the benefits of the suffering of Christ for us, thereby creating a people no longer under divine wrath. What God reveals, he truly bestows; and what we hear, we truly receive. Faith lays hold of Christ's righteousness which God bestows upon the ungodly in exchange for sin. "To preach," Vajta wrote, "is to make Christ contemporary so that his death and resurrection become our own and the redemption which he wrought becomes

---

[57] WA 51, 517 as cited in Fred W. Meuser, "Luther as Preacher of the Word of God," in *The Cambridge Companion to Martin Luther*, ed. Donald K. McKim (Cambridge: Cambridge University Press, 2003), 136.
[58] WA 10, I, 2, 51 as cited in Meuser, "Luther as Preacher of the Word of God," 137.
[59] LW 51, 76; WA 10, III, 15.
[60] LW 36, 340.

our righteousness."[61] The preacher speaks, and in his speaking the justifying action of God is accomplished. The Word of God bears "a performative authority" that has the power to transform lives and create new situations.[62] Here Rudolf Bultmann's words reflect accurately Luther's: "His works are his words [and] his words are his works."[63] By his own definition of the Word as deed, the Word accomplishes its own mission when it is preached and truly heard by the congregation.[64] The word spoken becomes the deed performed, if only we believe. Thus Luther avowed: "God has opened my mouth, and bidden me speak, and he supports me mightily . . . Therefore, I will speak and . . . not keep silent as long as I live, until Christ's righteousness goes forth as brightness, and his saving grace be lighted as a lamp."[65]

However by stressing the oral form of God's Word, Luther did not do away with the written form. As part of the worship order, Luther included "reading, interpreting, praising, singing, and praying."[66] But reading and exposition by the preacher takes precedence. Luther's view is very much at odds with the contemporary service that itches for the primacy of singing and praising. As regards singing, reading and instruction, Luther opted for the last as essential to the daily service. Even with singing and reading in both Latin and German services daily, he observed, churches remained an empty vessel.[67] Henceforth as a description of the German Mass of Wittenberg, he wrote: "Since the preaching and teaching of God's Word is the most important part of divine service, we have arranged for sermons and lessons as follows:

---

[61] Vajta, *Luther on Worship*, 73. See Henry S. Wilson, "Luther on Preaching as God Speaking," *Lutheran Quarterly* XIX: 1 (2005), 64–65. Karl Barth registered many of Luther's sayings on oral preaching in his *Church Dogmatics*, tr. George T. Thomson (New York: Charles Scribner's Sons, 1936), vol. 1:1, 137–40.

[62] Richard Lischer, *A Theology of Preaching* (Nashville: Abingdon Press, 1981), 71.

[63] Rudolf Bultmann, *Faith and Understanding* I, tr. L.P. Smith (London: SCM Press, 1969), 308.

[64] Richard Lischer, "Luther and Contemporary Preaching: Narrative and Anthropology," *Scottish Journal of Theology* 36 (1983): 487.

[65] LW 45, 347–48; WA 15, 24 as cited in Wilson, "Luther on Preaching as God Speaking," 64.

[66] LW 53, 13.

[67] LW 53, 89.

For the holy day or Sunday we retain the customary Epistles and Gospels and have three sermons."[68] He wanted "the Word of God (to) be given free reign to uplift and quicken souls so that they do not become weary . . . For the whole Scripture (i.e., Old and New Testaments) shows that the Word should have free course among Christians."[69] However the preacher does not present anything new to his congregation other than what has already been proclaimed and written by the Apostles. "It is impossible to derive the Word of God from reason; it must be given from above. Verily, we do not preach the human wisdom of philosophers, jurists, medics, or of any other profession . . . The apostles transmitted it to us, and thus it will continue until the end of the world."[70] There occurs in Luther a strong bond between the oral and written form of the Word. His sermon on John 6:45–46 is another proof of this:

> You are preserved by the words which you hear; they also illumine you, teach you, draw you, and bring you to Christ. First of all, you hear the Father speaking through the Son. You hear the Word or the voice. But this does not mean that you have already been drawn, for reason says that Christ is only human and that His speech is only human speech. But then, when you delight in occupying yourself with the Word, when you read it, hear it preached, and love it, the time will come when you will confess that God Himself uttered these words, and you will proclaim: 'This is truly the Word of God!' Thus faith is added.[71]

Faith arises as a result of reading and hearing the Word of God; both are in effect the power of God. "Above all, therefore, one must listen to and read the Word, which is the vehicle of the Holy Spirit. When the Word is read, the Holy Spirit is present; and thus it is impossible either to listen to or read Scripture without profit."[72] However Luther's emphasis on the instrumental causality of *fides ex auditu* the Word of promise led him to elevate preaching above mere reading and study alone. This is borne out in his

---

[68] LW 53, 68.
[69] LW 53, 12–14.
[70] LW 22, 477–78; WA 47, 187–88.
[71] LW 23, 97; WA 33, 147.26–148.1. For a study of an intimate relationship between the preached Word and Scripture, see Mark D. Thompson, *A Sure Ground on Which to Stand: The Relation of Authority and Interpretive Method in Luther's Approach to Scripture* (Carlisle: Paternoster, 2004).
[72] LW 30, 221; WA 20, 790, 24–27.

commentary on Romans 10:17: "The Word is the kind of thing which no one can grasp unless it is received by hearing and by faith."[73] For Luther, "to hear God's Word and believe it," Hughes Oliphant Old writes, "is the essence of worship."[74] Althaus quoted Luther in this aspect:

> When 'the soul firmly believes God's word, it considers him to be truthful, good and righteous. Thereby it pays him the highest honor it can: It admits that he is true and does not dispute the fact. Thus it honors his name. This also means that we can do no greater dishonor to God than not to believe him.'[75]

Christ's Testament: *Beneficium* and *Sacrificium*

Luther attached equal importance to preaching and sacraments, both are forms of the gracious and powerful word of God's promise. Just as God hides in the human agency of preaching to bestow grace, he too hides in the Eucharist, a designated place where he attaches the promise of his salvific and accessible presence. That Christ is bodily present in the Eucharist hinges on Luther's usage of the so-called *communicatio idiomatum*, according to which the ubiquity of Christ's divinity is communicated to his humanity.[76] However Christ's real presence in worship is not

---

[73] LW 25, 418: WA 56, 426–27. See Timothy George, "Martin Luther," in *Reading Romans Through the Centuries: From the Early Church to Karl Barth*, eds. Jeffrey P. Greenman and Timothy Larsen (Grand Rapids: Brazos Press, 2005), 110–11.

[74] Hughes Oliphant Old, *The Reading and Preaching of the Scriptures in the Worship of the Christian Church*. Vol. 4. *The Age of the Reformation* (Grand Rapids: Eerdmans, 2002), 42–43.

[75] WA 7, 25 as cited in Althaus, *The Theology of Martin Luther*, 45. Also quoted in Old, *The Reading and Preaching*, 42.

[76] See my article, "Chalcedonian Christology and Beyond: Luther's Understanding of the *Communicatio Idiomatum*," *Heythrop Journal* XLV (2004): 54–68; Joseph N. Tylenda, "Calvin's Understanding of the Communication of Properties," *Westminster Theological Journal* 38 (1975): 58–61; Wolfhart Pannenberg, *Jesus – God and Man* (Philadelphia: Westminster, 1977), 299. The main point of disagreement among Luther, Calvin and Zwingli concerns the usage of the doctrine of *communicatio idiomatum*. For Luther, there is a mutual Christological predication between the two natures: not only the divinity in Christ participates in

generated by good deeds, nor by the mental effort of remembering him, nor by transubstantiation. Rather it is effected by God's Word, through which "Christ comprehends himself in the bread."[77] Vajta commented: "The Word is the essence of his presence, for through the Word proclaimed, all the works of God are revealed."[78] Luther wrote:

> There stands the Word, and it says clearly and vividly that Christ gives his body to be eaten when he gives the bread. On this we stand, believe, and teach that truly and bodily the body of Christ is received and eaten in the Supper. But how this is effected, or in what manner he is in the bread, we do not know and are not supposed to know. We are to trust God's Word and not to limit him. Bread it is that we see with our eyes. But with our ears we hear that the body is there.[79]

Because hearing and believing God's Word is worship at its highest, it is impiety not to accept the perspicuity of his Word about Christ's real presence in worship, in which case the glory of God suffers diminution. Luther affirmed Christ's real presence in worship, even though the "how" of his presence remains a mystery. The decisive question is the "why" of his presence, and he found the answer in his doctrine of salvation, that God is presented in Christ as God for us (*pro nobis*). God reveals himself in a hidden manner, under the visible, earthly means of creation in order to effect his presence for us.

The nearness and accessibility of God are to be found in the Eucharist, for God has confined himself to it by his promise. Just as God is savingly present in human speech, so is he in the sacraments. The Eucharist thus conquers his own transcendence and distance, making his presence accessible and saving, if only we believe. Luther explained the Eucharist by the idea of Christ's testament, that the testator determines who will benefit from his last will, and the appointed heir, on the contrary, receives the estate not as something won by exertions but as an outcome of his

---

the suffering of humanity, but also the humanity in Christ participates in the ubiquity of divinity. Everything in Christ acquires "new" meaning. For Calvin and Zwingli, the predication is from natures to the person of Christ, not between two natures in Christ.

[77] WA 19, 493 as cited in Vajta, *Luther on Worship*, 90.
[78] Vajta, *Luther on Worship*, 90.
[79] WA 23, 87 as cited in *Luther on Worship*, 95.

promise. With this he underscored the reversal of direction as basic to the structure of worship, that the action proceeds from God, not from us. By stressing the causative character of the Word, Luther hailed Christ as the active giver who distributes his body and blood with the aid of the sacramental elements, but we the passive recipients apprehend these gifts through the responsive character of faith. In Hefner's words: "[Our] reception is fully embodied; its paradigm of intimacy is the eating and drinking, being fed by Christ's body and blood, as these are caught up in Christ's supreme act of obedience unto death."[80] Hence the Eucharist is not to be understood as a sacrifice, but as a sacrament. In worship, Luther elaborated:

> We do not presume to give God something in the sacrament, when it is he who in it gives us all things . . . We see, then that the best and greatest part of all sacraments and of the Mass is the word and promises of God, without which the sacraments are dead and are nothing at all . . . I accept for myself alone the blessing therein offered by God – and here there is no *officium* but *beneficium*, no work or service, but reception and benefit alone.[81]

In the Mass, two radically opposed views of God are brought into light. Luther's view of God and that of the Roman Church account for the divergent way in which each understands the Mass:

> When they [the Roman Church] sacrifice, they think it is necessary to placate God. But to wish to appease him is to believe that he is angry and unreconciled, and to believe that he is angry means to expect wrath rather than love, bad instead of good things. Yet if people would receive the Eucharist with profit, they must believe that God has long been reconciled, that out of his consummate love he gives in addition this most perfect gift. Nothing detracts as much from the proper celebration of the Eucharist or is as harmful to the conscience as this sacrilegious opinion of papists that God is angry and needs to be appeased with this sacrifice. If he were not so well reconciled and so full of love, he would never offer or bestow these great riches of his.[82]

---

[80] Cf. Philip J. Hefner, "The Church," in *Christian Dogmatics*, 2 vols., eds. Carl E. Braaten and Robert Jenson (Philadelphia: Fortress Press, 1984), vol. 2, 232.
[81] LW 35, 89–90.
[82] WA 8, 441 as cited in Vajta, *Luther on Worship*, 35.

For Luther, God's true deity consists in giving, not receiving. The reversal of direction applies to the nature of God – that it is part of God's *nature* that he give himself, totally, without any thought of return or reward. Luther intimated:

> For this is the true God who gives, but does not take; helps, but asks no help – in short, who does everything and gives everything, yet needs no one. And all this he does freely out of pure mercy and without merit for the unworthy and undeserving, even for the damned and lost. As such he wants to be remembered, confessed, and glorified.[83]

The Mass "is nothing else than a testament and sacrament in which God makes a pledge to us and gives us grace and mercy." Hence Luther calls the Mass a benefit, not received, but given (*beneficium, non acceptum sed datum*).[84] God does not benefit from us through the testament, which rather benefits us. In the Mass, we give nothing to God, but only receive from him. "For there is nothing there but a taking and receiving."[85] With Peter Lombard, Luther averred that it is not the sacrament, but faith in it that justifies.[86] Likewise with Augustine, he declared: "It justifies not because it is performed, but because it is believed."[87] The Mass is God's gift, and in it we encounter not an angry God who needs to be placated, but a merciful God, to whom praise and adoration are rightly due. Luther quoted Psalm 50:23: "Thanksgiving honors God," seeing thank offerings as the way to implement the First Commandment: this regards God as God and allows him to remain God.[88] This is true,

---

[83] LW 38, 107; WA 30, II, 603 (Admonition Concerning the Sacrament of the Body and Blood of our Lord, 1530) as cited in Vajta, *Luther on Worship*, 33.
[84] LW 35, 93. See Byran Spinks, *Luther's Liturgical Criteria and his Reform of the Canon of the Mass* (Notts: Grove Books, 1982), 15.
[85] LW 35, 94.
[86] Cf. P. Lombard, *Sententiae*, Book IV, Dist. 4, chs. 4–6, in J.-P. Migne, *Patrologia, Series Latina* 1800–1875 (Paris: Migne, 1844–1864), CXCII, 847–49 as cited in LW 29, 172; WA 57, III, 169.
[87] Cf. Augustine, *In Joannis Evangelium Tractatus*, CH. XV, Tr. LXXX, 3, in J.-P. Migne, *Patrologia, Series Latina*, 1800–1875 (Paris: Migne, 1844–1864), XXXV, 1840 as cited in LW 29, 172; WA 57, III, 169.
[88] LW 38, 107.

lofty, beautiful worship, namely his remembrance and the glory of the passion of Christ, which worship God himself established and to which he bore witness that he was indeed well-pleased with it. He has established it in such a way that it cannot be exhausted or observed enough, for who remembers God sufficiently? Who can praise him too much? Who can thank him too much? Who can honor Christ's passion too much? Why then have we mad saints raved so shamefully, as if there were no worship for us in this sacrament or as if we had long ago performed it and completely exhausted it?[89]

Contrarily the papists, by their sacrifice of works, strip God of divine glory. Their worship, according to Luther, is devoid of all reality, for internally in their hearts and externally in their works, they have no god. They invent another God for themselves, and thus are guilty of idolatry: "They commit idolatry as often as they sacrifice."[90] They do not glorify and praise God but want to earn merits through odious worship of their own devotion and self-chosen works. By turning worship into human performance, they denied or disgraced the true worship established by God. Rather than God's glory, self-satisfaction becomes the end (*telos*) of their worship. This is another abuse: "Such divine service was performed as a work where God's grace and salvation might be won. As a result, faith disappeared."[91] And when that happens, Christ – the object of mercy – also disappears, together with the adoring thankfulness to God that makes up the deeper pulse of worship. Piety is idolatrous when it attempts to worship a different God (i.e., an angry God who needs to be appeased) rather than the one revealed in the Mass (i.e., the merciful God who gives). It does not glorify God for who he is, namely, the Giver; nor does it thank him for the benefits received as an outcome of his promise. "[I]f a person desires to be of service," Luther thus argued, "he should demand and promote the worship of thanksgiving or he will be condemned together with all other works and merits with which one desires to win or to purchase God's grace."[92]

True worship is communion with God, which therein includes a humble, reverent, thankful appropriation of his sacramental

---

[89] LW 38, 105–06.
[90] WA 8, 442 as cited in Vajta, *Luther on Worship*, 33.
[91] LW 53, 11. See Moffart, "Luther," in *Christian Worship*, 127.
[92] LW 38, 108. See Frank C. Senn, "The Reform of the Mass: Evangelical, but Still Catholic," *The Catholicity of the Reformation*, ed. Robert W. Jenson

provision for our need of him. The sacrament is the place where God invests his glory and service so that we should thereby remember and worship him there. To remember Christ, he elaborated, is

> nothing other than to praise, listen to, proclaim, laud, thank, and honor the grace and mercy which God has shown us in Christ. Upon this Christ he has directed and concentrated all his glory and worship so that he does not wish to know of any glory or worship apart from Christ, yes, he does not even acknowledge it. Nor does he want to be anybody's God apart from Christ.[93]

Worship is integral to the *theologia crucis*, thus Luther declared: "God has his honor in this – that for our sakes he gives himself down to the utmost depth, into flesh and bread, into our mouth, heart and bosom, and more, for our sakes he suffers himself to be dishonorably treated both upon the cross and altar."[94] The cross reveals primarily not God's being but God's way of being in the world. It powerfully discloses the true identity of God as one who is not against us, but for us. That God is for us inspires the wounded worshippers to fix their gaze upon the crucified Christ from whom all consolations are derived. God is most Godlike in the suffering of the cross, sharing our deepest pain rather than remaining in his transcendent bliss. Hidden in the cross, where God is revealed not as most powerful but most weak, is the condition of the possibility of worship. So, Luther asserted,

> [T]o know Christ aright is to know him as the one who died for me and took upon himself my sin . . . There Christ is God and has put himself in my death, in my sin, and so gives me his living favor. There I recognize how he befriends me and the utter love of the Father is too much for any heart. Thus I lay hold of God where he is most weak,

---

(Grand Rapids: Eerdmans, 1996), 41–42; his *Christian Liturgy. Catholic and Evangelical* (Minneapolis: Fortress Press, 1997), 270–71.

[93] LW 38, 105.

[94] WA 23, 157, 30 (That these Words of Christ, 1527) as cited in Norman G. Nagel, "Martinus: Heresy, Doctor Luther, Heresy! The Person and Work of Christ," in *The Seven-Headed Luther: Essays in Commemoration of a Quincentenary 1483–1983*, ed. Peter N. Brooks (Oxford: Clarendon Press, 1983), 41.

and think, "Yes, this is God, this is his will and his good pleasure . . ." Therefore God is to be known alone in Christ.[95]

The Mediation of Christ

Christ's testament, not the priest's sacrificial offering, is the efficacy of worship. Priests could not bring a sacrifice – prayer, praise, and thanksgiving and ourselves – before God in their own person, but could only aid in the distribution of the testament. Luther made it clear in the *Treatise on the New Testament* that "we do not offer Christ as a sacrifice, but that Christ offers us. And in this way it is permissible, yes, profitable, to call the Mass a sacrifice; not on its account, but because we offer ourselves as a sacrifice along with Christ."[96] We could lay the sacrifices upon Christ, who in turn presents them for us before God, as St. Paul taught in Hebrews 13:15, "Let us continually offer up a sacrifice of praise to God," but only "through Christ." We approach God via the priesthood and mediation of Christ. As a godly Priest, Christ intercedes for us, receives our prayers, sanctifies them, and makes them pleasing to God in his own person. As further proof of this, Luther again referred to St. Paul, who said in Hebrews 9:24, "He has ascended into heaven to be a mediator in the presence of God on our behalf"; and in Romans 8:34, "It is Christ Jesus, who died, yes, who was raised from the dead, who sits on the right hand of God, who also makes intercession for us." This means that Christ our high priest takes up our cause, presents our prayers and praise, and offers them up to God in his person. "That is, we lay ourselves on Christ by a firm faith in his testament and do not otherwise appear before God with our prayer, praise, and sacrifice except through Christ and mediation."[97]

Luther accented the sole priesthood of Christ as the basis of our worship. The importance of Christ's priesthood and mediation consists in the fact that God comes to us in Jesus Christ as *man*, vicariously doing for us and in us what we cannot do for ourselves.

---

[95] WA 10, I, 277, 18ff as cited in Nagel, "*Martinus: Heresy, Doctor Luther, Heresy*," 41.

[96] LW 35, 98–99 as cited in Frank C. Senn, "Lutheran Spirituality," in *Protestant Spiritual Traditions*, ed. Frank C. Senn (New York: Paulist Press, 1896), 27.

[97] LW 35, 99.

Necessarily the reversal of direction entails the divinely ordained means by which we ascend to God, that is, not by way of Christ's divinity but his *lowly humanity*, *"that holy ladder."*[98] There is a movement in Luther's Christology: from below to above.[99] Ian Siggins elucidates Luther's Christological talk about God in his *theologia crucis*: "He who wants to encounter God must encounter Him where He may be grasped as He cannot be grasped in His majesty: in the Incarnate God, who lives in His mother's lap, and in the Crucified God. To cling solely to Christ as He goes through death to the Father is the only way to find God."[100] This Luther elaborated in his *Lectures on Hebrews* 1:2 (1517–18):

> One should also note that he mentions the humanity of Christ before he mentions His divinity, in order that in this way he may establish the well-known rule that one learns to know God in faith. For the humanity is the holy ladder of ours, mentioned in Gen. 28:12, by which we ascend to the knowledge of God. Therefore John 14:6 also says: "No one comes to the Father but by Me." And again: "I am the Door" (John 10:7). Therefore he who wants to ascend advantageously to the love and knowledge of God should abandon the human metaphysical rules concerning knowledge of the divinity and apply himself first to the humanity of Christ. For it is exceedingly godless temerity that, where God has humiliated Himself in order to become recognizable, man seeks for himself another way by following the counsels of his own natural capacity.[101]

Against Oecolampadius who said to Luther during the Marburg Colloquy, "You should not cling to the humanity and flesh of Christ, but rather lift up your mind to his divinity," Luther averred, "I do not know of any God except Him who was made flesh, nor do I want to have another."[102] The vicarious function of Jesus being the High Priest for humanity is the ground of worship, that

---

[98] LW 29, 111; WA 57, III, 99 (Italics are mine).
[99] Paul Althaus, *The Theology of Martin Luther*, tr. Robert C. Schultz (Philadelphia: Fortress, 1966), 186.
[100] Ian D. Siggins, *Martin Luther's Doctrine of Christ* (New Havens: Yale University Press, 1970), 84.
[101] LW 29, 111; WA 57, III, 99. Also cited in Kenneth Hagen, *A Theology of Testament in the Young Luther: The Lectures on Hebrews* (Leiden: E.J. Brill, 1974), 92.
[102] Quoted in Hermann Sasse, *This is My Body* (Minneapolis: Augsburg, 1959), 252–53.

in his person and act we, by faith in our person and act, enter the holy of holies. By stressing the soteriological significance of the person of Christ, Luther wanted to emphasize that we must "apply ourselves to the humanity of Christ" in faith in order that we might be caught up into "the love and knowledge of God." Commenting on Hebrews 4:14, Luther wrote: "For to those who have been terrified in consequence of the fear of that eternal judgment and that horrible cutting and division, no other refuge is left than that one sanctuary which is Christ, our Priest, in whose humanity alone we are protected and saved from a judgment of this kind, as in Ps. 91:4: 'He will cover you with His pinions, and under His wings you will find refuge'."[103] In our humanity, and for us, he offers a life of perfect obedience, worship and prayer to the Father.

The efficacy of our worship lies not in what we do nor how we feel, but what Christ does for us. Because of sin, we cannot offer acceptable worship to God, although we should. The gospel consists in this: that God provides for us, in our High Priest Jesus, the very worship that we could not offer. The worship which God requires of us, and which we could not offer, is already accomplished by Christ, our representative. Not our response, but Christ's response in which we share, is the basis of worship. Intrinsic to Luther's doctrine of the priesthood of Christ is the double meaning of grace: God gives himself to us, freely and unconditionally, to be worshipped; and he comes to us as man, freely and unconditionally, to mediate to us the efficacy of his worship via his priesthood in which we participate. In relation to us, God hides in Jesus' humanity to reach us; in relation to God, we too hide in his humanity by which we ascend to the heavenly sanctuary. Our worship is a participation in Christ's own act of perfect worship of the Father.

The Spirit as the Dynamic of Christ's Mediation

Being united with Christ, we participate in his relationship of open communion with the Father, and thus in Jesus' own sonship, that in him we too are the sons of God – this is known by divine revelation. Luther wrote in his *Lectures on Galatians*:

---

[103] LW 29, 167; WA 57, III, 164–65.

God has also sent the Spirit of His Son into our hearts, as Paul says here (Gal. 4:6). Now Christ is completely certain that in His Spirit He is pleasing to God. Since we have the same Spirit of Christ, we, too, should be certain that we are in a state of grace, on account of Him who is certain. So much for the internal testimony, by which the heart should believe with complete certainty that it is in a state of grace and that it has the Holy Spirit.[104]

Commenting on Hebrews 3:14, "For we become partakers of Christ," Luther explained: "For through faith Christ is called our 'substance', that is, riches, and through the same faith we simultaneously become His 'substance', that is, a new creature."[105] All that Christ is and has via the joyous exchange is imputed to us, thereby constituting us as a new creature, "a kind of beginning of His creation (cf. James 1:18)."[106] While God invites us to believe the gospel that only in Christ is God our true and dear Father, the Holy Spirit enters our hearts enabling us to cry "Abba Father." All three persons work together as one *ad extra* in the economy of salvation, drawing us into the inner sanctuary of the Godhead: "Working through the Spirit, Father and Son stir, awaken, call and beget new life in me and in all who are his. Thus the Spirit in and through Christ quickens, sanctifies, and awakens the spirit in us and brings us to the Father, by whom the Spirit is active and life-giving everywhere."[107]

The Spirit comforts, and causes our troubled hearts to believe with complete certainty that we are his beloved on account of Christ's certainty. The knowledge that we in Christ are in a state of grace is wrought by the Spirit, whose cry "vastly exceeds, and breaks through" the powerful and terrifying forces or cries of the Law, sin, death, and the Devil. The Spirit's cry conquers all cries of the contrary of the gospel, "penetrates the clouds and heaven, and it reaches all the way to the ears of God."[108] The Spirit intercedes for us with sighs too deep for words (Rom. 8:26), and bears witness with our spirit that we are his beloved. The Spirit confers upon our hearts the assurance that the work of Christ's mediation is completed, and that we in Christ are truly his, the designated

---

[104] LW 26, 378–79; WA 50, 575–77.
[105] LW 29, 157; WA 57, III, 153–54.
[106] LW 29, 156; WA 57, III, 152–53.
[107] LW 43, 28.
[108] LW 26, 381; WA 50, 580–81.

heir of divine estate. By the Spirit, we know what lies in God's heart concerning us, and thus are persuaded in our hearts that our salvation is treasured up *pro nobis*.[109] This idea appears in Luther's gospel sermon preached on a Pentecost Sunday, 1522:

> It is a faithful saying that Christ has accomplished everything, has removed sin and overcome every enemy, so that through him we are lords over all things. But the treasure lies yet in one pile; it is not yet distributed nor invested. Consequently, if we are to possess it, the Holy Spirit must come and teach our hearts to believe and say: I, too, am one of those who are to have this treasure.[110]

The Church's worship is that corporeal matrix in which God's grace in Christ flows to us in the dynamic of the Spirit. The work of the Spirit is related to the Word and the community of the Word, as Luther expressly said in his *Large Catechism*:

> The creation is past and redemption is accomplished, but the Holy Spirit carries his work unceasingly until the last day. For this purpose he has appointed a community on earth, through which he speaks and does all his work. For he has not yet gathered together all his Christian people, nor has he completed the granting of forgiveness. Therefore we believe in him who daily brings us into this community through the Word, and imparts, increases, and strengthens faith through the same Word and the forgiveness of sins.[111]

---

[109] See Anthony N.S. Lane, *Calvin and Bernard of Clairvaux: Studies in Reformed Theology and History* no: 1 (Princeton: Princeton Theological Seminary, 1996), 65, n. 481, where he made mention of the connection between Bernard's soteriology and Luther's. See my "Reaping the Right Fruits: Luther's Meditation on the Earnest Mirror, Christ," *International Journal of Systematic Theology* VIII.4 (2006): 382–410, where this connection is shown.

[110] See "Gospel Sermon, Pentecost Sunday," in *Luther's Church Postil: Pentecost or Missionary Sermons*, ed. John N. Lenker (Minneapolis: Lutherans in All Lands Co., 1907), vol. 12, 279, n. 16. Also cited in A.E. Carlson, "Luther and the Doctrine of the Holy Spirit," *Lutheran Quarterly* 11 (1959): 136–37. See also Luther's "The Large Catechism," in *The Book of Concord*, ed. Theodore Tappert (Philadelphia: Fortress Press 1959), 419, where Luther discussed the third article of faith.

[111] See "The Large Catechism," in *The Book of Concord*, 419.

The God who came to us in Christ is the same God who comes as the Holy Spirit. Luther expressly spoke of the Spirit as the efficacy of the grace of Christ in us:

> Although the whole world has sought painstakingly to learn what God is and what he thinks and does, yet it has never succeeded in the least. But here you have everything in richest measure. In these three articles God himself has revealed and opened to us the profound depths of his fatherly heart, his sheer, unutterable love. He created us for this very purpose, to redeem and sanctify us. Moreover . . . we could never come to recognize the Father's favor and grace were it not for the lord Christ, who is mirror of the Father's heart. Apart from him we know nothing but an angry and terrible judge. But neither could we know anything of Christ, had it not been revealed by the Holy Spirit.[112]

Both the Son and Spirit mutually coinhere in the mediatorial ministry on our behalf before the Father. Jesus the ascended High Priest through the interceding Spirit presents us to the Father. Not only does he minister the things of God to us, he too ministers the things of us to God – this does not occur apart from the Spirit, the power of efficacy. Then our faith is strengthened amid these terrors; it sighs to its Savior and High Priest, Jesus Christ. Causally we boldly come before heaven's throne of grace with confidence, knowing for sure that our being and act of worship will be acceptable on account of Christ's being and his act of worship in which we are sharing. Our prayers, praises and sacrifices do not *cause* God to act, but only *occasion* him to present himself for us in heaven so that along with Christ our worship and services are deemed acceptable to him.[113] This Luther explained by a helpful analogy:

> Not that we offer the sacrament, but by our praise, prayer, and sacrifice we move him and give him *occasion* to offer himself for us in heaven and ourselves with him. It is as if I were to say, I had brought a king's son to his father as an offering, when actually I had done no more than induce that son to present my need and petition to the king and made the son my mediator.[114]

---

[112] See "The Large Catechism," in *The Book of Concord*, 419.
[113] Italics are mine.
[114] LW 29, 111; WA 57, III, 99.

Christ is thus the chief worshipper, the one who worships on our behalf. He too is our worship leader, through whom our worship reaches the heavenly sanctuary.[115]

> For those who have the faith that Christ is a Priest in heaven before God, and who can lay on him their prayers and praise, their need and their whole selves, presenting them through him, not doubting that he does this very thing, and offers himself for them – these people take the sacrament and testament, outwardly or spiritually, as a token of all this, and do not doubt that all sin is there forgiven, that God has become their gracious Father, and that everlasting life is prepared for them.[116]

Human accretions are ineffectual, but by the priestly role of Jesus, the representative, we are drawn into the eternal riches of God's life. Not on its own account, but on account of the mediation of Christ is our worship made pleasing to God. Only in this fashion can worship be conceived of as an ordinance of grace, in which Christ is the mediator. By grace we share in Christ's priesthood, the efficacy of which is communicated to us through the agency of the Holy Spirit. Through the Spirit, Christ continues to intercede for us and with us, even as we do the same through him and in him. Worship thus is an event in which divine and human action coincide.

Conclusion

The key to Luther's theology of worship, as to his theology of atonement, lies in this "reversal": "Not that something is given to God, but that God gives something to us."[117] This basic structure of how God and humanity relate is the underpinning of Luther's view of worship, in virtue of which God comes to us with his gifts, and we by faith embrace him as a gracious God. This is made possible by the Holy Spirit, who is given to those who believe, causing them to perceive and receive his words and trust

---

[115] Cf. James B. Torrance, *Worship, Community and the Triune God of Grace* (Carlisle: Paternoster Press, 1996), 65.
[116] LW 35, 101. See David Fergusson, "Theology of Worship," *Scottish Bulletin of Evangelical Theology* 21 (2003): 13–14.
[117] Forde, "Luther's Theology of the Cross," 50.

him for good. The Holy Spirit draws us into the Father's bosom through Christ. The Spirit places us in Christ so that everything that the Son is and possesses via the joyous exchange is ours by faith. We in Christ are enabled to respond to God in praise because the Holy Spirit causes love for God to arise in our hearts (Rom. 5:5), stirring us to cry "Abba, Father!" The Spirit is the efficacy of Christ's priestly work in us. Worship is distinctively trinitarian, insofar as it is first and foremost what the Triune God does, and, in this, Luther accentuates grace as the chief motive of worship. The worship of the Church is the communion of the Holy Trinity with us his redeemed people. It is, Jünghans writes appropriately of Luther, "above all the gathering of the community in which God (i.e., the Triune God) serves the assembled people" with his gifts.[118] Worship is primarily what God does, only secondarily what we do in response to his act. It is efficacious on account of God's causative Word, through which God's deed is accomplished. It is not our attempt to impress God so as to earn divine favor; rather it is a graced response to God's unconditional love for us. For God's love precedes our worship, not vice versa. Worship does not cause God's love; rather God's love causes our worship. We worship him because he condescends and moves toward us with his lavish grace. The Church's worship, in which the Word is read, preached and celebrated, is the ordained place, where God hides the promise of his saving presence for faith. As such, "God cannot be anticipated or outmaneuvered, only enjoyed."[119] Worship then becomes a joyful response of God's redeemed to the bountiful gifts freely bestowed in Christ. Yet it is not on account of our response, but Christ's efficacious response imputed to us that our worship is deemed worthy. Our responsive worship of God is founded upon the causality of Christ's priesthood in which we partake. We cast all our activities (singing, praising, service, prayers, etc.) upon Christ, who through the Spirit presents them to the Father. By that, we enter the Sabbath, the rest which God gives not as a fitting reward, but purely out of his free grace. Worship is the gift of participating through the Spirit in the incarnate Son's

---

[118] Jünghans, "Luther on the Reform of Worship," 211.
[119] David Steinmetz, *Luther in Context* (Bloomington: Indiana University Press, 1986), 83.

mediation, his priestly ministry and open communion with the Father. Worship is, thus, purely God's causative work for us, in which we participate as passive recipients.

Chapter Five

The Trinitarian Dynamic of Worship in John Calvin's *Institutes* (1559)

Introduction

It is accepted knowledge that Calvin's theology of worship largely appears in his commentaries, sermons, and letters.[1] However it is arguable that Calvin's scholarship on this topic also occurs in his more polemical *Institutes* (1559). There he developed his theology within the limits of "piety," a term that designates our rightful orientation toward God in a manner that is worthy of him.[2] This includes a heartfelt worship, prayerful obedience, filial fear, and

---

[1] John D. Witvliet, *Worship Seeking Understanding* (Grand Rapids: Baker Academic, 2003), 127–48. See Pamela Ann Moeller, *Calvin's Doxology* (Allison Park: Pickwick Publications, 1997), whose treatment of Calvin's worship with a view to contemporary worship renewal is notable, though not trinitarianly constructed.

[2] Cf. Joel R. Beeke, "Calvin on Piety," in *The Cambridge Companion to John Calvin*, ed. Donald K. McKim (Cambridge: Cambridge University Press, 2004), 126–27; William J. Bouwsma, "The Spirituality of John Calvin," in *Christian Spirituality: High Middle Ages and Reformation*, ed. Jill Raitt (New York: Crossroad, 1987), 318-33; Lucien Joseph Richard, *The Spirituality of John Calvin* (Atlanta: John Knox Press, 1974); Serene Jones, *Calvin and the Rhetoric of Piety* (Louisville: Westminster John Knox Press, 1995).

reverential love toward him as he comes toward us with his grace and acceptance. Calvin's intention in writing the *Institutes*, as stated in his preface addressed to King Francis I, was "solely to transmit certain rudiments by which those who are touched with any zeal for religion might be shaped to true godliness (*pietas*)."[3] This he spelt out in Book II:

> True religion must come first, to direct our minds to the living God. Thus, steeped in the knowledge of him, they may aspire to contemplate, fear, and worship, his majesty; to participate in his blessings; to seek his help at all times; to recognize and by praises to celebrate, the greatness of his works – as the only goal of all the activities of this life.[4]

The aim here is to discern how the theological role of the Trinity serves as an overarching paradigm for worship in Calvin's thought.[5] As declared in the Creed, only when the gospel is understood in a fully trinitarian way can we truly appreciate the essential nature of salvation and worship. Basic to what Calvin calls "fitting worship" is an appreciation of the connection between worship and God's divine nature revealed in the incarnate Son along with his mediatorial activity toward us through the Holy Spirit.[6] Calvin's major preoccupation is not so much with the immanent relationships of three persons or with the problem of relating the three to the absolute simplicity of the Godhead, but rather with the way the Father, Son and Holy Spirit interact in making

---

[3] John Calvin, *Institutes of Christian Religion*, 2 vols., ed. John T. McNeill; tr. F.L. Battles (Philadelphia: Westminster, 1960), vol. 1, 9. Our discussion is based on the 1559 edition of the *Institutes*.

[4] *Institutes* 2.8.16.

[5] Philip W. Butin, "Church Ministry and Ours: A Trinitarian and Reformed Perspective on the Ministry of the Whole People of God," in *Calvin and Calvin Studies* VII, ed. John Leith (Grand Rapids: Calvin Society, 1994), 2. For Calvin's Trinity, see his *Revelation, Redemption and Response: Calvin's Trinitarian Understanding of the Divine-Human Relationship* (New York: Oxford University Press, 1994); Benjamin B. Warfield, "Calvin's Doctrine of the Trinity," in *Calvin and Augustine*, ed. Samuel Craig (Phillipsburg: Presbyterian and Reformed Publishing Co., 1980), 189-286; Thomas F. Torrance, "Calvin's Doctrine of the Trinity," *Calvin Theological Journal* 25 (1990): 165–90; Paul Helm, *John Calvin's Ideas* (Oxford: Oxford University Press, 2004), 35–57.

[6] *Institutes* 1.2.1.

the divine–human intimacy in worship possible and actual. Thus his articulation of the doctrine of the Trinity is predominantly economic and soteriological, focusing on the interactive roles of the three persons in the economy of salvation. The God with whom we have to do is simply and solely the God who is toward us, who reveals himself in creation, redemption, and who constitutes human response to him definitively in Jesus Christ, through the sanctifying agency of the Spirit. To know God aright is to know him only through participating in the Son's knowledge of the Father, and the revelation he offers us of himself through his Spirit. The weight of Calvin's thinking falls on the discussion of the economic Trinity in which the saving content of the divine–human relationship, thus worship, is located. His evangelical emphasis reinforces the way he should travel: to consider God primarily in terms of his saving work toward us, or in terms of faith's experience of God's redemptive acts. To "put it medievally, God in his *operations ad extra*, in his *potentia ordinata*."[7] The economic actions of the Triune God are Calvin's dogmatic starting point, and thus take priority in his *Institutes*. Worship, grounded in a trinitarian dynamic, is constituted by a double movement: the God–humanward movement as the efficient cause of our worship, and the human–Godward movement as the corresponding response of our faith. By the Spirit, we live in, and are nurtured by, the Triune God in Christ, the womb of the Church. Not on our own account, but on account of Christ's vicarious response and priesthood, is our worship made efficacious by the Spirit. Worship as a participation in the worship of the Father through the Son in the Spirit belongs intrinsically to Calvin's doctrine of reconciliation with God, and is of the very constitution of the gospel. The Church's worship Calvin understood as the visible enactment of God's grace and gratitude via the instruments of his gospel – Word and sacraments. Worship is a saving event in which the Church is most authentically the Church, as she hears his Word of promise enacted in preaching and the celebration of sacraments, and believes it. Through the Word, thus enlivened by

---

[7] John R. Loeschen, *Divine Community. Trinity, Church and Ethics in Reformation Theologies* (Missouri: Northeast Missouri State University, 1981), 18.

the Spirit, the Lord, not ideas nor memories about him, but he himself is truly manifested to the heart of worshippers.

The Knowledge of God the Creator: Worship Intended

Although Calvin distinguished between the knowledge of God the Creator and God the Redeemer, he endorsed Augustine's axiom that the one Triune God is the subject of both acts *ad extra*. Thus in book I, the pre-incarnate Christ is not excluded from the scene. Here Calvin was not speaking of the kind of knowledge with which sinners apprehend God the Redeemer in Christ, but only of the primal and simple knowledge to which every order of nature would have led us if Adam had remained upright.[8] In a long paragraph, Calvin elaborated the content and purpose of the knowledge of the Creator:

> [N]ot only does [God] sustain this universe (as he once founded it) by his boundless might, regulate it by his wisdom, preserve it by his goodness, and especially rule mankind by his righteousness and judgment, bear with it in his mercy, watch over it by his protection; but also that no drop will be found either of wisdom and light, or of righteousness or power or rectitude, or of genuine truth, which does not flow from him, and of which he is not the cause. Thus we may learn to await and seek all these things from him, and thankfully to ascribe them, once received, to him . . . For until men recognize that they owe everything to God, that they are nourished by his fatherly care, that he is the Author of their every good, that they should seek nothing beyond him – they will never yield him willing service. Nay, unless they establish their complete happiness in him, they will never give themselves truly and sincerely to him.[9]

The first article affirms God as the origin and goal of all that is. This knowledge sheds light on who God is in relation to us – that he is the Giver of all, and simultaneously illumines who we are in relation to him, that we are the recipients of all his gifts. Thus knowing God and knowing ourselves are mutually connected. "The sense of divinity" (*divinitatis sensus*) is ontologically constitutive of

---

[8] *Institutes* 1.2.1.
[9] *Institutes* 1.2.1. See Thomas Parker, *Calvin: An Introduction to His Thought* (London: Geoffrey Chapman, 1995), 15.

our creaturely status.[10] For God has not only implanted in all a certain understanding of his existence, but also discloses himself daily in the splendorous workmanship of his universe. So clear and so prominent is God's self-disclosure that none could take refuge in the pretense of ignorance. This innate knowledge of God is set within our perception, which God repeatedly renews by shedding "fresh drops" of his richest manifestations in nature and providence.[11] The enhanced knowledge of God revealed in nature serves to strengthen the faith of believers. "Therefore it was his will that the history of creation be made manifest, in order that the faith of the church, resting upon this, might seek no other God but him who was put forth by Moses as the Maker and Founder of this universe."[12]

The knowledge of God mediated by Scripture and the inner knowledge of God imprinted in each human being in creation both have worship as their intended goal. In a hermeneutical circle, Scripture invites us first to revere God, then trust in him, and finally, "by this we can learn to worship him."[13] This knowledge of God (the Father) as the fountainhead and source of all good begets "piety" – "that reverence joined with the love of God which the knowledge of his benefits induces." It too begets "pure and real religion," which for Calvin is "faith so joined with an earnest fear of God, a fear that both contains a voluntary reverence and also carries with it the true service and worship prescribed in the Law."[14] From this knowledge arises in the creatures the desire to cleave to him, to be loath at offending his glory, to love and revere God as "Father," worship and adore him as "Lord."[15] As object, God is worshipped as the Father and Lord of his creation.[16]

God so constitutes his creatures in such a way that they naturally possess the knowledge of him that leads them to revere

---

[10] *Institutes* 1.3.1. See Warfield, "Calvin's Doctrine of the Knowledge of God," in *Calvin and Augustine*, 32.
[11] *Institutes* 1.3.1. See Jones, *Calvin and the Rhetoric of Piety*, 163–64.
[12] *Institutes* 1.14.1.
[13] *Institutes* 1.10.2.
[14] *Institutes* 1.2.2.
[15] *Institutes* 1.2.2.
[16] Cf. *First Catechism* 1538, ed. & tr. Ford Lewis Battles (Pittsburgh: Pittsburgh Theological Seminary, 1972), 2; Ford Lewis Battles, "True Piety According to John Calvin," in *Interpreting John Calvin*, ed. Robert Benedetto (Grand Rapids: Baker Books, 1996), 290.

the origin of the good they experience. Fundamental to Calvin is the intrinsic unity of knowledge of God and worship, that when duly imbued with the knowledge of God, they may aspire to revere and worship his majesty, and make him the sole goal of all their actions. This is intimated in his commentary on Malachi 1:11: "We must bear in mind that God cannot rightly be worshipped except he is known."[17] As further proof, Calvin explained why Paul in his Areopagus sermon in Acts 17:24 "makes a beginning with a definition of God, so that he might prove from that how he ought to be worshipped, because the one thing depends upon the other."[18] The same appears in his *Institutes*:

> In seeking God, miserable men do not rise above themselves as they should, but measure him by the yardstick of their own carnal stupidity, and neglect sound investigation; thus out of curiosity they fly off into empty speculations. They do not therefore *apprehend God as he offers himself*, but imagine him as they have fashioned him in their own presumption. When this gulf opens, in whatever directions they move their feet, they cannot but plunge headlong into ruin. Indeed, whatever they afterward attempt by *way of worship or service of God*, they cannot bring as tribute to him, but they are worshipping not God but a figment and a dream of their own heart.[19]

God creates us with worship as our goal. To do otherwise is to degenerate from the law of our creation. "This was not unknown to the philosophers. Plato meant nothing but this when he often taught that the highest good of the soul is likeness to God, where, when the soul has grasped the knowledge of God, it is wholly transformed into his likeness."[20] We are born and live to the end

---

[17] CO 44.420 (Commentary on Mal. 1:11) as cited in Witvliet, *Worship Seeking Understanding*, 152.

[18] CO 48.410 (Commentary on Acts 17:25). See Carlos M.N. Eire, *War Against the Idols: The Reformation of Worship from Erasmus to Calvin* (Cambridge: Cambridge University Press, 1986), 197.

[19] Institutes 1.4.1 (Italics are mine).

[20] Institutes 1.2.3; see also 3. 25.2. Cf. William J. Bouwsma, *John Calvin: A Sixteenth Century Portrait* (NY: Oxford University Press, 1988), 103–04. Bouwsma finds that Calvin does not totally undermine the heritage of natural theology; he nevertheless concludes that the debate between Brunner, "for whom Calvin left a large place for the knowledge of God from nature," and Barth, "for whom he left little or none," "is futile because of Calvin's ambivalence; he can be cited on both sides of the

that we may know God, and worship him concomitantly. We are to direct our inbuilt sense of deity, not inwardly to the self, or outwardly to any creaturely beings or objects, but Godwardly to God in a reverential acknowledgment of him by which we fulfill the very objective for which we are created. Worship is vitiated when its object is not "God as he offers himself," but an imagination, an empty dream. The object of the knowledge of God cannot be a god who has no relation with us, but a God who intimately cares for us, and who therefore deserves our piety and worship.

That "God cannot be rightly worshipped except he is known" means that discourse on God's essence or majesty is forbidden. The speculative question "What is God?" (*quid sit Deus*), must give way to the revelatory question "What is God like?" (*qualis sit Deus*), that which accords with God's nature.[21] As Calvin explained, "Indeed, his essence is incomprehensible; hence, his divineness far escapes human perception. But upon his individual works he has engraved unmistakable marks of his glory."[22] The nature of God is to be apprehended in the act he performs for us – this is in line with the principle of correspondence between God's being and God's act, God's nature and God's operation. This too is evident in the preface of the Decalogue, leading into the First Commandment: "I am Jehovah, your God (*God's nature*), who brought you out of the Land of Egypt, out of the house of bondage (*God's deed*). You shall have no other gods before my face" (Ex. 20:2–3).[23] That God's essence is incomprehensible does not imply full-fledged agnosticism about God in himself; nor does knowing God only as he is toward us mean that our knowledge of God is only relational, completely devoid of metaphysical character. Here Benjamin B. Warfield errs when he says: "This much we know, [Calvin] says, that God is what His works and acts reveal him to be; though it must be admitted that his works and acts reveal not His metaphysical Being but His personal relations – not what he is *apud se* (in himself), but what he is *quoad nos* (toward us)."[24] In so doing Warfield drives a wedge between the immanent God *ad intra* and economic God *ad extra*, thereby confusing what God is to us with what he is in his outward relation with us. Contrarily,

---

issue (103, n. 51)."

[21] *Institutes* 1.2.2; 1.10.2; 3.2.6. See Helm, *John Calvin's Ideas*, 12.
[22] *Institutes* 1.5.1.
[23] *Institutes* 2.8.16.
[24] Warfield, "Calvin's Doctrine of God," in *Calvin and Augustine*, 154.

Calvin affirmed the close connection between God's nature and his essence in that his nature cannot but offer insight into his essence, even if that essence is beyond our reach.[25]

The true knowledge of God is always accompanied by reverential acknowledgment of him in that there is no speech about God without worship. Speaking against the impassive and idle deity of neo-Epicureans, Calvin asked: What profit is it to know such a God who lives in his transcendent bliss, a God with whom we have nothing to do? Such deity attracts no worshippers, for it has no dealings with people. Rather the knowledge of God, that by which we discern "what befits us and is proper to his glory, in short, what is to our advantage to know of him,"[26] is the condition of possibility of true worship. The only knowledge Calvin esteemed is that knowledge of God which effects piety. Governed by the primacy of the knowledge of God as he is "piously known,"[27] he considered it superfluous to advance any proofs for the existence of God. He too repudiated any attempt to understand the divine being in philosophical categories, but led us to Scripture, where God is shown "not as he is in himself, but as he is toward us so that this recognition of him consists more in living experience than in vain and high-flown speculation."[28] Not by the speculative knowledge, but by the pious knowledge of God – his outward relation with us – are we drawn to love and "worship him both with perfect innocence of life and with unfeigned obedience, then to depend wholly upon his goodness."[29]

---

[25] *Comm. Lam.* 3:8 as cited in Helm, *John Calvin's Ideas*, 15. The principle of correspondence requires that God cannot, in view of what he essentially is, negate what he has promised to do. Calvin wrote: "We may be content with this one thing, that when God claims to himself this prerogative, that he answers prayers, he intimates that it is what cannot be separated from his eternal essence and godhead, that is, that he is ready to hear prayer."

[26] *Institutes* 1.2.1.

[27] Dewey J. Hoitenga, Jr., "Faith and Reason in Calvin's Doctrine of the Knowledge of God," in *Articles on Calvin and Calvinism*, ed. Richard C. Gamble (New York: Garland Publishing, Inc., 1992), 33.

[28] *Institutes* 1.10.2.

[29] *Institutes* 1.10.2.

Thus Edward Dowey concludes: "To know God disinterestedly is, for Calvin, a contradiction in terms."[30]

The First Commandment: Pure Worship and Idolatry

Piety is idolatrous if it is directed to anyone or anything except the true God; it is also idolatrous if it attempts to worship God in any way other than that ordained by God:

> Then [God] defines lawful worship in order to hold mankind in obedience. He combines both [authority and form] under his law, first when he binds believers to himself to be their sole lawgiver, and then when he prescribes a rule whereby he is to be duly honored according to his own will.[31]

Whoever considers the First Commandment considers God alone as God. This is the purpose of this Commandment: God alone be exalted as pre-eminent among his people. By calling upon God, we make known the peculiar significance of his place and standing in our lives. That is, we allow God alone to be God, worthy of our adoration and trust. Worship, which flows from this Commandment, ultimately takes us back to it. If God is God in our lives, we worship God with true and zealous godliness as an obedience befitting his command. One cannot remain neutral when God's Word is spoken. God's command requires a response, but more importantly, the kind of response that accords with his nature: "As often as Scripture asserts that there is one God, it is not contending over the bare name, but also prescribing that nothing belonging to his divinity is to be transferred to another."[32] God claims for himself alone the glory of his divinity, which suffers diminution if it is attached to another. True worship thus must adhere to "this principle: God's glory is corrupted by an impious falsehood, whenever any form is attached to him."[33] Accordingly

---

[30] Edward A. Dowey, *The Knowledge of God in Calvin's Theology* (NY: Columbia University Press, 1952), 28.

[31] *Institutes* 1.12.1. For further study of Calvin's understanding of human images in relation to worship, see Randall C. Zachman, *Image and Word in the Theology of John Calvin* (Grand Rapids: Eerdmans, 2007), 373-77.

[32] *Institutes* 1.12.1.

[33] *Institutes* 1.12.1.

every pictorial representation of God commits an Athenian error which Paul refutes as a domestication of divine transcendence (Acts 17). It too is incongruous with the Second Commandment: "You shall not make for yourself, a graven image" (Ex. 20:4), which is an outflow of the First Commandment upon which "spiritual worship" of the invisible Deity is based.[34] The refusal to abide by the prescription of God and the audacity to corrupt God's command by devising material forms of worship are the roots of idolatry.

Calvin is no dualist. What he opposed was not the creaturely world, which by itself is of great dignity; but rather the prudence of human reason that refuses to worship God on his own terms, and at his level. The perversion of worship Calvin attributed to human attempts to reverse the order of divine reality, seeking to find the Creator in the created. In forbidding us to have strange gods, he meant that we are not to attach to another what rightly belongs to God. All impiety and superstition are diminution of the glory of Deity. To properly worship God is to render wholly to him "the things that are his," which include:[35]

> (1) "Adoration" I call the veneration and worship that each of us, in submitting to his greatness, renders to him. (2) "Trust" is the assurance of reposing in him that arises from the recognition of his attributes, when – attributing to him all wisdom, righteousness, might, truth, and goodness – we judge that we are blessed only by communion with him. (3) "Invocation" is that habit of our mind, whenever necessity presses us, of resorting to his faithfulness and help as our only support. (4) "Thanksgiving" is that gratitude with which we ascribe praise to him for all good things. As the Lord suffers nothing of these to be transferred to another, so he commands that all be rendered wholly to himself.[36]

Although Calvin's *Institutes* has established the basic theological framework for worship, the fullest statement is found in the 1543 apologetic treatise *The Necessity of Reforming the Church, addressed to the Emperor Charles V*, where Calvin exhorted all Christians to assume their primary duty in the maintenance of pure worship.[37]

---

[34] *Institutes* 2.8.17.
[35] *Institutes* 2.8.17.
[36] *Institutes* 2.8.17.
[37] Calvin, "The Necessity of Reforming the Church," see English

Quoting Luther and others, Calvin set forth a critique of late-medieval piety and a defense of the Protestant movement as the authentic expression of true piety.[38] He began by stating firmly two major constituents by which Christianity exists and maintains its truth: "a knowledge, first, of the right way to worship God; and secondly of the source from which salvation is to be sought. When these are kept out of view, though we may glory in the name of Christians, our profession is empty and vain."[39] These two "not only occupy the principal, but comprehend under them all other parts, and consequently, the whole substance of Christianity."[40] After these foundations come the sacraments and the Government of the Church, which were instituted for no other purpose than to preserve these doctrines, as the body serves the soul.[41] However, for Calvin correct worship is logically prior to true knowledge of salvation or righteousness in order of cognitive significance.[42]

Calvin then proceeded to describe what is meant by the due worship of God. Its chief foundation is the reverent acknowledgment of who God is, that he is the only source of all that is, and that therefore the glory and trust are ascribed to God.[43] Arising from this is prayer, praise and thanksgiving, these being attestations to the glory that is proper to him. Then there is the genuine hallowing of his name, which finds expression in corporate adoration and the attendant ceremonies performed to give bodily expression to the heart's worship. Next comes self-abasement, by which we are trained to obey him so that his fear might reign and regulate all aspects of our lives. Abiding in these things is the true and sincere worship which alone God approves. This knowledge is taught by the Holy Spirit throughout the Scriptures, and also, as previously discussed, known by the inborn dictate of piety.[44] Whoever desires to worship God aright must pay regard

---

translation in Calvin, *Tracts Relating to the Reformation*, vol.1, ed. Henry Beveridge (Edinburgh: Calvin Translation Society, 1844), 123–234.

[38] "The Necessity," 125. See Philip W. Butin, "John Calvin's Humanist Image or Popular Late-Medieval Piety and Its Contribution to Reformed Worship," *Calvin Theological Journal* 29 (1994), 425.

[39] "The Necessity," 126–27.

[40] "The Necessity," 126–27.

[41] "The Necessity," 126–27.

[42] *Institutes* 2.8.1. See Eire, *War Against the Idols*, 201.

[43] "The Necessity," 127.

[44] "The Necessity," 127.

to what God has commanded, or the Word which God employs as a bridle to keep us on a right path.[45] Thus it is forbidden of us to undertake a contrary course than his command, to add to his Word, or to debate with him about what constitutes right or wrong worship. Before God, the sole judge, "obedience is better than sacrifice" (I Sam. 25:22).

Calvin's theology of worship shines in his attack on late-medieval piety that has its basis in human initiative rather than in the desire to reverently obey what God commands in Scripture. His chief complaint about its image of worship is that it has undertaken a course that is at variance with God's command, and hence violated what Eire terms "the hermeneutic of transcendence."[46] Consequently the people, "forsaking the fountain of living waters, have learned, as Jeremiah tells us, to hew them out 'cisterns, broken cisterns, that can hold no water' (Jer. 2:13), . . . They say, indeed, that they seek salvation and every other good in God alone; but it is mere pretence, seeing they seek them elsewhere."[47] Their prayers are typically done as a religious obligation to satisfy God rather than as a fitting response to God's command and his promise attached therewith. They have turned the merciful God into an angry God who needs to be placated by human deeds, in which case the dignity of true worship is lost. Adoration is misdirected toward images and statues, including that of the saints and their relics. This robs God of his glory when it is transferred to the creatures. Medieval ceremonies are not attestations of divine worship, but are "superstitious," "fictitious," "frivolous" and "useless."[48] They are mixed with "numerous puerile extravagancies" and "impious rites" borrowed from the heathen, but adapted to "theatrical show," and thus are a mockery of God. True worship is also vitiated in individual Christian discipleship, in which one overlooks true repentance and devotes his attention to external deeds (as vigils, abstinences, etc.), which Paul calls "beggarly elements" of the world.[49] What makes this a pernicious error is the exchange in Christian self-abasement of "the shadow for the substance," seeing discipleship as little more than "external exercises of the body."[50]

---

[45] "The Necessity," 133.
[46] Eire, *War Against the Idols*, 201.
[47] "The Necessity," 129.
[48] "The Necessity," 129–39.
[49] "The Necessity," 132
[50] "The Necessity," 132.

The sacramental celebrations are not living exercises of piety because vernacular instructions are missing from them. Where the word is silent, nothing remains of significance and truth of the sacraments, except "showy ceremonies" and "empty figures."[51] Worship is "fruitless" when preaching is not central, and sermons consist of little more than old wives' tales and fictions. In short, human tradition, together with its inclination toward idolatry and its abuses, has replaced God's Word as the standard of medieval piety and worship.[52]

After a thorough critique of the errors of late-medieval piety, Calvin offered the rudiments that properly train congregants to a legitimate worship of God:

> [W]e exhort people to worship God neither in a frigid nor a careless manner . . . We proclaim the glory of God in terms far loftier than it was wont to be proclaimed before, and we earnestly labor to make the perfections in which His glory shines better and better known. His benefits towards ourselves we extol as eloquently as we can, while we call upon others to reverence His Majesty, render due homage to His greatness, feel due gratitude for His mercies, and unite in showing forth His praise. In this way there is infused into their hearts that solid confidence which afterwards gives birth to prayer; and in this way, too, each one is trained to genuine self-denial, so that his will being brought into obedience, he bids farewell to his own desires . . . Nor do we overlook external duties and works of charity, which follow on such renewal [by grace].[53]

The causative factor of worship is the wonder and glory of God *as God*, and the mercy and generosity of God as *our God*; the responsive character of worship is reverence, homage, gratitude, praise, and the confidence to recourse to him in every need, to surrender our lives to him for good, and serve our neighbors for their benefit. Worship, interlaced with faith, fear, reverence and love, is the fruit of the knowledge of God. What is striking in Calvin, as in Luther, is the link of worship with primary motifs

---

[51] "The Necessity," 138–39.
[52] "The Necessity," 132–33. Cf. 1539 "Letter to Sadolet," in Calvin, *Tracts*, 61.
[53] "The Necessity," 147.

– faith alone, Word alone, glory and praise of God, and Christian vocation.

The Mediation of Christ: Worship Restored

Sin averts "God's face away from the sinner; and . . . it is foreign to his righteousness to have any dealings with sin. For this reason . . . man is God's enemy."[54] And the pile of God's blessings remains at a distance, and cannot be enjoyed. The subjective condition of the soul negates the apparent possibility of knowledge, as Calvin explained: "As experience shows, God has sown a seed of religion in all men. But scarcely one man in a hundred is met with who fosters [the seed of religion], once received, in his heart, and none in whom it ripens – much less shows fruit in season" (cf. Ps. 1:3).[55] The seed of religion seldom takes root, and when it does, it tends to achieve the opposite of God's original intention. Instead of leading us upward to God, it leads us downward, toward death, blindness, and spiritual destruction. Scarcely anyone actuates this inclination toward God, and the one who does fosters it in a distorted manner, bearing dangerous and deformed fruits. The sinner can only respond to this desire erroneously, either by suppressing its effect or by perverting its intended purpose. The end result is that God's honor suffers disparagement, and we are separated further from the grace we desperately need. Yet God keeps this numinous awareness of himself perpetually alive, not so much to convince all without exception that God exists and is their Creator, as to condemn all without escape by their own testimony for failing to build on this awareness by worshipping him and consecrating their lives to his will. God intends the knowledge of his blessings in nature and history to lead us to him in worship, and obedience is now hindered by the fall. The actual knowledge of God framed within human apprehension is affected by the curvature of the soul. "The soul, being corrupted by sin, is dulled in its instinctive apprehension of God; and God's manifestation in nature and history is deflected in it."[56] Calvin is keenly cognizant of the fact of culpable human blindness. David Steinmetz writes correctly: "The difficulty is not with what is shown

---
[54] *Institutes* 3.11.21.
[55] *Institutes* 1.4.1.
[56] Warfield, "Calvin's Doctrine of the Knowledge of God," 32.

to fallen human reason through the natural order; the difficulty is with human misperception because of sin."[57] Because "the fault of dullness is within us," we are incapable of properly perceiving the ontological superiority of the Creator. We atomize the divine by creating a pantheon of fictitious creaturely deities: "Surely, just as waters boil up from a vast, full spring, so does an immense crowd of gods flow forth from the human mind, which each one, in wandering about with too much license, wrongly invents this or that about God himself."[58] Idolatry causes divine displeasure, and distances us from the purity of righteousness which is God. However, the worship that is lost due to sin is now restored by God the Son, who makes true worship possible, and abolishes the distance between God and us: "And that none may be deterred by difficulty of access, we proclaim that a complete fountain of all blessings is offered to us in Christ, out of which we may draw everything we need."[59] Calvin captured the Christological basis of worship in which the overwhelming sense of praise and adoration is the outcome of God's grace in Christ. The human response flows from the character of God's nature as revealed in the redemptive deed. Not on our own, but solely on account of Christ's efficacious act as the Mediator is our worship sanctioned as the true sacrifice.

For Calvin, justification is "the main thing on which religion turns."[60] Its material cause is Christ's vicarious obedience in his life and death, whereas its instrumental cause is faith without human works or credits. Justification occurs *extra nos*, outside ourselves, in Christ. That Christ might become ours entails this: the spotless righteousness of Christ – that of his perfect obedience – becomes ours in our justification. Contrary to the Roman Catholic view of

---

[57] David Steinmetz, *Calvin in Context* (NY: Oxford University Press, 1995), 29.

[58] *Institutes* 1.5.12. See Hughes Oliphant Old, "John Calvin and the Prophetic Criticism of Worship," in *John Calvin and the Church: A Prism of Reform*, ed. Timothy George (Louisville: Westminster John Knox Press, 1985): 230-46, where he argues how basic the prophetic critique of the temple worship is to the formation of New Testament worship.

[59] "The Necessity," 147.

[60] *Institutes* 3.2.1. Hence justification and sanctification are so closely linked that some Calvin scholars attribute to Calvin the doctrine of "double justification." See Bruce Demarest, *The Cross and Salvation* (Illinois: Crossway Books, 1997), 361.

justification as an infusion of grace, Calvin furnished a forensic interpretation:

> It is also evident that we are justified before God solely by the intercession of Christ's righteousness. This is equivalent to saying that man is not righteous in himself but because of the righteousness of Christ communicated to him by imputation . . . To declare that by [Christ] alone we are accounted righteous, what else is this but to lodge our righteousness in Christ's obedience, because the obedience of Christ is reckoned to us as if it were our own.[61]

That we are accepted freely by grace received in faith has direct implication for Calvin's understanding of worship. God accepts our worship freely in the person of his beloved Son, who in our name, in our humanity and on our behalf, has made the one offering to the Father which alone is sanctioned by God for all, and at all times.[62] The imputation of Christ's obedience and righteousness to the believer is the foundation of worship and salvation, the twin truths which define true Christianity. "As we ourselves, when we have been engrafted in Christ, are righteous in God's sight because our iniquities are covered by Christ's sinlessness, so our works are righteous and are thus regarded because whatever fault is otherwise in them is buried in Christ's purity, and is not charged to our account."[63] This insight of Calvin underscores the importance of worship as human action, nevertheless a responsive one sanctified by God's justifying grace. In this sense, worship is a gift of grace, and yet is an event in which both divine and human action coincide. God justifies not only the sinner, but also sanctifies (justifies) the believer's works – which works (including prayers, praises, etc.) demonstrate obedience to God. "In our sharing in Christ, which justifies us, sanctification is just as much included as righteousness."[64] To partake of Christ is to possess "a double grace": namely, the reconciliation with God through Christ's blessedness, and the sanctification by Christ's Spirit.[65]

---

[61] *Institutes* 3.11.23.
[62] *Institutes* 2.16.16.
[63] *Institutes* 3.17.10.
[64] *Institutes* 3.16.1.
[65] *Institutes* 3.2.1.

This is Calvin's rendering of the Pauline phrase: Christ is "our righteousness, holiness and redemption" (I Cor. 1:30).

Calvin spelt out at length the double emphasis of Christ's priestly office: reconciliation and intercession, under which worship is comprehended. "For under the law, also, the Priest was forbidden to enter the sanctuary (Heb. 9:7), that believers might know, even though the Priest as their advocate stood between them and God, that they could not propitiate God unless their sins were expiated (Lev. 16:2–3)."[66] But Christ fulfills the priestly role when, in his capacity as "a pure and stainless Mediator," he conquers "God's righteous curse" and makes perfect satisfaction for human sins. Moved by pure and free love, Christ descends to us clothed in our flesh, vicariously submits himself to the verdict of guilty and enters our condemnation. In so doing, he removes all cause for enmity and effects our reconciliation with God. He "wipes out all evil in us by the expiation set forth in the death of Christ."[67] "Therefore, by his love God the Father goes before and anticipates our reconciliation in Christ . . . But until Christ succors us by his death, the unrighteousness that deserves God's indignation remains in us, and is accursed and condemned before him. Hence, we can be fully and firmly joined with God only when Christ joins us with him."[68] In union with Christ, we may be assured that God is kindly disposed toward us, and we experience the joyous exchange of our sin, which stirs up God's wrath against us, for his righteousness, through which we are received into grace. Our praises or prayers could have "no access to God unless Christ, as our High Priest, having washed away our sins, sanctifies us and obtains for us that grace from which the uncleanness of our transgressions and vices debars us." Therefore we must "begin from the death of Christ in order that the efficacy and benefit of his priesthood may reach us."[69]

Integral to Christ's efficacious priesthood is Christ as "an everlasting intercessor" who, through his pleading obtains for us divine favor. In Christ, there was "a new and different order, in which the same one was to be both Priest and sacrifice." Christ assumes the priestly office, "not only to render the Father favorable

---

[66] *Institutes* 2.15.6.
[67] *Institutes* 2.16.3.
[68] *Institutes* 2.16.3.
[69] *Institutes* 2.16.3.

and propitious toward us by an eternal law of reconciliation, but also to receive us as his companions in this great office (Rev. 1:6). For we who are defiled in ourselves, yet are priests in him, offer ourselves and our all to God, and freely enter the heavenly sanctuary that the sacrifices of prayers and praise that we bring may be acceptable and sweet-smelling before God."[70] This is borne out in Christ's statement: "For their sake I sanctify myself" (Jn. 17:19). His sanctification is reckoned unto us: "For we, imbued with his holiness in so far as he has consecrated us to the Father with himself, although we would otherwise be loathsome to him, please him as pure and clean – and even as holy."[71] Whatever has been consecrated through the Mediator is acceptable to God.

At the heart of Calvin's view of worship is the basic distinction between "in ourselves" and "in Christ," the former being the condition in which we cannot access God, and the latter being the condition of efficacious worship. What we in ourselves could not offer, God himself provides in Christ. As God is comprehended in Christ, so is humankind, worship, and all else. Calvin declared: "Christ is the beginning, the middle, and the end,"[72] and "our whole salvation and all its parts [worship included] must be comprehended in Christ."[73] Calvin wrote:

> Therefore, that joining together of Head and members, that indwelling of Christ in our hearts – in short, that mystical union – are accorded by us the highest degree of importance, so that Christ, having been made ours, makes us sharers with him in the gifts with which he has been endowed. We do not, therefore, contemplate him outside ourselves from afar in order that his righteousness may be imputed to us because we put on Christ and are engrafted into his body – in short because he deigns to make us one with him.[74]

---

[70] *Institutes* 2.16.3.
[71] *Institutes* 2.16.3.
[72] Com. I Pet. 1:20 as cited in Charles Partee, "Calvin's Central Dogma Again," in *Calvin Studies* II, ed. John H. Leith (Davidson: Davidson College, 1986), 43. Cf. Dennis Tamburello, *Union With Christ: John Calvin and the Mysticism of St. Bernard* (Louisville: Westminster John Knox Press, 1994), 89 & 144.
[73] *Institutes* 2.16.19.
[74] *Institutes* 3.11.10. Partee, "Calvin's Central Dogma Again," 42–43; In his *Calvin and Classical Philosophy* (Leiden: E.J. Brill, 1977), 87–88, he argues that union with Christ is Calvin's central dogma. Whether that is the case or not remains debatable.

By an indivisible bond of fellowship, and with a marvelous communion, Christ becomes increasingly united to us, until he is completely one with us. His benefits would not profit us unless he first made himself ours.[75] The only bond of our union with God is union with Christ, in which imputation of Christ's benefits to us occurs. In worship, as in salvation, we are given a true participation in the cross of Christ. In Christ, we are fully endowed, and thus need not "seek outside him what we have already obtained in him and find in him alone."[76] Everything that Christ is (person) and does (work), which constitutes the basis of worship, is ours.

The *telos* of Christ's ministry is the reconciliation of wayward, broken sinners with God, and the restoration of pure worship. Christ continues to plead on our behalf so that we, in and through him, might be lifted up to reside with his Father in the heavenly realm, where we partake of all his innumerable benefits. It is to our great benefit that Christ ascended in his glorified humanity and resided at the right hand of his Father. For Christ to "reside" with his Father is for him to "preside" at the heavenly throne, from which he transfuses us with his power, and sanctifies us by his Spirit. "From this our faith . . . understands that the Lord, by his ascent to heaven, opened the way into the Heavenly Kingdom, which had been closed through Adam (Jn. 14:3). Since he entered heaven *in our flesh, as if in our name,* it follows, as the apostle says, that in a sense we already 'sit with God in the heavenly places in him' (Eph. 2:6), so that we do not await heaven with a bare hope, but *in our Head* already possess it."[77] What Calvin taught here is also found in his commentary on Hebrews 6:19:

> [B]ecause Christ has entered heaven our faith must also be directed there. This is the source of our knowledge that faith must not look anywhere else. It is useless for men to look for God in His majesty, because it is too remote and far from them: but Christ stretches out his hand to lead us to heaven, as was indeed foreshadowed earlier in the Law. The High Priest used to enter the holy of holies *not only in his own name, but in that of the people,* as one who in a way *carried all the twelve tribes on his breast* and on his shoulders, because twelve stones were woven into his breastplate and their names were engraved on the two onyx stones on his shoulders to be a reminder of

---

[75] *Institutes* 4.17.11.
[76] *Institutes* 3.24.5.
[77] *Institutes* 2.16.16 (Italics mine).

them, so that *they all went into the sanctuary together in the person.* The apostle is therefore right when he states that *our High Priest has entered heaven, because He has done so not only for Himself, but also for us.* There is therefore no cause for fear that the door of heaven may be shut to our faith, since it is never disjoined from Christ. Because it is for us to follow Christ who goes before us, He is called our Forerunner.[78]

Against Osiander, who saw Christ merely as the instrumental cause of our justification, Calvin repeatedly argued that Christ is the material cause and the minister of this great benefit – righteousness.[79] To conceive of Christ as Osiander did, Calvin contended, is to be led away "from the priesthood of Christ and His office of Mediator, to His eternal divinity."[80] In other words, Osiander bypasses the vicarious humanity of Christ – his life and obedience on our behalf – as the ground of our justification; he "obviously deprives the human nature of Christ of the office of justifying."[81] For Calvin, Christ is "the substance" – the sacrifice of propitiation, the "true priesthood,"[82] and the complete fulfillment of the priesthoods of old. "For Christ is the sole Pontiff and Priest of the New Testament [cf. Heb. 9], to whom all priesthoods have been transferred, and in whom they have been closed and terminated."[83] No Priests, except Christ whose priesthood is heavenly, could intercede efficaciously before God. Christ not only enters our death, and rises again in our humanity, but also returns to the Father as our eternal intercessor (Heb. 8:1). From this, it is clear that our prayers cannot be heard unless they are based on an intervening sacrifice. To enter the sanctuary with efficacy, we must not bypass Christ's humanity and his death, which alone sanctifies our prayers. "God will not hear us unless He is favorably inclined, and therefore He must first be appeased since our sins have made Him angry with us; and so there must of necessity be

---

[78] Comm. On Heb. 6:19 in Calvin Commentaries, vol. 12, 87 (Italics mine). Also quoted in James B. Torrance, "The Vicarious Humanity and Priesthood of Christ," in *Calvinus Ecclesiae Doctor*, ed. W. Neuser (Kampen: J.H. Kok, 1978), 71.
[79] *Institutes* 3.11.7–8.
[80] *Institutes* 3.11.8.
[81] *Institutes* 3.11.12.
[82] *Institutes* 2.15.6.
[83] *Institutes* 4.18.14.

a preceding sacrifice for our prayer to have any effect."[84] In our humanity, and in our name, Christ our Head offers a sacrifice that reaches the Holy of Holies, and whose efficacy extends to all at all times. "And it was done but once, because the effectiveness and force of that one sacrifice accomplished by Christ are eternal, as he testified with his own voice when he said that it was done and fulfilled (Jn. 19:30)." [85] Only through partaking of Christ, in union with him, can we partake of his nearness with God and its accompanying benefits, including his worship of, and his Sonly communion with the Father. The access through Christ to the heavenly sanctuary is a gift of grace:

> For, having entered a sanctuary not made with hands, [Christ] appears before the Father's face as our constant advocate and intercessor (Heb. 7:27; 9:11–12; Rom. 8:34). Thus he turns the Father's own eyes to his own righteousness to avert his gaze from our sins. He so reconciles the Father's heart to us that by his intercession he prepares a way and access for us to the Father's throne. He fills with grace and kindness the throne that for miserable sinners would otherwise have been filled with dread.[86]

Christ's mediation does not derogate human agency, but inspires it. Calvin's emphasis is this: "[Christ's] priesthood is *for us* in such a way that it recovers our own."[87] Such understanding animates the believer's active response to God in corporate worship, including our prayers, praises, thanksgivings, and whatever we venture to do in the worship of God:

> From this office of sacrificing, all Christians are called a royal priesthood (I Pet. 2:9), because through Christ we offer that sacrifice of praise to God of which the apostle speaks: "the fruit of lips confessing His name" (Heb. 13:15, Vg.). And we do not appear with our gifts before God without an intercessor. The Mediator interceding for us is Christ, by whom we offer ourselves and what is ours to the Father. He is

---

[84] John Calvin, *The Epistle of Paul the Apostle to the Hebrews and the First and Second Epistles of St. Peter*, Calvin's Commentaries, vol. 12, trs. William B. Johnston & eds. David W. Torrance and Thomas F. Torrance (Grand Rapids: Eerdmans, 1959), 106–07.

[85] *Institutes* 4.18.13.

[86] *Institutes* 2.16.16.

[87] John F. Jansen, *Calvin's Doctrine of the Work of Christ* (London: James Clarke & Co. Ltd, 1956), 44.

our Pontiff, who has entered the heavenly sanctuary (Heb. 9:24) and opens a way for us to enter (cf. Heb. 10:20). He is the altar (cf. Heb. 13:10) upon which we lay our gifts, that whatever we venture to do, we may undertake in him. He it is, I say, that has made us a kingdom and priests unto the Father (Rev. 1:6).[88]

Christ's priesthood has no other ground than his own person. In his person and in his name we all enter the sanctuary fearlessly. And because he enters the Holy of Holies "in our name," our worship "in the name of Jesus" also reaches the same place. His name bears us, sanctifies our being, hallows our lips which are otherwise defiled to sing hymns of praise, and leads our worship to heaven. We cannot invoke God and glorify his name except through Christ the Mediator alone, who performs the priestly office by standing before God in our name.[89] Through identifying completely with our humanity in order to act in our place, on our behalf, he not only ministers to us the things of God, but the things of us to God. As object, Christ is the one whom we worship as Lord and Head of creation and humanity; as subject, he is the one who, as Lord and Head, is the leader of our worship. As Calvin said, "Christ heeds our praises, and is the chief conductor of our hymns."[90] As the chief worshipper, Christ proclaims the praises of God amid his people (Heb. 2:12). In John Thompson's words: "Christ is the One who as the God–man comes as God, reveals himself, but is also representative man, being and doing in our place what we cannot be and do for ourselves."[91] True worship therefore consists chiefly not in what we do in our power, but rather in what Christ has done, and continues to do "in our name" as our great High Priest, the one true *Leitourgos* of the sanctuary (Heb. 8:2). In "the name of Christ" we are given a true participation in his communion with God which is understood as worship; and our being and earthly sacrifices have access to the heavenly sanctuary. The prime emphasis is not our response, but Christ's response imputed to us. Worship must be comprehended in Christ, not in

---

[88] *Institutes* 1.16.16.
[89] Comm. On Heb. 13:15 in *The Epistle of Paul the Apostle to the Hebrews and the First and Second Epistles of St. Peter*, 231.
[90] Comm. On Heb. 2:12 in *The Epistle of Paul the Apostle to the Hebrews and the First and Second Epistles of St. Peter*, 27.
[91] John Thompson, *Modern Trinitarian Perspectives* (Oxford: Oxford University Press, 1994), 99.

us; outside of us, not outside of Christ. God commands worship from us, but we in ourselves could not give. Yet God in Christ supplies what he commands. In Torrance's words:

> God draws near to us to give Himself freely to us in wonderful love and communion in an act where He draws us near to Himself in Christ. He accepts us in spite of our unworthiness, because He has provided for us a Worship, a Way, a Sacrifice, a Forerunner in Christ our Leader and Representative, and our worship is a joyful Amen to His Worship. The mystery, the wonder, and the glory of the gospel is that He who is God the Creator of all things, and worthy of the worship and praises of all creation, should become man and as a man worship God, and as a man lead us in our worship of God, that we might become the sons of God we were meant to be (Heb. 2:10), sharing with Him His Sonship and communion with the Father.[92]

The Dynamic of the Spirit: Worship Communicated

Like Basil, Calvin assigned to the Spirit, as his distinctive function, "the power and efficacy of [God's] activity."[93] The mutual interpenetration of the work of the Son and the Spirit is reflected in the transition from Book II to Book III, where Calvin did not move away from Christology, but rather simply proceeded to deal with how, through God the Spirit, the grace of Christ has efficacy in us. The basic question in view is "how we receive those benefits which the Father bestows on his only-begotten Son – not for Christ's own private use, but that he might enrich the poor and needy." As already discussed, humans are by nature worshipping creatures. But this basic instinct to seek God has been tragically misdirected by sin, and curved in on itself. To redirect and redeem the fallen creature, God became man in Christ. However "as long as Christ remains outside of us, and we are separated from him, all that he has suffered and done for the salvation of the human race remains useless and of no value for us. Therefore, to share with us what he has received from the Father, he had

---

[92] Torrance, "The Vicarious Humanity and Priesthood of Christ," 70.
[93] *Institutes* 1.13.18. Warfield, "John Calvin the Theologian," in his *Calvin and Augustine*, 484–85, attributed Calvin as the theologian of the Holy Spirit.

to become ours and to dwell within us."[94] Immediately following this, Calvin began to show how believers by the "secret energy" of the Spirit "come to enjoy Christ and all his benefits."[95] The Spirit's role in the believer's reception of the grace of Christ has its basis in the Pauline idea of the Spirit as the testimony and seal of his salvation in Christ. This theme found expression via Augustine in the Western formulation of the Spirit as the "bond of love" between the first two persons and between the believer and Christ.[96] Calvin showed his allegiance to the *filioque* tradition, that the Spirit proceeds from the Father *and the Son*, when he summed up the subsection with this: "The Holy Spirit is the bond by which Christ effectually unites us to himself."[97]

Abiding in Calvin's trinitarian dynamic, Butin recognizes, is a double movement: first from the Father, by the Spirit, to the Son (in the Spirit's temporal anointing of the incarnate Son); second, since the Spirit binds the redeemed to Christ, they (in Christ) appropriate God's gifts as a parallel movement from the Father, by the Spirit, for his Son's sake.[98]

> God the Father gives us the Holy Spirit for his Son's sake, and yet has bestowed the whole fullness of the Spirit upon the Son to be minister and steward of his liberality . . . For there is nothing absurd in ascribing to the Father praise for those gifts of which he is the Author, and yet in ascribing the same powers to Christ, with whom were laid up the gifts of the Spirit to bestow upon his people. For this reason he invites unto himself all who thirst, that they may drink (Jn. 7:37).[99]

The Spirit is called "the Spirit of Christ," not only by virtue of his essential oneness with the Father and the Son, but also by virtue of his character as our Mediator.[100] The unity of Christ and the Spirit means that Christ works "through" the Spirit: the Spirit is

---

[94] *Institutes* 3.1.1.
[95] *Institutes* 3.1.1.
[96] *Institutes* 3.1.1. The precise Latin term *vinculum* Calvin used reflects his Augustinian heritage. Cf. *Institutes* 4.17.12.
[97] *Institutes* 3.1.1.
[98] Butin, *Revelation, Redemption and Response*, 82.
[99] *Institutes* 3.1.2 as cited in Butin, *Revelation, Redemption and Response*, 82.
[100] *Institutes* 3.1.2.

the "bond" through which Christ unites us to himself; and the Spirit works "for" Christ: he leads us to an appropriation of those benefits which the Father bestows on his only-begotten Son.[101] Christ would have come in vain had he not been furnished with this power of efficacy, namely the Spirit. Likewise Christ's benefits would be of no use to us had he not furnished us with the same power of efficacy, by which we are made one with him. The Spirit communicates the unique life which Christ inspires in his own so that they might partake of his benefits. This has its basis in Paul's teaching on our "participation in the Spirit" (II Cor. 13:14). Without the Spirit none can taste the fatherly love of God, nor the beneficence of Christ. The dynamic of the Spirit in us thus means that we are no longer actuated by ourselves, but by his action and prompting, without which all of God's gifts are either perverted or misperceived (cf. Gal. 5:19–21). Accordingly whatever good things we possess are "the fruits of his grace."[102]

Just as we stand before the Son as sinners in need, we too stand before the Holy Spirit as sinners, to whom the benefits of the cross are applied. The Spirit is the efficacy of God's work in us. The position in which God places us is thus one of receiving what he bestows with lavish grace and generosity. Spiritual worship accepts that position in which God is the active giver, and we are the passive recipient. To properly worship is to apprehend him as he offers himself in Christ – this is by the revelation of the Spirit. Mckee is right in this: "For Calvin, the faith that directs piety to the true God is an 'existential acquaintance' with God's self-revelation and promises, a reverent knowing made possible by the Holy Spirit."[103] The reverent knowing of God in Christ by faith is the action of the Holy Spirit. Worship is initiated by God, just as the knowledge of God is obtained by the revelation of the Triune God. Calvin would have no difficulty with Hilary's position: "God cannot be apprehended except through God himself, and likewise God accepts no worship from us except through God himself . . . it is by God that we are initiated into the worship of God."[104]

---

[101] Jelle Faber, "The Saving Work of the Holy Spirit in Calvin," in *Calvin Studies VI: Calvin and the Holy Spirit*, ed. Peter De Klerk (Grand Rapids: Calvin Studies Society, 1989): 1–11.
[102] Ibid.
[103] McKee, "Contexts, contours and Contents," 176.
[104] *De Trinitate* 5:20 as cited in Philip W. Butin, *Reformed Ecclesiology. Trinitarian Grace According to Calvin*, in *Studies in Reformed Theology*

As the initiatory descent of worship, the Father moves freely and unconditionally toward us with extravagant grace through the Son by the Spirit. As the corresponding ascent of worship, we come to him with the sacrifice of praise, thanksgiving, prayers and service – these enacted responses of faith have the indwelling Spirit as the sole source. In the Spirit, all our responses – prayer, piety, obedience, service, praise – are rendered to the Father, the proper object of our worship, through his Son, the mediator of our worship. Hence worship too is an event in which divine and human action coincide, the former being the presupposition of the latter. The divine action is imputed to us by faith, which itself has no other source than the Spirit. Our corresponding action in worship is made efficacious through Christ in the dynamic of the Spirit. The pneumatological dynamic of Christ's mediation of the Church's worship is also borne out in Calvin's commentary on Hebrews:

> Because Christ suffered in the humility of the flesh, and taking the form of a servant made Himself of no reputation in the world, the apostle harks back to His ascension, by which not only the offense of the cross was removed, but also that humbling and inglorious condition which He took on Himself along with our flesh. It is by the power of the Holy Spirit which shone out in the resurrection and ascension of Christ that the dignity of Christ's priesthood is to be reckoned. He argues as follows – Since Christ has gone up to the right hand of God to reign graciously in heaven, he is the minister not of an earthly sanctuary, but of a heavenly one.[105]

For Calvin, as for Luther, the efficacy of Christ's heavenly priesthood is communicated to us by the ministry of the interceding Spirit – the dynamic of Christ's mediation. By Christ's ascension, his worship is imputed to us by faith in the power of efficacy. In the Son, by the Spirit, God enters the lives of individuals and the community, sanctifying our being and doing (e.g., worship). The Spirit who effectually unites us to Christ also effectually binds us to Christ's ascended position, in which we feel the power and efficacy of his closeness with his Father. The work of the Son

---

and History, ed. David Willis-Watkins (Princeton: Princeton Theological Seminary, 1994), 26, n. 81.
[105] See Comm. Hebrews 8:1; cf. Comm. Heb. 9:14; 10:19–23 in *Calvin's Commentaries*, eds., Torrance (s), 104.

and the Spirit are mutually related in the economy of salvation. Without the Son we know nothing of the fatherly embrace of God; and without the Spirit we know nothing of the efficacy of Christ's mediation. A proper theology of worship takes into consideration the two divine movements in Trinity: the God-humanward movement – God from the Father through the Son by the Spirit to us, and conversely, the human-Godward movement – we by the Spirit through the Son to the Father. This is not an *ordo essendi*, of essence, but an *ordo cognoscendi*, of experience. For Calvin, the Spirit is the efficacy of both sides of the direction of divine–human relation.[106] In the former, the Spirit is "the witness to us of the free benevolence of God with which God the Father has embraced us in his beloved only-begotten Son" as his own.[107] In the latter, the Spirit "supplies the very words so that we may fearlessly cry, 'Abba, Father!'" (Rom. 8:15; Gal. 4:6), and causes our hearts to be enflamed with the love of God and with a reverent devotion.[108] The descending movement of the Son is from the Father by the Spirit, but his homecoming is his ascending movement that draws our humanity up into communion with the Father by the Spirit. We are given the gift of "the Spirit of adoption" (Rom. 8) by which our identity as sons is forged, and we are exalted to share by grace in the incarnate Son's intimate communion with his Father.

Thus, constitutive of the theme of Christ's vicarious humanity is the doctrine of the joyous exchange wrought by, and in, Christ between God and us, of which the Spirit is its causative agency. Inculcated in our hearts is this: Christ's atoning benefits belong to us in a joyous exchange for our sinful plight and its disastrous end. Calvin expanded at length on how the Spirit unfolds to us and in us the richness of God's grace, which we inherit in Christ.

> We see that our salvation and all its parts are comprehended in Christ (Acts 4:12). We should therefore take care not to derive the least portion of it from anywhere else. If we seek salvation, we are taught by the very name of Jesus that it is "of him" (I Cor. 1:30). If we seek any other gifts of the Spirit, they will be found in his anointing. If we seek strength, it lies in his dominion; if purity, in his conception; if gentleness, it appears in his birth. For by His birth He was made

---

[106] Butin, *Revelation, Redemption and Response*, 84.
[107] *Institutes* 3.1.3.
[108] *Institutes* 3.1.3. Cf. Hughes Oliphant Old, *Guides to the Reformed Tradition* (Atlanta: John Knox Press, 1984), 154.

like us in all respects (Heb. 2:17) that He might learn to feel our pain (cf. Heb. 5:2). If we seek redemption, it lies in his passion; if acquittal, in his condescension; if remission of the curse, in his cross (Gal. 3:13); if satisfaction, in his sacrifice; if purification, in his blood; if reconciliation, in his descent into Hell; if mortification of the flesh, in his tomb; if newness of life, in his resurrection; if immortality, in the same; if inheritance of the heavenly kingdom, in his entrance into heaven; if protection, if security, if abundant supply of all blessings, in his Kingdom; if untroubled expectation of judgment, in the power given to him to judge. In short, since rich store of every kind of good abounds in him, let us drink our fill from this fountain, and from no other.[109]

In Christ, all that he is and has become ours so that, by grace, his life is our life; his death our death, his victory our victory, his resurrection our resurrection, his righteousness our righteousness, his heavenly kingdom our heavenly kingdom, and his eternal prayers and self-offering to the Father our prayers and offering to the Father's throne; his priesthood our priesthood; his altar our altar; his worship our worship – all these are communicated by faith in the dynamic of the Spirit. We are accepted in the Beloved Son whose being is one with the Father, and by the Spirit, we come to enjoy the benefits of Christ's eternal priesthood, even his efficacious worship of the Father.

The Church's Celebration: The Context of the Spirit's Communication

That which makes the Church most truly the Church is her faithful worship of God in the celebration of the Word and the sacraments. The Church's visible worship is the context of the Spirit's communication of Christ's mediating grace. Calvin put it: "It is therefore certain that the Lord offers us mercy and the pledge both in his sacred Word and in his sacraments."[110] Preaching is an instrument of divine power, through which God's triune grace is enacted visibly and actually in the Church. In preaching, "we hear his ministers speaking just as [God] himself spoke," via the interaction of the Word and Spirit: "God breathes faith into us

---

[109] *Institutes* 2.16.19.
[110] *Institutes* 4.14.7.

only by the instrument of his gospel, as Paul points out that 'faith comes by hearing.' Likewise the power to save rests on God; but He displays and unfolds it in the preaching of the gospel."[111] In preaching, "God himself appears in our midst," as he did to "the holy patriarchs in the mirror of his teaching in order to be known spiritually."[112] God willed that holy assemblies be held at the sanctuary in order that proclamation by the Priest might foster agreement in faith. Both in Old and New Testaments, we are exhorted to "seek the face of God in the sanctuary."[113] Thus believers find no greater help than public worship, where the Word of God is heard, and where, as Paul said in II Corinthians 4:6, "the glory of God shines in the face of Christ." For Luther, as it is for Calvin, God's Word is God's action; it is of the power of the preached Word to do its own mission, as it were, to effect what God commands and promises.[114]

Accompanied by the Word and the efficacious power of the Spirit, sacraments are "mirrors" in which we contemplate the riches of God's grace which resides in them. They are "pillars" or "columns" that sustain faith which has the Word as its ultimate foundation: "For by them he manifests himself to us . . . as far as our dullness is given to perceive, and attests his good will and love toward us more expressly than by the Word."[115] The sacraments have the Word of promise as the content, the Spirit as the efficacy, and a tangible, visible support for faith as the intent. Yet the power of the sacraments to accomplish their intent is supplied by the economic operation of the Triune God in them:

> Therefore, Word and Sacraments confirm our faith when they set before our eyes the good will of our heavenly Father toward us, by the knowledge of whom the whole firmness of our faith stands fast

---

[111] *Institutes* 4.1.5.

[112] *Institutes* 4.14.7.

[113] *Institutes* 4.14.7. Hughes Oliphant Old, *The Reading and Preaching of the Scriptures in the Worship of the Christian Church*, vol., 4: *The Age of the Reformation* (Grand Rapids: Eerdmans, 2002), 133.

[114] See Comm. On Rom. 3:4 as cited in Ronald S. Wallace, "The Preached Word as the Word of God," in *Readings in Calvin's Theology*, ed. Donald McKim (Grand Rapids: Baker Book House, 1984), 236: "He says in words He fulfills the same in deed; for He so speaks that His command immediately becomes His act."

[115] *Institutes* 4.14.10.

and increases its strength. The Spirit confirms it when by engraving this confirmation in our minds, he makes it effective. Meanwhile, the Father of lights [cf. James 1:17] cannot be hindered from illuminating our minds with a sort of intermediate brilliance through the Sacraments, just as he illuminates our bodily eyes by the rays of the sun.[116]

The "perichoretic" unity of the Son and Spirit in the same Godhead accentuates the central role of the Spirit as the efficacy of God's action in Christ, rendering tangible and real the presence of Christ in the Lord's Supper.[117] In speaking of our participation in Christ, Calvin related "its whole power to the Spirit."[118] He deemed it "utterly unlawful" to drag Christ's body, which is contained in heaven, under the "corruptible elements."[119] Calvin's defense of the participation in Christ through the Spirit follows closely Chrysostom's:

> And there is no need of this for us to enjoy a participation in it, since the Lord bestows this benefit upon us through his Spirit so that we may be made one in body, spirit, and soul with him. The bond of this connection is therefore the Spirit of Christ, with whom we are joined in unity, and is like a channel through which all that Christ himself is and has is conveyed to us. For if we see that the sun, shedding its beams upon the earth, casts its substance in some measure upon it in order to beget, nourish, and give growth to its offspring – why should the radiance of Christ's Spirit be less in order to impart to us the communion of his flesh and blood?[120]

With Augustine, Calvin did not conceive of the Supper as an empty figure or a simple remembrance, but as the symbol by which the reality of the thing signified surely abides there.[121] By the Spirit, our faith recognizes that in the mystery of the Supper, Christ is truly present through the symbols by which our souls are fed elegantly, and that the power of his vicarious obedience in

---

[116] *Institutes* 4.14.10.
[117] See Butin, "Christ's Ministry and Ours," 3, notes that although the term *perichoresis* did not appear in Calvin's *Institutes*, its meaning abided.
[118] *Institutes* 4.17.12.
[119] *Institutes* 4.17.12.
[120] *Institutes* 4.17.12. Cf. *Sermon on the Holy Spirit* in Chrysostom's *Opera* (Basel, 1530), V, 379 as cited in *Institutes* 4.17.12, n. 35.
[121] *Institutes* 4.17.10. Cf. Benjamin Charles Milner, Jr., *Calvin's Doctrine of the Church* (Leiden: E.J. Brill, 1970), 128.

obtaining righteousness for us is truly felt by us. Christ "testifies and seals in the Supper . . . by manifesting there the effectiveness of his Spirit to fulfill what he promises. And truly he offers and shows the reality there signified to all who sit at that spiritual banquet, although it is received with benefit by [faith] alone."[122] Regarding how this happens, Calvin confessed, "I rather experience than understand."[123] But he was persuaded concerning the basis for that experience:

> Even though it seems unbelievable that Christ's flesh, separated from us by such great distance, penetrates to us, so that it becomes our food, let us remember how far the secret power of the Holy Spirit towers above all our senses, and how foolish it is to wish to measure his immeasurableness by our measure. What, then, our mind does not comprehend, let faith conceive: that the Spirit truly unites things separated in space.[124]

The Spirit unites us to Christ, and renders possible for us a true participation in his flesh and blood. He accomplishes this, not by pulling Christ down to us but rather by raising us to him, ushering us into the exalted position in which Christ is now seated. Worship thus centers on this most glorious action of the sacrament performed in heaven, not on earth. As criticism of the Roman and Lutheran views of the real presence, Calvin wrote:

> But greatly mistaken are those who conceive no presence of the flesh in the Supper, unless it lies in the bread. For thus they leave nothing to the secret work of the Spirit, which unites us to Christ. To them, Christ does not seem present unless he comes down to us. As though, if he should lift us to himself, we should not as much enjoy his presence![125]

Calvin's critique springs not only from the Christological standpoint, but also from the pneumatological standpoint. The antithesis between "the coming of Spirit and the ascent of Christ" in Calvin best captures the true meaning of sacramental worship. The Spirit descends to us in order to elevate us to Christ, to his exalted

---

[122] *Institutes* 4.17.10.
[123] *Institutes* 4.17.32.
[124] *Institutes* 4.17.10.
[125] *Institutes* 4.17.31.

position with his Father.[126] The Spirit places us in Christ, to enjoy him and all his benefits which he accomplishes and inherits from his Father. Through the Spirit, we are "sharers in His Ascension,"[127] and hence partake of Christ's worship of, and his Sonly communion with, his Father. Because we are raised by the Spirit to the place of his ascension, "it was established of old that before consecration the people should be told in a loud voice to lift up their hearts."[128] The upward movement of the Eucharistic worship is the domain of the Spirit, by which the believer rises up in reverent contemplation to those lofty mysteries which lie hidden in the elements.[129] Thus to worship him aright is to worship him spiritually in heavenly glory. The lawful veneration and worship are to be directed not to the sign below but to Christ above. What is communicated to us is not so much Christ's body, but rather the plentitude of life from his body that is promised in the Supper. The ascended Christ "from the substance of his flesh breathes life into our souls – indeed, pours forth his very life into us – even though Christ's flesh itself does not enter us."[130] By "breathes," a supposedly pneumatological image, Calvin ascribed the vivifying power both to the Son and the Spirit in a differentiated unity. Having elevated us to be with Christ, the Spirit from heaven imparts into us the very life-giving power from the flesh of Christ.[131] The Spirit is the effective agency of this action that we are made "partakers of his substance that we may also feel his power in partaking of all his benefits."[132]

Calvin detested the practice of the papists who, not content with Christ's priesthood, attempt daily to sacrifice Christ anew. Such action is sacrilegious as it conceives the Mass as the appeasement of God's wrath. Christ alone is the sacrifice of propitiation, which secures for us a righteous standing before God. Accordingly, what we could offer is precisely the "sacrifice of praise and reverence," that "veneration and worship of God, which believers both owe and render to him."[133] By the Spirit's grace, the Supper enables us

---

[126] *Institutes* 4.17.31.
[127] Sermon on Acts 1:9–11 as cited in Torrance, "The Vicarious Humanity and Priesthood of Christ," 70.
[128] *Institutes* 4.17.36.
[129] *Institutes* 4.14.5.
[130] *Institutes* 4.17.32.
[131] *Institutes* 4.17.32.
[132] *Institutes* 4.17.10.
[133] *Institutes* 4.17.32.

as a royal priesthood to lay upon Christ – the altar – our being and doing as living sacrifices that are acceptable to God. The Supper thus is the liturgical enactment of grace and gratitude, which lies at the core of Calvin's worship.[134]

Conclusion

Worship, like salvation, is primarily God's gift *a priori*, i.e., prior to and independent of our act of worship. In the ruin of mankind no one now worships God as Father or as the Author of salvation, until Christ the Mediator appears as our sin-bearer, by whom we are restored to grace. Only in the face of Christ (II Cor. 4:6) can we behold God the Redeemer, through whom we ascend to the heavenly throne. In order to worship God aright, we must enter into a saving relationship with him in his incarnate Son, for it is only through reconciliation to God by the blood of Christ that we may draw nigh to him and have access to him. The reconciliation and the access to God find their gracious fulfillment in Christ's priestly office. What was necessary to recover the Father's favor and the proper worship of him has been completed by that one unique, perfect sacrifice of his. Christ is the sole remedy of perverted worship, and the complete fountain of blessings – this is revealed to worshippers by the Spirit. The Spirit is the efficacy of Christ's priesthood in us, that his priesthood is ours; his worship is our worship expressed in prayers, praises and adorations. In worship, God can only be enjoyed as we bow in adoration and praise for his inestimable gifts, which the Spirit inculcates in us via the instruments of divine power – preaching and sacramental forms. Calvin's trinitarian understanding of worship incorporates the soteriological import of the vicarious humanity of Christ and the dynamic agency of the Spirit. The effective force of that one sacrifice – Christ's sinless offering of holiness to the Father – is eternal. Christ is thus the one true eternal worshipper, "the one for the many,"[135] who through his representative humanity gathers up all humanity in himself. By the Spirit, we partake of the efficacious worship and response Christ offers to the Father. Ours is a response to Christ's, nevertheless an actuated response of the Holy Spirit:

---

[134] Brian A. Gerrish, *Grace and Gratitude: The Eucharistic Theology of John Calvin* (Minneapolis: Fortress Press, 1993), 19–20.
[135] Thompson, *Modern Trinitarian Perspectives*, 100.

he enables this, and so fulfills what he demands, drawing us into the incarnate Son's worship of the Father, something which we in our defiled selves could not offer. Calvin's ability to steer away from the danger of objectivism, and foment the subjective aspect of revelation that accentuates a person's willful and free response to Christ's is praiseworthy.

Bibliography

Books

Althaus, Paul. *The Theology of Martin Luther*. Translated by Robert C. Schultz. Philadelphia: Fortress Press, 1966.

Ayres, Lewis. *Nicaea and Its Legacy: An Approach to Fourth-Century Trinitarian Theology*. Oxford: Oxford University Press, 2004.

Badcock, Gary D. *Light of Truth and Fire of Love: A Theology of the Holy Spirit*. Grand Rapids: William B. Eerdmans, 1997.

Barth, Karl. *Protestant Theology in the Nineteenth Century: Its Background and History*. Valley Forge: Judson, 1973.

———. *Church Dogmatics*. Vol. 1/1. Translated by George T. Thomson. New York: Charles Scribner's Sons, 1936.

Basil the Great. *On the Holy Spirit*. Translated by David Anderson. Crestwood: St. Vladimir's Seminary Press, 1980.

———. *De Spiritu Sancto*. Translated by Blomfield Jackson. Vol. 8. In *The Nicene and Post-Nicene Fathers*, 2nd Series. Edited by Philip Schaff and Henry Wace. Edinburgh: Clark, 1989.

Battles, F. Lewis. *Interpreting John Calvin*. Edited by Robert Benedetto. Grand Rapids: Baker Books, 1996.

Bernard of Clairvaux. *On the Song of Songs*. Translated by Kilian Walsh and Irene Edmonds. 4 vols. Cistercian Fathers Series. Kalamazoo: Cistercian, 1971–80.

Brecht, Martin. *Martin Luther*. Vol 2: *Shaping and Defining the Reformation 1521–1532*. Translated by James L. Schaaf. Minneapolis: Fortress Press, 1990.

Brooks, Peter N., ed. *The Seven-Headed Luther: Essays in Commemoration of a Quincentenary 1483–1983*. Oxford: Clarendon Press, 1983.

Butin, Philip W. *Reformed Ecclesiology: Trinitarian Grace According to Calvin.* Princeton: Princeton Theological Seminary, 1994.

———. *Revelation, Redemption, Response: Calvin's Trinitarian Understanding of the Divine-Human Relationship.* New York: Oxford University Press, 1995.

Calvin, John. *Institutes of Christian Religion.* Vol. 20–21. The Library of Christian Classics. Edited by John T. McNeil; translated by Ford Lewis Battles. Philadelphia: Westminster Press, 1960.

———. *The Epistle of Paul the Apostle to the Hebrews and the First and Second Epistles of St. Peter.* Translated by William B. Johnston; edited by David W. Torrance and Thomas F. Torrance. Calvin's Commentaries, vol. 12. Grand Rapids: William B. Eerdmans, 1959.

Casey, Michael. *Athirst for God. Spiritual Desire in Bernard of Clairvaux's Sermons on the Song of Songs.* Kalamazoo: Cistercian Publications, 1988.

Davies, Brian and Brian Leftow, eds. *The Cambridge Companion to Anselm.* Cambridge: Cambridge University Press, 2004.

Eire, Carlos M.N. *War Against the Idols: The Reformation of Worship from Erasmus to Calvin.* Cambridge: Cambridge University Press, 1986.

Elder, E. Rozanne, ed. *The Chimaera of His Age: Studies on Bernard of Clairvaux.* Kalamazoo: Cistercian Publications, 1980.

Evans, G.R. *The Mind of St. Bernard.* Oxford: Oxford University Press, 1983.

———. *Bernard of Clairvaux.* New York: Oxford University Press, 2000.

———, ed. *The Medieval Theologians: An Introduction to Theology in the Medieval Period.* Oxford: Blackwell Publishers Ltd., 2001.

Fedwick, Paul J., ed. *Basil of Caesarea: Christian, Humanist, Ascetic: A Sixteenth-Hundredth Adversary Symposium.* 2 vols. Toronto: Pontifical Institute of Medieval Studies, 1981.

Feuerbach, Ludwig. *The Essence of Faith According to Luther.* Translated by George Eliot. New York: Harper & Row, 1957.

Forde, Gerhard O. *The Preached God: Proclamation in Word and Sacrament.* Edited by Mark C. Mattes and Steven D. Paulson. Grand Rapids: Wm. B. Eerdmans, 2007.

Foxgrover, David, ed. *The Legacy of John Calvin.* Grand Rapids: Calvin Study Society Papers, 1999.

Gamble, Richard C., ed. *Articles on Calvin and Calvinism.* Vol. 1: *The Biography of Calvin.* New York: Garland Publishing, Inc., 1992.

———. *Articles on Calvin and Calvinism.* Vol. 2: *The Organizational Structure of Calvin's Theology.* New York: Garland Publishing, Inc., 1992.

George, Timothy, ed. *John Calvin and the Church. A Prism of Reform.* Louisville: Westminster John Knox Press, 1985.

———. *Theology of the Reformers.* Nashville: Broadman Press, 1988.

Gerrish, Brian. *Grace and Gratitude: The Eucharistic Theology of John Calvin.* Minneapolis: Fortress Press, 1993.

Gilson, Etienne. *The Mystical Theology of St. Bernard*. New York: Sheed & Ward, 1940.

Greenman, Jeffrey P. and Timothy Larsen, eds. *Reading Romans Through the Centuries: From the Early Church to Karl Barth*. Grand Rapids: Brazos Press, 2005.

Gribomont, Jean. *The "Unwritten" and "Secret" Apostolic Tradition in the Theological Thought of St. Basil of Caesarea*. Edinburgh: Oliver and Boyd, 1965.

———. *Word and Spirit: A Monastic Review. In Honor of Saint Basil the Great*. Still River, Mass.: St. Bede's Publications, 1979.

Gunton, Colin E. *Father, Son and Holy Spirit*. Edinburgh: T&T Clark, 2003.

Hagen, Kenneth. *A Theology of Testament in the Young Luther: The Lectures on Hebrews*. Leiden: E.J. Brill, 1974.

Hall, Christopher A. *Learning Theology with the Church Fathers*. Illinois: InterVarsity Press, 2002.

Hanson, Richard P.C. *The Search for the Christian Doctrine of God: The Arian Controversy 318–381*. Edinburgh: T. & T. Clark, 1988.

Hasting, James ed. *Encyclopedia of Religion and Ethics*. New York: Scribner's Sons, 1917.

Haykin, Michael A.G. *The Spirit of God: the Exegesis of 1 and 2 Corinthians in the Pneumatomachian Controversy of the 4th Century*. Leiden: E.J. Brill, 1994.

Helm, Paul. *John Calvin's Ideas*. Oxford: Oxford University Press, 2004.

———. *Faith and Understanding*. Grand Rapids: William B. Eerdmans, 1997.

Heron, Alastair. *The Holy Spirit*. Philadelphia: Westminster Press, 1983.

Hogg, David S. *Anselm of Canterbury: The Beauty of Theology*. Aldershot: Ashgate Publishing Limited, 2004.

Hopkins, Jasper. *A Companion to the Study of St. Anselm*. Minneapolis: University of Minnesota, 1972.

Jansen, John F. *Calvin's Doctrine of the Work of Christ*. London: J. Clark, 1956.

Jenson, Robert W., ed. *The Catholicity of the Reformation*. Grand Rapids: William B. Eerdmans, 1996.

———. *Systematic Theology*. Vol 2: *The Works of God*. Oxford: Oxford University Press, 1999.

Jocobs, C.M, ed. *Works of Martin Luther*. 6 vols. Philadelphia: Muhlenberg Press, 1930–1943.

Jones, Serene. *Calvin and the Rhetoric of Piety*. Louisville: Westminster John Knox, 1995.

Kärkkäinen, Veli-Matti. *Pneumatology. The Holy Spirit in Ecumenical, International, and Contextual Perspective*. Grand Rapids: Baker Academic, 2002.

Kelly, John N.D. *Early Christian Doctrines*. London: Harper & Row, Publishers, 1978.
Klerk, Peter De, ed. *Calvin Studies VI: Calvin and the Holy Spirit*. Grand Rapids: Calvin Studies Society, 1989.
Klotsche, Ernest Heinrich. *The History of Christian Doctrine*. Grand Rapids: Baker, 1979.
Kopecek, Thomas A. *A History of Neo-Arianism*. 2 vols. Cambridge: Philadelphia Patristic Foundation, 1979.
Lane, Anthony N.S. *Calvin and Bernard of St. Clairvaux: Studies in Reformed Theology and History*. Princeton: Princeton Theological Seminary, 1996.
———, *John Calvin: A Student of Church Fathers*. Edinburgh: T.&T. Clark, 1999.
Leaver, Robin A. *Luther's Liturgical Music. Principles and Implications*. Grand Rapids: Wm. B. Eerdmans, 2006.
Leclercq, Jean. *Bernard of Clairvaux and the Cistercian Spirit*. Translated by Claire Lavoie. Cistercian Studies Series 16. Kalamazoo: Cistercian, 1976.
———, *The Love of Learning and the Desire for God: A Study of Monastic Culture*. 3rd ed. Translated by Catharine Misrahi. New York: Fordham University Press, 1982.
Letham, Robert. *The Holy Trinity: In Scripture, History, Theology, and Worship*. Phillipsburg: Presbyterian and Reformed Publishing, 2004.
Loeschen, John R. *Divine Community: Trinity, Church and Ethics in Reformation Theologies*. Missouri: Northeast Missouri State University, 1981.
Loewenich, Walther von. *Luther's Theology of the Cross*. Translated by Herbert Bouman. Minneapolis: Augsburg Publishing House, 1982.
Lohse, Bernhard. *Martin Luther's Theology: Its Historical and Systematic Development*. Minneapolis: Fortress Press, 1999.
Luther, Martin. *Luther's Works*. American Editions. 55 Vols. Edited by Jaroslav Pelikan and Helmut T. Lehman. St. Louis: Concordia Publishing House; Philadelphia: Fortress Press, 1955–67.
———. *Martin Luthers Werke: Kritische Gesamtausgabe*. 100 vols. Weimar: Hermann Bohlau Nachfolger, 1883–.
———, *D. Martin Luthers Werke. Kritische Gesamtausgabe. Briefwechsel*. 11 vols. Weimar: Herman Bohlau Nachfolger, 1906–61.
———, *D. Martin Luthers Werke: Kritische Gesamtausgabe. Tischreden*. Hermann Bohlau Nachfolger, 1912–21.
Maag, Karin and John Witvilet, eds. *Worship in Medieval and Early Modern Europe: Change and Continuity in Religious Practice*. Notre Dame: University of Notre Dame Press, 2004.
Maschke, Timothy, Franz Posset and Joan Skocir, eds. *Ad Fontes Lutheri: Toward the Recovery of the Real Luther: Essays in Honor of Kenneth Hagen's Sixty-fifth Birthday*. Milwaukee: Marquette University Press, 2001.

Maxwell, William D. *A History of Christian Worship*. Grand Rapids: Baker Book House, 1982.
McDonnell, Kilian. *John Calvin, the Church, and the Eucharist*. Princeton: Princeton University Press, 1967.
McGinn, Bernard. *The Growth of Mysticism: Gregory the Great through the 12th Century*, vol. 2 of *The Presence of God: A History of Western Christian Mysticism*. New York: Crossroad Publishing House, 1994.
McGuire, Brian P. *The Difficult Saint: Bernard of Clairvaux and his Tradition*. Kalamazoo: Cistercians, 1991.
McKee, Elsie, A., ed. *John Calvin: Writings on Pastoral Piety*. New York: Paulist Press, 2001.
McKim, Donald K., ed. *Reading in Calvin's Theology*. Grand Rapids: Baker Book House, 1984.
———, ed. *The Cambridge Companion to Martin Luther*. Cambridge: Cambridge University Press, 2004.
———. *Understanding the Medieval Meditative Ascent: Augustine, Anselm, Boethius, and Dantes*. Washington: The Catholic University of America Press, 2006.
Meredith, Anthony. *The Cappadocians*. London: Geoffrey Chapman, 1995.
Micklem, Nathaniel, ed. *Christian Worship: Studies in Its History and Meaning*. London: Oxford University Press, 1936.
Milner, Benjamin C. *Calvin's Doctrine of the Church*. Leiden: E.J. Brill, 1970.
Moeller, Pamela A. *Calvin's Doxology: Worship in John Calvin's 1559 Institutes With a view to Contemporary Worship Renewal*. Allison Park: Pickwick Publications, 1997.
Moltmann, Jürgen. *The Spirit of Life: A Universal Affirmation*. Minneapolis: Fortress, 1993.
Müller, Richard A. *The Unaccommodated Calvin: Studies in the Foundation of a Theological Tradition*. Oxford: Oxford University Press, 2000.
Neuser, W., ed. *Calvinus Ecclesiae Doctor*. Kampen: J. H. Kok, 1978.
Ngien, Dennis. *The Suffering of God According to Martin Luther's* Theologia Crucis. New York: Peter Lang, 1995.
———. *Apologetic for* Filioque *in Medieval Theology*. Milton Keynes: Paternoster, 2005.
———. *Luther as a Spiritual Adviser: The Interface of Theology and Piety in Luther's Devotional Writings*. Milton Keynes: Paternoster, 2007.
Niesel, Wilhelm. *The Theology of Calvin*. Translated by H. Knight. Philadelphia: Westminster Press, 1956.
Oberman, Heiko. *Luther: Man Between God and the Devil*. Translated by E. Walliser-Schwarzbart. New York: Image Books, 1992.
Old, Hughes Oliphant. *The Patristic Roots of Reformed Worship*. Zurich: Theologischer Verlag, 1975.

———. *The Reading and Preaching of the Scriptures in the Worship of the Christian Church*. 5 volumes. Grand Rapids: William B. Eerdmans, 1998–2002.
Olson, Roger E. *The Story of Christian Theology. Twenty Centuries of Tradition and Reform*. Illinois: InterVarsity Press, 1999.
Olson, Roger E., and Christopher A. Hall. *The Trinity*. Grand Rapids: William B. Eerdmans, 2002.
———. *The Mosaic of Christian Belief: Twenty Centuries of Unity and Diversity*. Illinois: InterVarsity Press, 2002.
Parker, Thomas H.L. *The Oracles of God: An Introduction of the Preaching of John Calvin*. London: Lutterworth, 1947.
———. *Calvin's Doctrine of the Word and Sacrament*. Grand Rapids: William B. Eerdmans, 1957.
———. *Calvin: An Introduction to His Thought*. Louisville: Westminster/John Knox Press, 1995.
Pelikan, Jaroslav. *Luther's Works, Companion Volume: Introduction to Exegetical Writings*. St. Louis: Concordia Publishing House, 1959.
———. *The Mystery of Continuity: Time and History, Memory and Eternity in the Thought of Saint Augustine*. Charlottesville, Va.: University Press of Virginia, 1986.
Pennington, M. Basil, ed. *Saint Bernard of Clairvaux: Studies Commemorating the Eighth Centenary of His Canonization*. Kalamazoo: Cistercian Publications, 1977.
———. *The Last of the Fathers: The Cistercian Fathers of the Twelfth Century*. Still River: St. Bede's Publications, 1983.
Plass, Edward. *What Luther Says: A Practical In-Home Anthology for the Active Christian*[10th]. St. Louis: Concordia, 1994.
Posset, Franz. *Pater Bernhardus: Martin Luther and Bernard of Clairvaux*. Kalamazoo: Cistercian Publications, 1999.
Rainey, David Lloyd. "The Argument for the Deity of the Holy Spirit According to St. Basil the Great, Bishop of Caesarea." ThM Thesis, Vancouver School of Theology, 1991.
Reuver, Arie de. *Sweet Communion. Trajectories of Spirituality from the Middle Ages through the Further Reformation*. Translated by James D. De Jong. Grand Rapids: Baker Academic, 2007.
Richard, Lucien. *The Spirituality of John Calvin*. Atlanta: John Knox Press, 1974.
Rousseau, Philip. *Basil of Caesarea*. Berkeley: University of California Press, 1994.
Schufreider, Gregory. *Confessions of a Rational Mystic*. Indiana: Purdue University Press, 1994.
Senn, Frank C. *Christian Liturgy: Catholic and Evangelical*. Minneapolis: Fortress Press, 1997.

Senn, Frank C., ed. *Protestant Spiritual Traditions*. New York: Paulist Press, 1986.

Shannon, William H. *Anselm: The Joy of Faith*. New York: The Crossroad Publishing Company, 1999.

Shepherd, Victor. *The Nature and Function of Faith in the Theology of John Calvin*. Macon: Mercer University Press, 1983.

Siggins, Ian D. *Martin Luther's Doctrine of Christ*. New Havens: Yale University Press, 1970.

Sommerfeldt, John R. *The Spiritual Teachings of Bernard of Clairvaux*. Cistercian Fathers Series 125. Kalamazoo: Cistercian Publications, 1991.

Sommerfeldt, John R., ed. *Bernardus Magister: papers presented at the nonacentenary celebration of the birth of Saint Bernard of Clairvaux*, sponsored by the Institute of Cistercian Studies, Western Michigan University, 10–13 May 1990. Kalamazoo: Cistercian Publications, 1992.

Southern, Richard. *Saint Anselm: A Portrait in a Landscape*. Cambridge: Cambridge University Press, 1990.

Spinks, Bryan. *Luther's Liturgical Criteria and His Reform of the Canon of the Mass*. Notts: Grove Books, 1982.

Steinmetz, David C. *Luther in Context*. Bloomington: Indiana University Press, 1986.

———. *Calvin in Context*. New York: Oxford University Press, 1995.

Studer, Basil. *Trinity and the Incarnation: The Faith of the Early Church Fathers*. Translated by Matthias Westerhoff; edited by Andrew Louth. Collegeville: Liturgical Press, 1993.

Swanson, Robert N., ed. *Continuity and Change in Christian Worship: Studies in Church History* vol. 35. Suffolk: Boydell Press, 1999.

Swete, Henry B. *The Holy Spirit in the Ancient Church*. Grand Rapids: Baker Book House, 1912.

Tamburello, Dennis E. *Union With Christ: John Calvin and the Mysticism of St. Bernard*. Louisville: Westminster John Knox Press, 1994.

Tappert, Theodore G., tr. and ed. *The Book of Concord*. Philadelphia: Muhlenberg Press, 1959.

Thompson, John. *Modern Trinitarian Perspectives*. Oxford: Oxford University Press, 1994.

Thompson, Mark D. *A Sure Ground on Which to Stand: The Relation of Authority and Interpretive Method in Luther's Approach to Scripture*. Carlisle: Paternoster, 2004.

Torrance, James B. *Theological Foundations for Ministry*. Grand Rapids: William B. Eerdmans, 1979.

———. *Worship, Community and the Triune God of Grace*. Carlisle: Paternoster, 1996.

Torrance, Thomas F., ed. *The Incarnation*. Edinburgh: Handsel Press, 1981.

———. *The Trinitarian Faith: The Evangelical Theology of the Ancient Catholic Church*. Edinburgh: T. & T. Clark, 1988
———. *The Christian Doctrine of God: One Being, Three Persons*. Edinburgh: T.&T. Clark, 1996.
Vajta, Vilmos. *Luther on Worship*. Philadelphia: Fortress Press, 1958.
Wendel, Francois. *Calvin: The Origins and Development of His Religious Thought*. Durham: Labyrinth Press, 1987.
Wengert, Timothy J., ed. *Harvesting Martin Luther's Reflections on Theology, Ethics, and the Church*. Grand Rapids: William B. Eerdmans, 2003.
Williams, Watkin Wynn. *The Mysticism of St. Bernard of Clairvaux*. Burns, Oats & Washbourne, 1931.
———. *Saint Bernard of Clairvaux*. Manchester: Manchester University Press, 1935.
Willis, E. David. *Calvin's Catholic Christology*. Leiden: E.J. Brill, 1966.
Wingren, Gustaf. *The Living Word: A Theological Study of Preaching and the Church*. Translated by V.C. Pogue. Philadelphia: Fortress Press, 1960.
Witvilet, John D. *Worship Seeking Understanding: Windows into Christian Practice*. Grand Rapids: Baker Academic, 2003.
Wood, A. Skevington. *Captive to the Word: Martin Luther, Doctor of Sacred Scripture*. Grand Rapids: William B. Eerdmans, 1969.
Zachman, Randall C. *Image and Word in the Theology of John Calvin*. Notre Dame: University of Notre Dame Press, 2007.

Journal Articles

Akin, Daniel L. "Bernard of Clairvaux: Evangelical of the 21st Century." *Criswell Theological Review* 4 (1990): 327–50.
Amand de Mendieta, Emmanuel. "The Pair Kerygma and Dogma in the Theological Thought of St. Basil of Caeserea." *Journal of Theological Studies* 16 (1965): 129–42.
Battles, F. Lewis. "God was Accommodating Himself to Human Capacity." *Interpretation* 31 (1977): 19–38.
Bell, T.M.A.C. "*Testimonium Spiritus Sancti* – An Example of Bernard-Reception in Luther." *Bijdragen, Tijdschrift voor Filosofie en Theologie* 53 (1992): 62–72.
Butin, Philip. "Constructive Iconoclasm: Trinitarian Concern in Reformed Worship." *Studia Liturgica* 19 (1989): 133–42.
———. "John Calvin's Humanist Image of Popular Late-Medieval Piety and Its Contribution to Reformed Worship." *Calvin Theological Journal* 29 (1994): 419–31.
Campbell, Richard. "Anselm's Theological Method." *Scottish Journal of Theology* 32 (1979), 541–62.

Carlson, Arnold E. "Luther and the Doctrine of the Holy Spirit." *Lutheran Quarterly* 11 (1959): 135–46.

Chen, Sheryl Frances. "Bernard's Prayer Before the Crucifix that Embraced Him: Cistercians and Devotion to the Wounds of Christ." *Cistercian Studies* 29 (1994): 23–54.

Crouse, Robert D. "Anselm of Canterbury and Medieval Augustinians." *Toronto Journal of Theology* 3 (1987): 60–68.

Decorte, Jos. "Saint Anselm of Canterbury on Ultimate Reality and Meaning." *Ultimate Reality and Meaning* 12 (1988): 177–90.

Eastman, Patrick W.H. "The Christology in Bernard's *De Diligendo Deo*." *Cistercian Studies* 23 (1983): 119–27.

Evans, Gillian R. "Making the Theory Fit the Practice: Augustine and Anselm on Prayer." *Epworth Review* 18 (1991): 78–81; 19 (1992): 57–68.

———. "St. Anselm and Knowing God." *Journal of Theological Studies* 28 (1977): 430–44.

Fergusson, David. "Theology of Worship." *Scottish Bulletin of Evangelical Theology* 21 (2003): 7–19.

Hanson, Richard P.C. "The Divinity of the Holy Spirit." *The Church Quarterly* 1(1969):

———. "Basil's Doctrine of the Tradition in Relation to the Holy Spirit." *Vigiliae Christianae* 22 (1968): 241–55.

Haykin, Michael A.G. "And Who is the Spirit? Basil of Caesarea's Letters to the Church at Tarsus." *Vigilae Christianae* 41 (1987): 377–85.

———. "'In the Cloud and In the Sea' Basil of Caesarea and the Exegesis of I Cor. 10:2." *Vigiliae Christianae* 40 (1986): 135–44.

Johnson, Oliver. "God and St. Anselm." *Journal of Religion* 45 (1965): 326–32.

Larson, Mark J. "A Re-examination of *De Spiritu Sanctos*: Saint Basil's Bold Defence of the Spirit's Deity." *Scottish Bulletin of Evangelical Theology* 19 (2001): 65–84.

Lischer, Richard. "Luther and Contemporary Preaching: Narrative and Anthropology." *Scottish Journal of Theology* 36 (1983): 487–504.

McDonnell, Kilian. "Spirit and Experience in Bernard of Clairvaux." *Theological Studies* 58 (1997): 3–18.

McKee, Elsie Anne. "Context, Contours, Contents: Toward a Description of Classical Reformed Teaching on Worship." *Princeton Theological Seminary Bulletin* 16 (1995): 173–201.

Morreall, John. "The Aseity of God in St. Anselm." *Sophia* 23 (1984): 35–44.

Morris, Anne. "The Trinity in Bernard's Sermons on the Song of Songs." *Cistercian Studies* 30 (1995): 35–57.

Mousnier, R. "St.Bernard and Martin Luther." *American Benedictine Review* 14 (1963): 448–62.

Nichols, Aidan. "Anselm of Canterbury and the Language of Perfection." *Downside Review* 103 (1985): 204–17.

Noble, Tom A. "Gregory Nazianzen's Use of Scripture in Defense of the Deity of the Spirit." *Tyndale Bulletin* 39 (1988): 101–23.
Posset, Franz. "St. Bernard's Influence on Two Reformers: John von Staupitz and Martin Luther." *Cistercian Studies* 25 (1990): 175–87.
———. "Recommendations by Martin Luther of St. Bernard's *On Considerations*." *Cistercian Studies* 25 (1990): 25–36.
———. "The Elder Luther on Bernard." *American Benedictine Review* 42 (1991): 25–52; 179–201.
Raitt, Jill. "Calvin's Use of Bernard of Clairvaux." *Archiv Für Reformationsgeschichte* 72 (1981): 98–121.
Read, D.H.C. "The Reformation of Worship. I. The Dislocation of Worship in the Modern World." *Scottish Journal of Theology* 7 (1954): 393–407.
———. "The Reformation of Worship. II. The use of Our Heritage." *Scottish Journal of Theology* 8 (1955): 64–79.
———. "The Reformation of Worship. III. The Direction of Worship." *Scottish Journal of Theology* 8 (1955): 272–87.
Reid, Stanley. "Bernard of Clairvaux in the Thought of John Calvin." *Westminster Theological Journal* 41 (1978): 127–45.
Rena, Thomas. "*The Song of Songs* and the Early Cistercians." *Cistercian Studies* 27 (1992): 39–49.
Rogers, Katherin. "Anselm on Praising a Necessarily Perfect Being." *International Journal for Philosophy of Religion* 34 (1993): 41–52.
Scholl, Edith. "The Sweetness of the Lord: Dulcis and Suavis." *Cistercian Studies* 27 (1992): 359–66.
Schonbeck, Oluf. "Saint Bernard, Peter Damian, and the Wounds of Christ." *Cistercian Studies* 35 (1995): 275–84.
Schwarz, R. "Luther's Inalienable Inheritance of Monastic Theology." *American Benedictine Review* 39 (1988): 430–50.
Sibley, Laurence C. "Late Have I Loved You: Augustinian Spirituality in Book 10 of the *Confessions*." *Westminster Theological Journal* 65 (2003): 69–81.
Tinker, Michael. "John Calvin's Concept of Divine Accommodation: A Hermeneutical Corrective." *Churchman* 118 (2004): 325–58.
Torrance, Thomas F. "Calvin's Doctrine of the Trinity." *Calvin Theological Journal* 25 (1990): 165–90.
Tylenda, Joseph. "Christ the Mediator: Calvin versus Stancaro." *Calvin Theological Journal* 8 (1973): 5–16; 131–57.
Wright, David. F. "Basil the Great in the Protestant Reformers." *Studia Patristica* 17 (1982): 1149–55.
Yamamura, Kei. "The Development of the Doctrine of the Holy Spirit in Patristic Philosophy: St. Basil and St. Gregory of Nyssa." *St. Vladimir's Theological Quarterly* 18 (1974): 3–21.
Zona, James W. "'Set Love in Order in Me': Eros-Knowing in Origen and Desiderium-Knowing in Saint Bernard." *Cistercian Studies* 34 (1999): 157–82.

General Index

Althaus, Paul, 128
Amand de Mendieta, Emmanuel, 4
Aristotle, 117
ascending movement, 32, 64, 162
ascension, xii, xvii, 101–102, 161, 167
aseity, 52–53
Athanasius, 3, 6, 10, 17, 19, 31
Augustine, 38, 41, 48, 56, 64, 72–75, 79, 124, 137, 139, 165
Anselm of Canterbury, ix, xi, xv, xvi, 35–62

Badcock, Gary, 3
Barth, Karl, 38–39, 40, 42, 110, 141
Basil of Caesarea, ix, x, xv, xvi, xvii, 1–32
Battles, Ford L., 140
Bernard of Clairvaux, ix, x, xv, xvi, xvii, 63–104, 110
bond of love (*vinculum caritatis*), 72, 75, 95
Bouwsma, William J., 141
Bray, Gerald, 58
Brecher, Robert, 41
Brecht, Martin, 112
Brunner, Emil, 141

Burgess, Stanley, 81
Butin, Philip W., 29, 146, 159–160, 162, 165

Calvin, John, ix, xi, xv, xvii, 27, 122, 136–169
Campbell, Richard, 39
Casey, Michael, 85, 88, 100
Chrysostom, John, 165
Colle, Ralph Del, xii, xiii
communicatio idiomatum, 121
compunction, 47, 87
constitutive kiss, 63
Croix, Richard E La, 40
Crouse, Robert D., 34

Daley, Brian E., 75
Davies, Brian, 34, 36–37, 40, 42, 44, 46, 49–53, 56, 60
Decorte, Jos, 37–38, 41, 51
deification, 19
descending movement, 32, 162
Dreyer, Elizabeth, 72, 81

Ebeling, Gerhard, 109
economic, 2, 13, 23, 32, 101, 138, 142, 164–165
economic Trinity, 138

General Index

efficacy, xvi, 9, 48, 94, 103, 108–109, 129, 112, 115, 129, 152, 158, 160, 162, 168
Eire, Carlos M. N., 113, 141, 146–147
Eucharist, 121–123
Evans, Gillian R., 34, 38, 43, 55, 92

faith, 37, 42, 60–62, 101, 107–110, 120, 132, 134, 140, 148, 154, 160–161, 164–165
Feuerbach, Ludwig, 109
Filioque, ix, 56–58, 75–76, 159
First Commandment, 107–108, 111, 142, 144–145
Forde, Gerhard O, 106, 133

George, Timothy, 110, 116, 121
Gerrish, Brian A., 168
God's act, 142
God's being, 142
God's essence, 142
God's love, 87–88, 90–92, 95–96, 97, 134
Gonzalez, Justo, 4, 34
Gunton, Colin, 28
Gilson, Etienne, 84
Gregory of Nazianzus, 3, 19
Gregory the Great, 79, 87–88, 99
Gribomont, Jean, 3

Hagen, Kenneth, 128
Hall, Christopher A., 13
Hanson, Richard, 3–4, 32
Hefner, Philip, 123
Helm, Paul, 137, 144–143
Heron, Alasdair, 3
hidden God, 44–46, 99–100
hiddenness, 45
Hilary of Portier, 29, 160
Hogg, David S., 36, 42
homoousios 2–3, 33
Hopkins, Jasper, 34, 37, 47, 51, 55, 59, 61–62
Haykin, Michael A. G., 9

humanity of Christ, xi, xvi, 64, 68, 71, 90–103, 106–107, 127–129, 155

idolatry, 5, 71, 109, 111, 125, 144
impassibility, 49–50, 96
immanent, 2, 13, 23, 64, 74, 77, 83, 101 137, 142
immanent Trinity, 2, 73, 76

Jansen, John f., 156, 167
Jenson, Robert, 116, 123
Jones, Serene, 136, 140
joy, xvi, 37, 54, 60–61
Jünghans, Hans, 112, 135
Justification, 150, 155

Kalam, Cyril, 3
Kärkkäinen, Veli-Matti, 72
kenosis, 98

Lane, Anthony N. S., 131
Larson, Mark J., 3–4
Leclercg, Jean, 88, 102
Leftow, Brian, 49
Lischer, Richard, 119
Loewenich, Walther von, 105
Lombard, Peter, 124
Lohse, Bernhard, 109
Lord's Supper, 108, 112, 165, 167–168
Luther, Martin, ix, x, xv, xvii, 105–135, 148

Malcolm, Norman, 40
McDonnell, Kilian, 63, 80
McGinn, Bernard, 89, 96
McGuire, Brian Patrick, 94
McKee, Elsie, 111, 160
McMahon, Robert, 57, 60
Meredith, Anthony, 33
Moeller, Pamela A, 136
Moffat, James, 111
Moltmann, Jürgen, 31–32
Morris, Anne, 72, 78

mystical union, xi, xvi, 83–90, 103

Nagel, Norman G., 126–127
Ngien, Dennis, ix, vi, x, xi, xii, 58, 91, 1–6–107, 116, 121, 131
Nicaea, 2, 5
Nichols, Aidan, 39
Norris, Frederick, 3

O' Collins, Gerald, 74
Old, Hughes O., 63, 150, 162, 164

Pannenberg, Wolfhart, 121
participated kiss, 80–81
Pelikan, Jaroslav, 5, 7, 17, 30, 114, 116–117
Pennington, M. Basil, 71
Plato, 41, 117, 141
Posset, Franz, 70, 90–100
prayer, x, 61, 119, 127, 129, 133–134
preaching, 115, 117–119, 138, 141, 163–164
priesthood of Christ, 127, 129, 133, 152, 155–157, 167–168
pro me, pro nobis, 107, 109–110, 122, 131

Rainey, David, 25
real presence, 122, 166
reconciliation, 68, 138, 142, 151–152, 154, 168

sabellianism, 25
sacrament, xi, 115, 118–119, 123–125–126, 138, 164–166
Sasse, Herman, 128
Schonbeck, Oluf, 94, 97
Scholl, Edith, 79
Schufreider, Gregory, 42
Second Commandment, 145
Senn, Frank C., 125, 127
Sense of divinity (*divinitatis sensus*)
Sermon, 114–115, 120
Siggins, Ian D., 128
simplicity, 20, 56, 137

Spinks, Byran, 124
Sommerfeldt, John R., 94
Southern, Richard, 38
Staupitz, Johann, 117
Steinmetz, David, 134, 150
Stiegman, Emero S., 84, 92
Studer, Basil, 8
subordinationism, 7, 25
Swete, Henry B., 17

Tamburello, Dennis E., 66, 153
Tertullian, 75
testament, 121, 124
the mediation of Christ, xvii, 127–129, 133, 127–129, 133, 156, 162
Thompson, John, 157, 168
Thompson, Mark D, 120
theology of the cross (*theologia crucis*), xi, xvii, 105–106, 126, 131
Torrance, James B., 133, 156, 158
Torrance, Thomas F., 3, 16, 28, 32, 137
transubstantiation, 122

Vilmos, Vajta, 107, 115, 119, 122, 125

Ward, Benedicta, 34, 37–38, 40–42, 45–49, 55, 61
Warfield, Benjamen B., 137, 150, 142, 149, 158
Watkin-Jones, Howard, 72, 76
Wilson, Henry, 119
Witvliet, John, 136
Word of God, xi, xv, 88, 86, 108, 112, 114, 116–117, 119–120, 122, 131, 138, 144, 163–165
wounds of Christ, 90–103
Wright, David, 34

Yamamura, Kei, 6

Zachman, Randall C., 144